The Lost Territories

Southeast Asia

POLITICS, MEANING, AND MEMORY

David Chandler and Rita Smith Kipp

SERIES EDITORS

The Lost Territories

Thailand's History of National Humiliation

SHANE STRATE

UNIVERSITY OF HAWAI'I PRESS *Honolulu*

Paperback edition 2022

Printed in the United States of America

Library of Congress Cataloging-in-Publication Data

Strate, Shane, author.
The lost territories : Thailand's history of national humiliation / by Shane Strate.
pages cm — (Southeast Asia: politics, meaning, and memory)
Includes bibliographical references and index.
ISBN 978-0-8248-3891-1 (hard cover: alk. paper)
1. Nationalism and collective memory—Thailand. 2. Thailand—History. 3. Thailand—Historiography. I. Title. II. Series: Southeast Asia—politics, meaning, memory.
DS578.S83 2015
959.3—dc23
2014023204

ISBN: 978-0-8248-9341-5 (paperback)

University of Hawaiʻi Press books are printed on acid-free paper and meet the guidelines for permanence and durability of the Council on Library Resources.

To Kaddi

CONTENTS

ACKNOWLEDGMENTS

This book is the product of many treasured associations, both personal and professional, which deserve recognition. I began thinking of this topic in 2001, back when I was a student of European history and Southeast Asia remained shrouded in Oriental mystery. Rodney Bohac first helped me formulate theoretical connections between Europe and Asia. Without guidance from Eric Dursteler and Michael Murdock, I would never have stayed with the project or chosen to become a historian. In the early stages of writing this book, I learned from Anne Raffin, Shawn Miller, Mary Richards, Michael Farmer, Heather Arnita, Julie Radle, Ignacio Garcia, David C. Wright, Elizabeth Sage and many others.

My introduction to Southeast Asian history began when I arrived at the University of Wisconsin-Madison. Working with Thongchai Winichakul remains one of the great honors of my short career. I continue to be inspired by both his scholarship and his commitment to building a more democratic Thailand. A special thank you to Al McCoy, whose inexhaustible knowledge base helped transform me into a Southeast Asianist. Katherine Bowie, Larry Ashmun and Louise Young provided valuable feedback at various stages of research and writing.

Several people and institutions assisted me with funding and employment, which allowed me to pursue my degree and support a small family. First and foremost, I offer my sincere appreciation to the U.S. Department of Education for granting me a Fulbright-Hays research award. Their generous funding meant I did not have to be separated from wife and children while conducting research in Bangkok. I deeply appreciate the financial support I received from the UW-Madison Department of History and the Center for Southeast Asian Studies. Thank you to Michael Cullinane, Erin Crawley, Jim Schlender, Mary Jo Wilson, Nancy Turner, and Robert Patterson for your assistance in obtaining various forms of financial support.

I am grateful to Ian Wendt for providing a map that allowed me to avoid the pitfalls and find the oases in the wilderness of graduate school. I have fond memories of stimulating conversations with Francis Bradley, Sorasak Ngamcachonkulkid, Heidi Fischle, and Thanapol Limapichart, and of trading anxieties with Mary Sutphin during late-night bus rides home from the Memorial Library. In Madison, our life away from the university was enriched by our association with the Davis, Miller, Schaefer, and Lindquist families. While in Thailand, the Poulsen, Selway, Nielson, and Gibbons families helped make Nichada Thani feel like home.

The research for this book took me to a number of libraries and archives. I appreciate the patience and assistance of staff at the National Library of Thailand and the Library of the National Assembly of Thailand. Special thanks to the printing office of the Assumption Cathedral in Bangkok for granting me access to their private collection of memoirs and materials. Most of the documents cited here originated in the National Archives of Thailand in Bangkok, which also granted me permission to publish several images. In France, I owe a great deal of thanks to the document supervisors at the Archives nationales d'outre mer. I appreciate the staff at the National Archives II in College Park, Maryland, for their help in locating State department materials.

Several scholars made contributions, both direct and indirect, to the conceptual framework of this book. In Thailand, I was fortunate to meet Chalong Soontravanich, who allowed me to present my work to one of his classes. I am grateful to the students at Chulalongkorn University, who suggested that I investigate the rash of Anti-Catholic incidents in the 1940s. Thanet Aphornsuvan and Somsak Jeamteerasakul provided guidance as I worked through difficult theoretical constructs. Aaron Skabelund and Tim Davis offered critical advice. I am indebted to William Callahan, Zheng Wang, and others for developing adroit phrases that gave expression to concepts that I struggled to articulate. E. Bruce Reynolds and David Chandler read drafts of the manuscript and corrected errors. Thank you, Eric Hyer, for an opportunity to present an early version of this research.

I have been fortunate to learn from so many outstanding colleagues at several institutions. I especially want to thank Jim Tueller, Michael Murdock, and Troy Smith at BYU-Hawaii; also Joe Blankenau, Pamela Everett, Karen Mecseji, and Don Hickey at Wayne State College. Many thanks to my new colleagues here at Kent State University for welcoming me to the department. And of course, the true friendship and camaraderie of Cory Crawford and Michael Mackay will never be forgotten. For two agonizing and glorious years we worked together, sneaking away from our uncompleted manuscripts and teaching responsibilities whenever possible to walk down the hill towards Steve's Crest.

I am grateful that this book has found a home with University of Hawaii Press, and I wish to express my appreciation to series editors David Chandler and Rita Smith Kipp. I feel blessed to work with Pamela Kelley and her outstanding editorial staff. Their efforts, along with the important contributions of an anonymous reviewer, have improved this manuscript in ways too numerous to mention. Any errors that remain are my responsibility alone.

Finally, this book represents a return, however small, on the substantial investment made by a number of family members. At every stage of my life, my parents, Morgan and Denise Strate, have provided broad shoulders for me to stand on. My wonderful in-laws offered continuous emotional and temporal support. My children have changed schools and bid farewell to friends as they trailed my professional pursuits around the globe. Most of all, I have been blessed by the love and devotion of my wife, Kaddi. How fortunate that I convinced her to marry me years ago, before she realized what she was getting into.

Introduction

The Idea of "Loss" in Thai Historical Narratives

At the beginning of 2001, Thailand found itself struggling to overcome the lingering effects of the Asian financial crisis, which originated with the collapse of the Thai financial markets. By March of that year, the government announced a series of urgent priorities designed to help the country stabilize its economy. After reviewing the government's plan, opposition leaders criticized the apparent exclusion of education from the agenda. Among the harshest critics was former Permanent Secretary for University Affairs Vijit Srisa-an, who viewed education funding as a top priority for revitalizing the nation. "Without a clearer education policy," he warned, "we will never be able to get away from western colonialism."[1]

Vijit's statement speaks to the ambivalent nature of Thailand's relationship with the West. The country's history, as it is traditionally written, insists that the country adapted to the Western-dominated world order more successfully than other Southeast Asian kingdoms. Thai leaders proved very receptive to foreign ideas and technology and adapted their policies to suit changing geopolitical conditions. According to many observers, this flexibility allowed Thailand to avoid becoming a European colony. Yet despite their country's proud history of independence, some Thai leaders continue to view the West as a threat. Vijit did not explain how Western colonialism continues to endanger Thailand's well-being, but his remarks illustrate an important ambiguity within its nationalist rhetoric. If Thailand was so successful at maintaining its independence, why do leaders like Vijit still feel a pressing need to get away from Western colonialism?

Recent attempts to answer this question have led historians to abandon the binary model that classifies nonwestern societies as either independent or colonized and instead recognize that Thailand, like other regions, displayed characteristics of both categories as early as the nineteenth century.[2] Thai history is marked by successful adaptation and diplomacy, but the country has also witnessed continuous, sometimes violent confrontations with Western powers. These clashes produced complex results. Growing European influence in mainland Southeast Asia jeopardized the country's independence and the supremacy of the Thai elite. Ultimately, Western imperialism reached a form of accommodation with the Chakri monarchy and created conditions that helped ensure the dynasty's survival. So while Thailand did not become a colony of either Britain or France, its ongoing struggle against and accommodation with the West influenced the development of a modern national identity.

This study seeks to understand the formation of that identity by examining the way Thai leaders shaped perceptions of the country's relationship with the West. Thai nationalist discourse is a coin with two sides. The side most often presented to the world depicts Thailand's bold efforts to confront the Western challenges of modernity. It celebrates the state's unique ability to preserve the country's independence. There is also an alternate side, a darker narrative that commemorates moments of national shame. Throughout the twentieth century, these episodes of victimization have been incorporated into what Marc Askew labels "the nation in danger" discourse, used to legitimize military expansion, ethnic chauvinism, political witch hunts, or religious persecution.[3] This study examines the origins and history of this second narrative as an important thread in the fabric of identity formation and Thailand's ambivalent attitudes towards the West.

GATEWAYS TO THAI HISTORY: VICTORS AND VICTIMS

Thai historiography contains a series of premises or themes that shape the production of all historical knowledge. These issues have become what Thongchai Winichakul called "gateways" to Thai history, established dogmas intended to reaffirm contemporary political and social agendas.[4] The first and most important of these themes is the idea that *Siam was never colonized.* For decades, historians accepted this conclusion as an indisputable fact given that Siam, unlike each of its neighbors, never became a European colony. The assumption was that the monarchy used bureaucratic reforms and an agenda of modernization to successfully fend off European attempts at colonization. Ultimately, the skillful diplomacy of the Thai rulers saved the kingdom and preserved its identity.[5] Although this formula was intended to explain Siam's confrontation with the West, it also became the historical framework for previous eras. In his official history of Ayutthaya,

Prince Damrong depicted the kingdom as constantly under siege from the Burmese, the archenemies of the Siamese. Certain plays of Luang Wichit Wathakan, former minister of fine arts during the first administration of Prime Minister Phibun (1938–1944), also advanced this idea.[6] To this day, the trope that *Siam was never colonized* functions as an important source of political legitimacy for the monarchy and its allies. It suggests that the primary function of the state is to protect the kingdom's independence and territory and encourages the nation to rally around the standard of the king, who will guide the country through any future crisis, just as he has always done in the past.

If the first theme celebrates the country's survival from colonialism, a second theme identifies the costs and consequences of survival, often portraying Siam as victim rather than victor. I refer to this theme as *lost territory* because discourses that include it often use maps to convey an overall sense of injustice, dishonor, or humiliation that resulted from Western intervention in Thai affairs. This is the theme's main purpose: to communicate the extent of past injuries sustained by the body of the nation. It achieves this goal by identifying specific regions that once belonged to the Thai state but that were taken away by hostile powers through deceit or aggression. Like the first theme, *lost territory* rests on a series of ahistorical assumptions. It projects modern conceptions of boundaries into the past to designate a geographical space, and the people within it, as Thai. The extent of this imagined territory fluctuates depending on the period, but once defined within a discourse the boundaries become sacred and inviolable. The borders of the nation-state are perceived as eternal, an inheritance from an ancient past (rather than a recent construction); therefore it naturally follows that the areas in question rightfully belong to the kingdom and have indeed been lost. After quantifying the extent of the nation's injury, the next step in this discourse is to assign blame. *Lost territory* is a tool for delegitimizing state leadership, as the government in question failed in its primary duty to secure the kingdom's borders. An effective way to discredit political opponents is to associate them with territorial loss. Conversely, a demonstrated ability to restore (or expand) national space is a powerful method for asserting one's right to rule. Either way, this second theme acts as an important reminder of the dangers that can befall the nation if it fails to unify behind proper leadership.

The themes of *Siam was never colonized* and *lost territory* exist in a binary tension. Any history written on Thailand must account for both ideas, but because one simultaneously complements and contradicts the other, each must be modified if they are to coexist within a single coherent narrative. A theme must be assigned either a dominant or a subordinate role in order to alleviate the inherent conflict. Because historians of Thailand have traditionally sought to congratulate its leaders for defending its independence, they designate *Siam was never colonized* as the dominant theme of their works while relegating *lost territory* to a subordinate role. It is important to note that the act of subordinating a theme does not deny its existence. The two ideas exist in a dichotomy; therefore eliminating one theme entirely would destroy the context of its opposite. Even narratives that celebrate how the country survived the 1893 Franco-Siamese crisis must acknowledge that Siam signed the unequal treaties and surrendered its claim to the Lao territories. Instead, subordination involves sanitizing and transforming a theme into something that reinforces, rather than threatens, its alternate. Siam's territorial concessions prove only that the kingdom's very existence was threatened, which in turn elevates the heroism of the leaders who saved the majority of the country from being colonized.

Under the right political conditions, however, the subordinate theme can compete for the position of dominance and reconstruct the entire narrative. This work argues that the 1940 border negotiations between Thailand and French Indochina provided the ideal atmosphere for this type of inversion. The prospect of enlarging the country's boundaries offered the military elite something they desperately needed to prevent the monarchy from returning: a source of political legitimacy. The Phibun government's irredentist rhetoric relied heavily on the theme of *lost territory* while reassigning *never colonized* to a subordinate role. In order to construct an anti-imperialist discourse that would mobilize an entire nation, the government downplayed Siam's legacy of independence and instead interpreted the Franco-Siamese crisis of 1893 as a defeat that robbed the nation of both its territory and its honor. The leaders of Thailand provoked the 1941 war with French Indochina because they felt confident that avenging the loss from a half century earlier would allow the military to replace the monarchy in the role of national savior.

COMPETING NARRATIVES: ROYAL-NATIONALISM VS. NATIONAL HUMILIATION

Themes are important because they are manipulated to construct narratives. Not surprisingly, the theme of survival occupies the dominant role in these narratives, whose purpose is to credit the heroism or diplomatic genius of the monarchy for preserving national autonomy. Let us examine the two most common forms of narrative used to analyze Thai history. The most common narrative in Thai historiography is Royal-Nationalism. One example of this narrative is the historiography on the 1855 Bowring Treaty and the coming of the West. Prior to the 1850s, Siamese rulers relied on the junk trade with China and refused Western requests to increase economic exchange. After the Opium Wars, however, many in Bangkok became convinced of the superiority of Western arms and shipping technology. Following his ascension to the throne, Rama IV invited John Bowring, Britain's governor of Hong Kong, to negotiate a change in trade relations. The resulting treaty ended royal monopolies, limited Siamese tariffs on British goods, and granted extraterritorial privileges for British citizens.[7] This landmark agreement with Britain was the first of many similar treaties with other European powers. If we analyze the Bowring Treaty through the lens of Royal-Nationalism, Mongkut is a hero for initiating Siam's entrance into the world capitalist economy. The king's intrepid leadership allowed Siam to reach a gradual accommodation with the West by eliminating any pretext for a military conflict with Britain. He had the foresight to appropriate Occidental influence and technology instead of clinging to the old ways and suffering the fate of the Qing dynasty.

The Bowring Treaty also contains several elements connected to the theme of *lost territory*. Extraterritorial clauses lowered tariffs, limited Siamese sovereignty, and marked the beginning of Siam's inferior relationship with the West. Generally speaking, Royal-Nationalist narratives acknowledge these aspects, but they do so in a way that subordinates them. Because the treaty's unequal aspects have the potential to undermine royal valor and destabilize the overall narrative, the memory of these concessions must be neutralized by the sense of a "nation in danger." Royal-Nationalist historians depict the Bowring Treaty as a choice between accommodation and invasion. Forced to decide between granting extraterritoriality on one hand and British colonization on the other, Mongkut chose the lesser of two evils. Thus, the Royal-Nationalist narrative evaluates the success of foreign interaction primarily in terms of survival. Its adherents interpret even the worst foreign policy disasters as victories as long as the country maintains some semblance of independence.

For this reason, Royal-Nationalist historians embrace the concept of *bamboo diplomacy*—the idea that Thai foreign policy is firmly rooted but flexible enough to bend in favor of prevailing political winds.[8] In one example, Thamsook Numnonda argues that Phibun used bamboo diplomacy to help the country emerge comparatively unscathed from World War II. Setting aside the four-year Japanese occupation and the postwar reparations forced on Thailand by the Allies, she interprets Thailand's wartime strategy as a form of victory through endurance. "The Thai art of diplomacy had once again saved the nation," Thamsook comments. "And this, of course, has always been the way the Thais have met and overcome every crisis."[9]

Royal-Nationalist history has been well documented in other studies. The purpose of this book is to explore its mirror image, a narrative that I have labeled "National Humiliation" discourse. In this alternate history, *lost territory* assumes the dominant role, while *never colonized* has been subordinated to a position of secondary importance. Although National Humiliation history is most commonly associated with irredentism, it encompasses much more than the issue of stolen land and ethnic diasporas. It structures modern Thai history as an act in two parts. First, the arrival of Western imperialism in Southeast Asia causes the gradual decline of Thai prestige and the erosion of its sovereignty. In the second act, a strong, modern, confident Thailand emerges under the leadership of the military, which restores the nation's territory and its international status. Although the theme of *lost territory* surfaces among the royal elite following the 1893 crisis, the narrative of National Humiliation did not find full expression until after the 1932 military coup that ended the absolute monarchy and brought the People's Party into power. The brainchild of Wichit Wathakan, this discourse became the basis of the irredentist campaign that led to war with French Indochina in 1941.

National Humiliation discourse reinterprets the history of Thai-West relations as a series of emasculating encounters. Not surprisingly, the Bowring Treaty looks very different when viewed through its lens. The narrative argues that, far from saving the country from British colonization, the 1855 negotiations marked the beginning of Siam's gradual descent from regional empire towards European client-state. As we will see in chapter 1, this viewpoint resulted in part from the anachronistic application of modern Western legal concepts. Once twentieth-century Siamese legal scholars began thinking in Western terms such as "sovereignty," "boundary," and "jurisdiction," they projected these ideas onto past events in order to reevaluate their significance.[10] By twentieth-century standards, the Bowring Treaty represented a clear loss of sovereignty, as Mongkut had given away the right to set duties on imports and granted Europeans exemption from Siamese law. Furthermore, when historians placed the treaty in the context of territorial adjustments that occurred between 1890 and 1910, it became the first in a long series of diplomatic and military assaults on Siamese autonomy. By using National Humiliation discourse to construct a new historical memory of the "unequal treaties" (as agreements with the European powers became known), Thai leaders hoped to mobilize support for the stated goal of reducing Western interference in the country's affairs.[11]

To increase public antipathy towards colonial powers, National Humiliation narratives strove to subordinate the *never colonized* theme without renouncing it. The post-1932 military regimes never argued that the country had been colonized; only that it had lost pieces of territory and sacrificed aspects of sovereignty that its new leaders would restore. In its irredentist propaganda, the Phibun government had to carefully negotiate the royal legacy while quantifying the damage sustained by the nation and assigning blame. William Callahan's research on the People's Republic of China demonstrates how Chinese politicians explain loss by accusing specific internal groups of having "sold out the nation."[12] In Thailand this process requires subtlety, because the largest losses of territory and sovereignty occurred during the reigns of Mongkut and Chulalongkorn—the twin pillars of Royal-Nationalist historiography. These two kings were so respected by the people that the military regime was reluctant to criticize them. In state propaganda of the 1940s, the scapegoat for territorial loss was Thai Catholics, not Chulalongkorn or Mongkut. In the discussion of the Bowring Treaty, Mongkut appears as the victim of Western imperialist treachery. Rather than target individual kings, the narrative blames the institution of the monarchy for the loss of the kingdom's territory. The implied conclusion is that royal foreign policy was outdated and therefore unable to meet the challenges of the modern era. Such accusations also provided an opening for the Thai junta to assert its own right to rule, provided it could restore the territory lost by the monarchy. This seemingly generous treatment of the Thai kings also served a larger strategy. The military leaders of the 1930s wanted to displace the monarchy while simultaneously appropriating its legacy of leadership. They reinforced the belief that the country had always been free, and it would always remain free.

THE FRANCO-SIAMESE CRISIS AND THE BIRTH OF MODERN THAI HISTORIOGRAPHY

The two ideologies described above were each a response to the state's need for a discourse to account for the country's changing role in the modern world. The creation of the modern geobody of Thailand involved a series of territorial concessions to colonial powers from 1867 to 1909. From the perspective of the Thai elite, the birth of the nation-state was a painful and traumatic procedure that resulted in a drastic reduction of both the size and prestige of the kingdom. The pivotal event in this process of spatial construction was the 1893 Franco-Siamese crisis. Siam's humiliating defeat also commenced its decline as an imperial power. Over the next two decades, Chulalongkorn authorized a series of foreign treaties that conceded both territory and privileges to Britain and France. The defeat of 1893 came to be viewed as a scar on the body of the nation and a stain on its honor. By the twentieth century, the Siamese elite recognized the need for a historical narrative that would facilitate the grieving process by explaining the nature of the country's loss. If we are to understand the function of these discourses, we must recount the event that made them necessary.

At the end of the nineteenth century, the Kingdom of Siam participated in what might be called the "scramble for Southeast Asia." With Britain encroaching from Burma and Malaya and France expanding west from Cochin China and Tonkin, Bangkok raced to extend its control over areas that it considered vassal states. The increased proximity of French and Siamese garrisons along the Mekong River eventually led to sparring between the two armies. Instead of yielding to a superior military power as it had done in the past, Chulalongkorn and his advisors determined to hold firm. A new generation of leaders, which Battye refers to as "Young Siam," pivoted away from the country's traditional strategy of territorial appeasement. Encouraged by the success of recent modernization efforts and confident they would receive British assistance, the Royal Council determined to "act like Europeans" and insist on their rights under international law.[13] The decision to risk military confrontation had dire consequences. France responded to Siamese brinkmanship by engineering a naval blockade of the Chao Phrya River. With French gunships docked near the Grand Palace and Bangkok on the verge of riot, Chulalongkorn agreed to end the standoff by signing a series of ultimatums.

The speed of Siam's collapse and its aftermath became a defining moment in Thai history, commonly referred to as "RS 112."[14] In the final settlement, Siam renounced its claim to the left bank of the Mekong, an area comprising roughly one-third of the total territory of the kingdom. France also insisted on a twenty-five kilometer demilitarized zone along the new border with French Indochina, a war indemnity of three million francs, and the extension of extraterritorial privileges to all Asiatic protégés living in Siam. As a final degradation, French troops would occupy the Siamese town of Chantaburi (and later Trat), located a mere two hundred kilometers southeast of Bangkok, until authorities in Indochina were satisfied that Siam had fully complied with all clauses of the agreement.

Before addressing interpretations of this event, several other points must be examined. First, the conflict was the result of Siamese efforts to compete with the French in the game of colonial expansion, not to preserve its own independence. The crisis grew out of an initial dispute over territory in the Sip Song Chu Thai, located in the space between the empires of Siam and French Indochina. What began as a preliminary border conflict escalated into a significant threat to the kingdom largely due to the overconfidence and blundering of the Siamese elite. Siam's military strategy backfired. It achieved nothing except to provide the French with a pretext for further expansion at Siam's expense. Finally, the Franco-Siamese crisis was not the result of anticolonial attitudes; it helped give birth to such attitudes. In particular, Britain's refusal to get involved in the dispute exposed the futility of Siamese diplomatic strategy and engendered enormous resentment against both the French and British. Given the factors listed above, the true casualty of the 1893 Franco-Siamese conflict was not territory, soldiers, or even sovereignty; it was the prestige of the monarchy. The Siamese elite were devastated by the defeat. They could not accept that they had been defeated so easily and forced to concede so much. The formerly powerful empire had been rendered completely helpless when confronted with a modern European military force. A new historical narrative was required to repair the monarchy's image and help Siam's rulers come to terms with their place in the new Asia.[15]

In order to salvage the country's prestige and assert a form of moral authority, Royal-Nationalist historians explained Siam's collapse by portraying it as the victim of an illegal invasion. This required the acceptance of a series of geographical anachronisms. Thai scholars never acknowledged that Siam in the 1890s had been a confederation of vassal states loosely held by a system of allegiance to rulers in Bangkok. Instead, they used twentieth-century understandings of linear boundaries and political jurisdiction, implying that regions such as the Sip Song Chu Thai had already been integrated into the nation-state of Siam. In their eyes, the 1893 crisis represented a French violation of the borders of a sovereign country, rather than a contest to establish sovereignty over the largely autonomous Lao territories along the Mekong River valley. For several decades the Siamese government downplayed its claim to these lands, having learned a costly lesson regarding the consequences of needlessly provoking the French, but the overall narrative clearly implied that the regions were "stolen."

From the beginning, Royal-Nationalist historians set out to vindicate Chulalongkorn's foreign policy and uphold the monarchy's role as the defenders of the nation. They argued that France had succeeded in stealing territory but failed in its ultimate goal of making all of Siam part of French Indochina. Despite their duplicity and overwhelming technological advantage, France had been thwarted by the diplomatic genius of the king, who understood that territorial concessions were necessary to preserve overall independence. He had sacrificed a finger in order to save the hand. Moreover, by standing his ground and provoking an international crisis, the king initiated the process of multilateral peace negotiations. As David Wyatt describes the outcome, "The 1893 crisis was not the end of Siam's struggle for national sovereignty, but it marked the beginning of Siam's attempt to salvage what it could from an impossible situation. It was the last occasion on which the kingdom had to give up territory without compensation, and it was the point at which Britain and France began to face up to the necessity of coming to terms in Southeast Asia."[16]

This new historiography redeemed Chulalongkorn's legacy. History might have depicted him as the monarch who unwisely pursued a military solution, mismanaged the conflict, and was forced to meekly accept the crushing terms of reparation. Instead, he emerged as a hero who achieved a lasting peace. Refusing to acknowledge that the kingdom had been defeated, this narrative lauded Siam as the only Southeast Asian country to withstand European imperialism. This perspective evolved into the *king saved the country* trope that continues to be the basis of Thai historiography.

The 1932 military coup that ended absolute monarchy in Siam created conditions that allowed the National Humiliation discourse to emerge and eventually challenge Royal-Nationalism's control over the nation's historiography. The new military elite needed a narrative that would convince the populace of its right to rule the country. The regime's chief ideologue, Wichit Wathakan, reevaluated the significance of the 1893 confrontation with France. While deemphasizing the preservation of the kingdom, the new historiography focused on the country's loss of sovereignty and honor. The military junta accused the old regime of allowing Britain and France to treat Siam like a colony, citing issues such as extraterritoriality and loss of control over tariffs and taxation. Lao and Khmer regions ceded to French Indochina became known as the *lost territories,* a powerful symbol of Siam's diminished status. As part of its irredentist foreign policy, Phibun's government produced anachronistic maps identifying areas of French Indochina that had once been part of Thailand, while Wichit penned editorials comparing these territories to limbs that had been amputated from the body of the nation. Whereas Royal-Nationalist historiography sought to distract focus away from the embarrassment of the monarchy/nation, this new narrative on the *lost territories* celebrated episodes of humiliation. By doing so, the military regime hoped to transform the disgrace of the Siamese elite in 1893 into a collective trauma that would bond citizens to the new state.

By the 1940s, National Humiliation proponents began openly discussing the Franco-Siamese crisis as symptomatic of Siam's inequality with the West. They analyzed why Siam had been defeated and asked who was to blame. The resulting explanation for the loss was twofold. Rather than criticize Chulalongkorn directly, the military elite took a more circuitous route, suggesting that Siam had been defeated because it was insufficiently modern and lacked adequate technology. The royal cabinet had assumed international law would offer their country some protection; but France behaved like a barbaric country that understood only the violent language of fire and steel. In a contest determined entirely by brute force, even the remarkable fighting spirit of Siam's soldiers could not negate the advantage of France's modern weaponry. The second factor explaining Siam's defeat involved the betrayal of its supposed ally, Great Britain. For years Siam adopted a pro-British foreign policy, granting the British concessions on the understanding that their influence could at some point be a useful deterrent to French intervention. Yet when French gunboats threatened the Siamese capital, the British consul refused to involve his country, advising Chulalongkorn only to seek the best terms possible. The Thai military elite saw British neutrality as a form of betrayal, one they would remember when it came time to choose sides during World War II.

EFFECTS OF NATIONAL HUMILIATION DISCOURSE

Following the 1932 coup d'etat, the Thai military formed a new state and also created a new sense of historical memory. The fledgling government designed its narrative to provide a much-needed form of political legitimacy, while also discrediting the monarchy's right to rule. The National Humiliation narrative is, at its core, a state history. From its inception, it represented the military elite's vision of the new state and its role in guiding the country forward into a new age. That new role was based on the state's reconstruction of the Franco-Siamese crisis as a type of *chosen trauma*—a historical grievance that is the inheritance of every Thai person. The chapters that follow discuss the origins of this discourse and examine its circulation. In the process, this work demonstrates how the imagery of tragedy and loss has affected national identity and explains why these ideas resonated with the people of Thailand at particular moments in history.

First, this new historiography served to bond the citizen with the state by converting royal shame into national agony. As chapter 2 argues, the Franco-Siamese crisis would have been of little or no concern to the average Siamese peasant living in 1893. The clash of French and Siamese armies on the left bank of the Mekong diminished royal prestige but did not affect the day-to-day affairs of commoners. By 1941, a much larger percentage of the population was aware of the existence of a Thailand, with its corresponding concepts of citizenship, boundaries, and sovereignty. National Humiliation discourse applied these ideas retroactively to past events, rewriting the story of 1893 as a Western attack on the nation-state rather than a case of injured royal pride. Ordinary people expressed a sense of outrage that Thailand had suffered the indignity of having territory, which they now perceived as Thai, stolen by France. Once this new historical memory gained widespread acceptance, the state was better able to convince citizens that a bright future could be created for the nation once the grievances of the past had been resolved.

Since this is a loss-based narrative, it required new methods for communicating a sense of injury to generations far removed from the actual event. The Thai state employed chronology to achieve this goal. In the 1940s, Thai historians generally used the Buddhist (and occasionally the Christian) calendar when referring to past dates. The Franco-Siamese crisis, however, was always expressed as "RS 112," the 112th year of the Rathanakosin period, dated from the founding of the Chakri dynasty. This unique timetable accorded the event a special stature within the overall chronology of Thai history and served as a subtle reminder of the monarchy's role in the tragedy.[17] The most important symbol of loss was the image of the *lost territories* themselves. The color-coded maps printed and distributed by the Phibun government in the late 1930s reinforced perceptions that France had not just taken land; it had also sullied the nation's honor. These maps reconstructed the Thai past as a timeline of painful territorial concessions.

The maps also illustrate a second consequence of National Humiliation: it is an attempt to narrowly redefine Thai identity based on the model of the state-as-victim. In the new narrative, the state has replaced the monarchy as the hero. It is heroic not because it won the confrontation with French imperialism but because it lost. Herein lies the discourse's central paradox. In the state's version of history, it functions as both victim and hero, because in the anticolonial atmosphere of Southeast Asia in the 1940s heroism was associated with injustice or tragedy. It was the product of being a political prisoner, experiencing racism, or suffering from European imperialist occupation. The imagined loss of the Franco-Siamese conflict became the basis of the state's persecution complex, which claims that national survival is constantly threatened by enemies from without and within. In such a hostile world, the path forward requires all citizens to rally around the state's leadership and conform to its definition of "Thainess." Political factions such as the PAD use the map plotline of the *lost territories* to intimidate opposition, as if to say, "This is what happens when the nation is not united."

Just as National Humiliation assists in redefining the national character, it also provides a footing from which to project the new identity onto an enlarged geographical space. Wichit's concept of a "Greater Thailand," which was based on his own cartographical sequence of the *lost territories*, used the idea of loss in an attempt to forge bonds between peoples divided by the 1893 borders. Thais who embraced this narrative gradually began to view the Lao and Khmer peoples of French Indochina as part of their larger nation. The border regions were reimagined as occupied areas of Thailand. The "left-bank Thais," as they came to be known within the discourse, were portrayed as fellow victims of the Franco-Siamese crisis. They lived under French colonial oppression, deprived of the constitutional freedoms now enjoyed by the people of Thailand. Despite such rhetoric, this study argues that National Humiliation is in fact a form of irredentism and neo-imperialism disguised as a movement to liberate peoples and redeem the country's honor.

As a final consequence, National Humiliation historiography glorifies the military as the saviors of the nation. By the 1940s, the Phibun regime had successfully linked the image of *lost territories* to the growing perception that—in terms of technology, living standards, and international status—Thailand had more in common with colonies than colonizers. Extraterritoriality, customs duties, and especially the failing border negotiations with French Indochina (all results of the Franco-Siamese crisis) helped sell the idea that the country was being held back from modernity by the collective efforts of the West. With the monarchy in exile, the only institution capable of diagnosing the nation's ills and prescribing the necessary remedy was the military. Phibun's cultural programs were part of the military's overall direction towards modernity, and this required exorcising the demons of past loss and defeat. This discourse established 1893 as the year of Thailand's fall; 1941 was supposed to mark its redemption.

THE *CHOSEN TRAUMA*

In identifying the traumatic effects of the Franco-Siamese crisis on national identity in Thailand, I refer to a phenomenon that Vamik Volkan calls "The Chosen Trauma." This term refers to the creation of collective memory regarding a perceived tragedy that once befell a group's ancestors. It does not imply that people choose to be victimized but rather that nations, religious communities, or ethnic groups can develop a sense of solidarity through the reconstructed memory of an ancestor's trauma.[18] The sense of loss remains powerful even if an extended period of time separates the victimized generation and its descendants. In some cases, the memory lies dormant for several decades, all the while being silently acknowledged through various elements of popular culture, only to reemerge later under suitable conditions. The appearance of a charismatic political leader is the most common method for awakening the *chosen trauma*. Once it has been reactivated, the historical truth of the loss is no longer important because the function of the memory has changed. While the original episode was humiliating, the shared mental representation of that event now serves to link individual members to the group, paradoxically lifting their self-esteem and infusing them with a common purpose: to remove the disgrace of their forefathers.[19] If the *chosen trauma* is reactivated under stressful circumstances, for example a potential attack on the community, the community may experience what Volkan refers to as a "time collapse." The group begins to make conscious and unconscious connections between the *chosen trauma* and the current crisis. An event that occurred centuries ago may seem to have happened only yesterday. The group's claim to what was lost becomes exaggerated. Even if historical circumstances do not permit the group to reverse the humiliation, the mental image of the events still allows individuals to bond together "under a large tent of victimhood."[20]

I argue that the purpose of National Humiliation discourse was to transform the Franco-Siamese crisis into Thailand's *chosen trauma*. Chapter 1 describes the Thai government's efforts to publicize the notion of *lost territory* and the resulting groundswell of support for confronting French Indochina over the border question. Ordinary citizens pledged to sacrifice their possessions and even their lives in order to avenge a defeat they projected onto their ancestors. Volkan's argument that nations form this sense of victimization unconsciously does not apply to Thailand in the 1940s. Without question, there was a coordinated effort by members of the Phibun administration to promote National Humiliation imagery and communicate it to the masses. In doing so, however, the military elite benefited from preexisting narratives or cultural markers that they appropriated into their larger historiography of victimization. One goal of this book is to describe that process.

Even before 1932, the Siamese elite carefully managed historical memory of its defeat by the French. To protect royal dignity and maintain stable relations with France, the monarchy did not permit open discussion of the *lost territories* or the naval defeat at Pak Nam. Despite their efforts to act as gatekeepers to history, memories of the loss began to find expression using a variety of methods and interpretations. For example, visitors to Chantaburi Province can visit Khuk Khikai (Chicken Dung Prison). In 1893, the French constructed the prison to hold Siamese patriots who opposed their occupation. French wardens kept chickens on the wire-mesh roof of the jail so that bird droppings would fall down onto the prisoners below. After Chantaburi was returned to Siam, the prison became an important historical reminder of the region's ordeal. In similar fashion, the people of Trat Province celebrate "Trat Independence Day," an annual four-day festival marking the end of the French occupation (1904–1907). City residents display hundreds of royal flags bearing a white elephant on a red background to commemorate their province's return to Siamese sovereignty. Such monuments and rituals preserved memories of a traumatic event in the kingdom's past, which in turn provided fertile ground for the seeds of anticolonialism and irredentism planted during the first Phibun regime.

Ostensibly, these events are celebrations of royal leadership and independence, but embedded within the ritual lies resentment towards unwelcome Western influence within Thailand. The novel *Thawiphob* (or *Tawipob*) tells the story of a woman named Maneejan who mysteriously transports back and forth between her late-twentieth-century world and the Siam of the nineteenth century.[21] As she reconnects with her heritage and falls in love with a patriotic court official, Maneejan grows indignant at the unrestrained westernization of her modern Thailand. Rachel Harrison has analyzed the novel and the imagery of its corresponding movie, *Siamese Renaissance,* to suggest that both convey a very direct message. Thais must be flexible in adopting Western ideas that complement but do not jeopardize "Thainess."[22] As the storyline develops, it becomes clear that the author's anxieties about contemporary Thai culture are rooted in past interactions. During Maneejan's first visit to the past, she observes the Bowring Treaty, which marks the beginning of European influence in Siamese affairs and later plays a role in the Franco-Siamese crisis. Both events symbolize the subordination of Siam to Western power. The movie adaptation includes a reenactment of the infamous episode where French consul Gabriel Aubaret assaulted a Siamese official, grabbing the prince by his hair and throwing him down a flight of stairs.[23] Outraged at this insult, Maneejan proceeds to assassinate Aubaret. This event leads to an alternate reality in which Siam becomes a French colony and a giant replica of the Eiffel Tower looms over the banks of the Chao Phrya River.

Thus, even as novels such as *Thawiphob* advocate Royal-Nationalist discourse, they also address the theme of *lost territory* in ways that preserve its importance in the historical memory. This memory lies dormant within Thai society until it can be activated under the right political conditions by a leader capable of reformulating a new discourse to exploit it.

NATIONAL HUMILIATION WITHIN THE HISTORIOGRAPHY

The central issue of Thai historiography in the twentieth century has been Thailand's search for its place within the new global order created by the West. The writings of Prince Damrong, younger brother of Chulalongkorn and the father of Thai history, provided an initial framework for the debate. Damrong's story of Siam focused on the monarchy as the dominant tradition that connects the modern kingdom back through Ayuthaya to the golden age of Sukothai. The king was the father of the nation, who protected his people from external threats and allowed them to follow Buddhist precepts.[24] This leadership style, which was unique to the Siamese monarchy, had been embraced by all of the Chakri monarchs since the dynasty's founding. According to Damrong, these rulers brought progress to the country and guarded it against all enemies, allowing Siam to enter the twentieth century as a proud, independent nation. For decades, Western historiography on Siam's entry into the modern world was heavily influenced by Damrong's work. Even so, scholars were divided on the driving force behind Siam's transformation. On one side, Walter Vella and other scholars stressed the importance of colonial encroachment in the reform of the political system, while others such as David Wyatt credited the creativity of the Siamese elite for the kingdom's success.[25] Despite differences, these Western perspectives reaffirmed Damrong's narrative. Siam appeared as an exceptional country where the monarch gave birth to the nation, limited Western influence, and formulated an alternate path to a uniquely Thai modernity.

In the 1950s, Thai scholars produced the first serious challenge to Damrong's royalist methodology by rewriting the country's history within a Marxist framework. Udom Srisuwan argued that there had been nothing "revolutionary" about the 1932 Revolution, which lacked mass support and left Thailand mired in a semifeudal society. His analysis of Thai economic production questioned the trope of continued independence, suggesting instead that Thailand shared the semicolonial characteristics of prerevolutionary China.[26] Western academics took longer to begin questioning the nature of "independence." In the 1970s, Benedict Anderson noted that Thailand's exceptional status was always assumed and celebrated but never concretely analyzed. This lack of analysis demonstrated that many historians accepted the existence of an unbroken thread of Siamese independence during the colonial era, which in turn proved the overwhelming success of the Royal-Nationalist narrative. Instead of assuming that independence vaulted Thailand forward on the path to modernity, Anderson speculated that Thailand was perhaps further behind for having been "indirectly colonized."[27]

In the past two decades, a number of scholars have challenged the mythology of Thai independence and in the process called into question the usefulness of the entire independent versus colonized paradigm. These studies point to a number of factors that suggest Western influence may have exceeded royal influence in shaping the development of the Thai nation-state. This includes the role of Western imperialism in establishing Thailand's current geopolitical boundaries, the impact of colonial influence on Thai judicial and economic systems, and the westernization of the cultural forms of the royal elite themselves.[28] Scholars such as Kasian and Peleggi have examined how the Thai elite solidified their position as rulers through mimicry of Western material culture and ideas of civilization.[29] Thongchai, along with Baker and Pasuk, acknowledge that colonial forces played a lead role in defining the boundaries of the nation-state, while their restraint allowed the monarchy to exercise suzerainty over the territory that remained. As a result, "colonialism engendered—rather than endangered—modern Siam as a political entity."[30] In her work on the southern provinces, Tamara Loos focuses on the pluralistic legal system employed by the monarchy to demonstrate that the Thai elite acted as both colonizer and colonized. Each of these revisions challenges Damrong's model of Siamese exceptionalism.

As the paradigm defining Siam's place in the modern world continues to take shape, scholars continue to debate the appropriate terminology for accurately describing Siam's connection to Western imperialism. Like Udom, Peter Jackson finds the Maoist concept of semicolonialism useful to describe the Thai elite's collaboration with demands of the global economy. Michael Hertzfeld prefers "crypto-colonialism," suggesting the Thai elite purchased "nominal political independence at the expense of massive economic dependence." Loos argues that both these terms are counterproductive because they further entrench the binary form of analysis that scholars should be attempting to dismantle. Moreover, the emphasis on the "colonized" aspect of Thai society ignores the imperialist activities of the Thai elite themselves. At present, a workable language for discussing the scope of Euro-American centrism remains elusive.[31]

Like the works mentioned, this book seeks to further undermine the binary classification of nonwestern states as "colonized" or "noncolonized" and provide additional insight into Thailand's accommodation with Western influence and its influence on Thai identity. Deconstructing the ideas embedded within National Humiliation discourse provides additional tools to analyze, rather than simply celebrate, the notion of Thai uniqueness. Long before Udom's idea of semicolonialism, other historians had begun to challenge Damrong's conception of Thai history as an unbroken chain of unblemished sovereignty. In the late 1930s, newspapers regularly published articles debating whether Thailand was completely independent in the modern sense. An article by Wichit Wathakan argued that the country had made great strides politically and eliminated the unequal treaties, but it did not control its own banks, insurance companies, ports, and other large corporate interests. Foreign control of the economy, he argued, meant Thailand might one day lose its political and judicial autonomy as well.[32] Led by Phibun, the new military elite characterized independence as an objective that had yet to be realized. Imperialism became an enemy that helped create the nation-state, but it did so in a way that retarded Thailand's progress. Like their Chinese counterparts, Thai writers portrayed the nation body as having been asleep for centuries, awakening only in reaction to imperialist powers constantly nibbling at its extremities. Damrong utilized Royal-Nationalist narratives to placate the masses, encouraging them to take pride in their country and accept the leadership of the monarchy. Wichit employed National Humiliation discourse to rouse the country to anger over its subservient status and promised that Phibun would restore Thailand's international prestige.

National Humiliation discourse also leads to a reinterpretation of the militarism and expansionism that occurred during World War II. Royal-Nationalist accounts have had great difficulty dealing with the rise of Thai fascism because the theme of *lost territory* becomes ascendant and destabilizes the narrative framework. In conventional histories, the irredentism of the Phibun era exists as an anomaly, an attempt to imitate the world's fascist regimes that ends immediately after Japan's defeat. Thamsook Numnonda attempts a different approach, portraying Phibun as the gifted leader who saved the nation through deft diplomacy. She argues that Phibun's alliance with the Japanese upheld Thai independence during the war, and following his downfall the maneuverings of the Seri Thai shielded the country from

Allied reparations. This dogmatic insistence that Thailand remained unoccupied throughout the global conflict requires a remarkably flexible concept of independence.[33] Royal-Nationalist writers interpret events in this manner to preserve the all-important sense of chronological continuity that must exist between premodern and modern worlds.

Narratives based on National Humiliation invert this model by depicting the crisis of 1893 as a rupture in the historical continuum, one that compromised contemporary notions of territorial integrity and royal sovereignty. It became a moment of death and rebirth. The Thai elite mourned the loss of territory and prestige while struggling to reimagine the boundaries and government of the emerging nation-state. Future generations developed a new language to express that loss. Thongchai has convincingly described the creation and function of the geobody but did not examine the imagined effects of loss or injury to that body. By the late 1930s, the Thai military elite had reconceptualized the Franco-Siamese crisis as the violent amputation of a limb from the body of the nation, then they successfully sold that concept to the nation. The resulting irredentist campaigns proved enormously successful in rallying citizens in support of government action against foreign countries. Of course, not everyone in Thailand accepted the new historiography. During the 1940 border crisis, Pridi and his clique denied that Thailand had just cause to attack French Indochina. Even at the height of the Preah Vihear dispute in 1962, there were many within Thai elite circles who privately recognized the controversy for what it was—the state's attempt to bully Cambodia into ceding a potential World Heritage site to Thailand.

Today, National Humiliation historiography continues to be utilized by an aspiring statesman seeking an explanation for the latest predicament. Its ideas have been prominent in the recent surge of Thai nationalism. Since the 1997 economic crisis, public intellectuals have recast Western capitalism as the greatest threat to the nation's well-being. This dialogue draws on a well-established tradition of anticolonial motifs (economic imperialism, Thais as the slaves of foreigners, and Western robber barons) in order to make Thailand's foreign debt appear just as illegitimate as its previous territorial losses. It also creates cohesion within the political community. As William Callahan has pointed out, political factions who disagreed about most issues were drawn together by their common opposition to the International Monetary Fund.[34] The history of National Humiliation discourse is a study of Thai resentment and suspicion directed towards the West.

CHAPTER SUMMARIES

The first chapter explores the roots of National Humiliation discourse, which emerged from Siam's efforts to repeal the unequal treaties. These negotiations conceded that the country's status within the international community had diminished and attributed that fact to Western intervention. The debate began a process of historical revision. Having concluded that Siamese sovereignty had been compromised, legal scholars searched the historical record for the event or persons most responsible. Since extraterritoriality and tariff concessions originated with the 1855 Bowring Treaty, this era received the most attention. It was not until after the 1893 crisis that the Siamese elite began to interpret the Bowring Treaty as a threat to their control over the kingdom. In 1855, Mongkut conceded certain aspects of Siamese sovereignty but benefited enormously from the resulting commercial trade relationships. In the 1900s, Chulalongkorn ceded territory to obtain a more modern type of sovereignty, a necessary concession due to the increased number of foreigners living in Siam. The negotiation over the unequal treaties was an important step in the eventual formation of National Humiliation historiography because it raised the issue of Siam kowtowing to Western powers.

Chapter 2 moves forward to the 1930s to explain how the Thai government constructed National Humiliation rhetoric and provoked a border conflict with French Indochina, all in order to bolster credibility for Phibun's growing dictatorship. Wichit used modern geography to define the *lost territories,* a symbol that effectively communicated a sense of victimization that masked Thai neo-imperialist ambitions in Southeast Asia. Maps, radio broadcasts, and newspaper articles demanded the return of these lands to restore national pride and liberate those left-bank Thais allegedly living under French oppression. State propaganda was very successful, as evidenced by the massive support for the government in the form of mass demonstrations and monetary donations. Although the terms of the Tokyo Peace Accord were disappointing, the lands ceded to Thailand supported the state's claims that the country had "defeated" France, regained its national honor, and therefore made great progress towards modernity.

National Humiliation discourse seeks to unify the country against foreign threats as well as against those within Thailand who seek to sell out the country. Chapter 3 examines the government's efforts to link Catholicism with French imperialism and expel the Church from Thailand beginning in 1940. The state's attempt to make Buddhism the national religion included government-sponsored harassment of minority religions. Muslims and Protestants were also affected by this policy, but Catholics were the primary target. For decades, missionaries had effectively used extraterritoriality to operate above the law. During the reign of Chulalongkorn, Thai rulers reacted cautiously as friars exercised political and judicial influence and defied the rule of provincial authorities while spreading a foreign religion. In 1940, Thai propaganda depicted the actions of these priests as evidence of colonial influence within their country. Because Phibun's fascist policies promoted external expansion and internal purification, the government attempted to break the Church's influence in Thailand. Thai Blood Party leaflets identified Catholics as enemies of the true faith. The government arrested clergy, banned meetings, and sanctioned mobs that attacked Catholics and destroyed Church property. The state maintained that the elimination of this foreign faith was necessary in order to achieve complete independence.

The Japanese invasion and occupation of Thailand forms the subject of chapter 4. It argues that Phibun blended National Humiliation discourse with Pan-Asianism in an effort to maintain the illusion that the Japanese occupation did not compromise Thai independence. During the war, the military elite acted as the buffer between the Japanese imperialists and the Thai people, appropriating Pan-Asian ideology and reformulating it for domestic consumption. In speeches and radio propaganda, Phibun drew on the theme of past suffering in an effort to establish continuities between the recent skirmish with French Indochina and Japan's larger war in East Asia. The Thai military had just finished a war to drive the French out of the Golden Peninsula; the next step was to help Japan eliminate Western imperialism in Asia. Thailand's official declaration of war on the Allies directly referenced National Humiliation, faulting Britain and the United States of failing to help during the Franco-Siamese crisis. Thus, narratives of loss formed the basis of a military partnership with Japan and of relations with those countries soon to be liberated. By supporting the Japanese, the Thai military elite hoped to secure a privileged position within the emerging hierarchy of East Asia.

Chapter 5 is a discussion of the postwar fallout. It challenges the narrative that Thailand escaped serious consequences from its dalliance with Japan, arguing instead that the Thai state was demoralized and disgraced by defeat. By focusing on the political debate within the National Assembly, this section demonstrates how the postwar regime attempted to distance itself from National Humiliation discourse and collaboration with Japan. In 1946, the new civilian government faced a serious dilemma over the fate of the four provinces obtained in 1941. After years of irredentist propaganda, it would have been difficult for any Thai government to give up land without sacrificing legitimacy. The government's ultimate decision to cede the provinces back to French Indochina raised a complex issue. Did its action represent a rejection of Thai irredentism, or was it simply bending to international will? Regardless, the transfer of the provinces to French Indochina in 1946 reopened the wound of past humiliation. For many, the loss of territory confirmed the National Humiliation perspective, just as the government was attempting to move away from that discourse. Royal-Nationalist narratives reinterpreted the military regime's legacy and cast Phibun in the role of the usurper. The memory of the *lost territories,* however, remained a much more complex issue.

The final chapter examines National Humiliation rhetoric in Bangkok's press coverage of the Thai-Cambodian dispute over Preah Vihear. The border tensions from 1958 to 1962 illustrate how this discourse can lie dormant for many years, only to erupt under the right conditions to transform Thai politics. From the Thai standpoint, this eleventh-century Hindu temple will be forever associated with the theme of *lost territories.* Preah Vihear was unknown to most Thais until 1941, when newspaper articles celebrated its "liberation" from France. Within National Humiliation discourse, Preah Vihear represented the four provinces ceded to French Indochina in 1946 and an opportunity to denounce the duplicitous diplomacy of the West. This chapter also explains why the Thai saw themselves as losing Preah Vihear in 1962, when in reality it had been part of French Indochina since 1904. This sense of grief triggered a massive wave of nationalist sentiment. The demonstrations, newspaper campaigns, and donations of money to the Sarit government were all part of a reenactment of the 1940 effort to recover the *lost territories.* Preah Vihear's significance now transcends its association with architecture, culture, or religion. It has become a discursive symbol of National Humiliation.

SOURCES

The research for this work made use of several archival collections found in the National Archives of Thailand in Bangkok. The Ministry of Interior catalogue contained a host of useful documents related to government strategies to build nationalism and limit French influence (including the Catholic Church) within Thailand. The Foreign Ministry, Ministry of Education, and other collections were also valuable. Since this projection is primarily an effort to understand how nationalists communicated ideas of loss to a larger populace, the majority of sources involve some form of popular media. Vernacular newspapers from the late 1930s and early 1940s provide an invaluable source of commentary and debate on relevant issues, allowing historians to sketch the mentalité of the era. The National Library of Thailand contains a diverse though sporadic array of newspapers. Clippings of related newspaper articles are also hidden within various files in the Ministry of Interior and *suan bukhon* collections at the National Archives of Thailand. Transcripts of speeches and programs broadcast over the radio occasionally appeared in newspapers or were published by the Department of Publicity. Most of Phibun's official speeches can be found on microfilm at the Chulalongkorn University Library. The Ministry of Interior also contains several copies of anti-French handbills distributed throughout Thailand. An important source of the Pan-Thai propaganda spread throughout French Indochina is the *Archives Nationale d'Outre Mer* in Aix-en-Provence, France. Records of the parliamentary debates from 1941 and 1946 were obtained from the library at Thailand's National Assembly. I am also indebted to the staff of the Assumption Cathedral archives in Bangkok for granting me access to unpublished personal accounts of Catholics who suffered religious persecution during the 1940 Franco-Thai conflict.

1 Constructing Loss

Repealing the Unequal Treaties in Siam

In creating National Humiliation discourse, Wichit and Phibun utilized imagery from the Siamese campaign to revise the unequal treaties. Prior to the invention of *lost territories*, the unequal treaties best illustrated Siam's struggle to reassert itself in a twentieth-century world dominated by Western norms and values. The issue helped create a forum wherein scholars could discuss the gap between Siam and the West, while denouncing European efforts to undermine sovereignty and slow national progress. Like the irredentists of the 1930s, treaty revisionists created a narrative that identified a critical moment of loss in Siamese history. They saw themselves as working to reverse that loss. Unlike Wichit's chronology, however, these reformers identified the 1855 treaty with Britain as Siam's *chosen trauma,* the event responsible for Siam's gradual decline. As we will see, the rhetoric of revision incorporated themes of betrayal and anticolonialism that proved anachronistic to Mongkut's negotiations with the British. In actuality, the language and narrative that Thai legal scholars employed to denounce the Bowring Treaty of 1855 was far better suited to the 1893 Franco-Siamese crisis.

THE UNEQUAL TREATIES IN SIAM

In the latter half of the nineteenth century, Siam signed a series of trade agreements with European countries that opened its economy to global capitalism. The negotiations were patterned after existing European treaties with China and Japan, which eventually became known as the "unequal treaties" because they placed two important restrictions on Asian countries. The treaties limited the amount of tariffs that could be placed on European imports, often to only 3 percent per annum. More importantly, the agreement exempted westerners from local law. The Bowring Treaty anticipated the influx of British immigrants to Siam, and because Europeans viewed Asian legal practices as both irregular and excessively cruel, they had serious reservations about allowing themselves to be subject to Asian law. Furthermore, Christian Europeans resented the prospect of having to obey the laws of a non-Christian nation.[1] The enforcement of this immunity required the establishment of a foreign consul in Bangkok, whose powers were defined by treaty. Foreign law in Siam was enforced solely at the discretion of this consul. This meant the consul was under no obligation to punish an offending Englishman in Siam, even if it could be proved he had violated British law.[2] In addition, extraterritoriality ensured that foreigners paid a reduced rate of taxation on any land they chose to purchase.[3]

Thais are not as familiar with the definitions of extraterritoriality as they are with the well-publicized struggle to repeal these European privileges. Lysa Hong argues that the Thai collective memory of extraterritoriality focuses exclusively on the heroic efforts to modernize the Thai state and elevate the country to a status on par with European nations.[4] The general public's perception of these inequalities has been shaped by the arguments of Royal-Nationalist historians. Prince Damrong first propagated the narrative that the British had forced King Mongkut to sign a series of humiliating concessions in order to preserve the nation's independence. This explanation appears in Damrong's book, *Khondi thi khapachao ruchak,* and for decades it was accepted by the general scholarship. Writing in the 1920s, Damrong projected his concerns regarding the unequal aspect of the Bowring Treaty onto the era of Mongkut. If we are to understand the evolution of public perception regarding the unequal treaties, we should begin with an analysis of the nationalist historiography that emerged following World War I.

Siamese legal scholars of that decade produced volumes of literature arguing for the removal of the unequal treaties. One prominent example is Luang Nathabanja's *Extra-territoriality in Siam.* Published in 1924, the book argued that extraterritoriality is a custom with medieval origins that no longer applied to a modernized, civilized nation such as Siam. Nathabanja, a graduate of Columbia Law School, began his case by expounding on the foundational principles and customs of international relations. First among these was the concept of sovereignty, that nations with accepted boundaries are independent entities with the right to establish "whatever form of government it wishes; it may form its social institutions upon any model; and it being a necessary result of independence that its will shall be exclusive and supreme over its territory."[5] States consequently have a corresponding right of jurisdiction; to decide what acts shall be deemed acceptable within its dominions, which extends over both citizens and their property. Individuals entering into foreign territory enter into a contract with the state, to obey its laws and maintain order and tranquility within the realm. Since law enforcement is the exclusive duty of the state sovereign, no nation should be able to exercise its own law within the borders of another nation. Foreign jurisdiction can operate only with the consent of the host country, which must be obtained either by legislative acts or by international treaty. Infringement of these rules violates the independence of the nation and places the offender "beyond the pale of the civilized community."[6]

According to Nathabanja, the great powers observed the above principles in their diplomatic relations with each other but denied the same courtesies to weaker polities such as Siam. Europeans believed that the laws of civilization did not apply to such backward countries, where local laws and institutions were deemed insufficient to maintain the requisite level of security. Siamese punishments, for example, were viewed as excessively cruel and barbaric. Finally, Europeans held that the principle of full sovereignty applied only to Christian states and that the citizens of these states should not be subjected to the laws and customs of non-Christian kingdoms. Nathabanja dismissed these justifications as a pretext for imperialist aggression.[7] He further suggested that the concessions made by states such as Siam only appeared to be voluntary, but in reality they were "wrested from the local state by threats or by sheer forces of arms."[8]

Nathabanja described the Bowring Treaty as the origins of Siam's humiliation at the hands of the Western powers. He argued that the treaty created a two-tiered legal system, one where "aliens began to enjoy even more rights and privileges than the citizens did. The national sovereignty was shorn off to some extent in favor of foreigners who came to seek wealth and pleasure in her domain!"[9] Another historian, writing much later, agreed with this assessment. Vichitvong Na Pombhejara argued that Mongkut's decision to grant Europeans consular jurisdiction was a major blow to Siamese absolute authority within the kingdom. His brief discussion of extraterritoriality reconstructed Siamese history since 1855 as a crusade fought by Royal-Nationalists to limit all forms of foreign aggression and intervention in Siam. By using twentieth-century legal principles to evaluate treaties from the mid-nineteenth century, scholars such as Vichitvong and Nathabanja created a narrative that associated the Bowring Treaty with inequality and humiliation. The history of the unequal treaties was transformed into a heroic struggle to regain lost sovereignty.

SIGNING THE BOWRING TREATY

Kullada Kesboonchoo Mead's work on the rise of royal absolutism in Siam presents the Bowring Treaty in a very different light. Arguing against Charles Tilly's "war makes states" thesis, Kullada follows Anderson's suggestion that Southeast Asian states centralized to better serve the expansion of the global capitalist system. Pressures and opportunities created by the world economy, not war, created the modern state in Siam.[10] The Bowring Treaty, therefore, played a critical role in the formation of the Siamese state. The government decided to abandon the traditional system of royal trade monopolies and tax farms in favor of entering the world economy and a policy of accommodation with the West. In doing so, it did not lose its sovereignty but developed a different conception of the term.

Nathabanja's narrative suggested that the British forced their way into Siam and strong-armed the monarchy into giving up sovereignty over the country. In actuality it was the Siamese, led by a group of young reformers, who initiated the negotiations that gave birth to the Bowring Treaty.[11] Mongkut's decision to embrace the West, however, was not without controversy. The prospect of entering into a trade agreement with Britain divided the Siamese court into two factions. In 1850, when Bowring's predecessor Sir James Brooke arrived in Bangkok intent on securing a trade pact, he perceived the court to be split "into the King's party and the Prince's party, and it may be generally taken for granted that the Princes themselves and the party adhering to their cause are favorable to Europeans, whilst the King and the opposite party are opposed to them."[12] These parties, with Rama III leading the more conservative group and Mongkut at the head of the pro-Western clique, split mainly over how the treaty would affect their personal fortunes. Conservatives had a vested interest in maintaining both the trade monopolies run by the Chinese and the tax farming system; while members of the pro-Western faction understood how to profit from the growing world economy and the new technology that would accompany it.[13] Even though the king's party prevailed and the court rejected the Brooke mission, most parties involved realized Siam was merely delaying the inevitable.

After Rama III died in 1850, the balance of power between the two parties shifted towards the young reformers. Mongkut became king due to the support of the pro-Western noble families, who pressed him to reconcile with the British as soon as circumstances would allow. When Sir John Bowring arrived in 1855, he found a Siamese elite determined to conclude an agreement, although serious differences still remained. Conservative nobles rallied to prevent the abolition of tax farms, causing the pro-Western faction to reformulate their argument and claim the abolition was necessary because the tax farms oppressed the common people.[14] Monopolies were abolished except for opium and firearms, both of which continued to be controlled by the king.[15] Many nobles also opposed Britain's requests for access to exported rice and the establishment of a British consul in Bangkok, a practice that would lead other foreign powers to follow suit. But the British also made small concessions. Bowring agreed to Mongkut's request that he extend his mission to Vietnam, so that Siam could avoid giving the impression it had lost its position regarding Laos and Cambodia by conceding to the British.

Kullada's work demonstrates that the Bowring Treaty was not a case of the British bullying Siam, as Nathabanja suggested. In spite of their limited bargaining power, the Siamese elite proved tough negotiators and profited a great deal from the resulting treaty. In Kullada's words, the majority faction within the Bangkok court "saw the potential benefits from the trade treaty and *welcomed* the British demands. Their perception and hard work brought about the conclusion of the treaty. The expansion of trade and production provided the basis for the establishment of the absolutist state under King Chulalongkorn."[16]

Obviously, this is not to argue that the Bowring mission refrained from the threat of force to enhance its bargaining position; rather that the Siamese elite benefited from the proceedings also. The treaty with Britain greatly enhanced Mongkut's position and created a new basis of political legitimacy. It was proof that the monarchy could preserve Siamese independence by negotiating with Western powers while adapting their technology and practices to local culture. Contrary to the accusations of legal historians, the monarchy was not humiliated by the imposed restrictions. During the negotiations, the issue of extraterritoriality was not a point of contention. As there were few British residents in Siam at the time, Mongkut did not view extraterritoriality as a potential threat to his authority within the kingdom. Instead, it was a natural concession for a Siamese monarch to make. The kings of Ayuthaya had granted extraterritoriality privileges to European merchants beginning in the seventeenth century.[17] The consensus among the Siamese elite at the time was that the king had strengthened the country's international position rather than weakened it.

ADAPTING TO THE UNEQUAL TREATY SYSTEM (1855–1893)

The Siamese found their new association with the West more rewarding than their previous relationship with the Qing dynasty. Prior to the Anglo-Chinese wars, Siam regularly sent tribute missions to China, acknowledging the emperor's status as the preeminent political authority in Asia and seeking trade opportunities within his realm. The Chinese rarely reciprocated these acts of diplomacy. For the West to actively court Siam, traveling to Bangkok several times to establish a trade relationship with Rama III and later Mongkut, proved gratifying to the Siamese elite. Constance Wilson points out that the Siamese enjoyed the foreign interest in their kingdom and took great pride in becoming a diplomatic center at a time when their political rivals in Mandalay, Hué, and Phnom Penh did not.[18] Mongkut understood that Siam was the lesser partner in the relationship (as it had been with the Chinese) and was prepared to tolerate another legal system operating within his country. Unlike China, Siam succeeded in avoiding a continual escalation of unequal clauses. The country ceded no territory until 1867 and did not pay a war indemnity until the conflict with France in 1893.

Far from undermining the monarchy, extraterritoriality helped Bangkok strengthen control over its network of vassals. In the 1880s, the Kingdom of Siam was still an extremely complex, fluid system of tributary relationships held together by the Chakri dynasty. A vassal state acknowledged the superiority of the Siamese monarchy by providing a recurring form of tribute in return for the overlord's protection and patronage. Vassal rulers aspired to regional autonomy, sometimes submitting to the authority and protection of multiple sovereigns in order to counterbalance competing claims and thus establish a form of independence.[19]

The 1855 Bowring Treaty forced the transformation and clarification of the overlord-vassal relationship. The British questioned whether the Lao kingdoms, which had not been signatories nor even participated in the negotiations, would honor the new agreement. As an important supplier of teak to British Burma, Lan Na received particular attention in this regard. A substantial population of foreigners already resided at the capital of Chiang-Mai. In 1860, British consul Robert Schomburgh journeyed to Chiang-Mai to make contact with teak traders and ascertain the political climate in Lan Na. The sovereign, Kawilirot, viewed the teak forests surrounding Chiang-Mai as his own private reserves and did not consider his natural resources subject to free trade regulations. He informed Schomburgh that he would not abide by the Bowring Treaty and requested that the British sign a separate pact with Lan Na. Schomburgh refused this request, referring the matter instead to the Siamese court. In 1863, a Burmese trader who qualified for extraterritorial privileges as a British subject filed a breach of contract suit against Kawilirot resulting from a teak transaction. In a consular court, the British judge decided Kawilirot had not been abiding by the rules of free trade. As a result, Mongkut summoned Kawilirot to the Grand Palace and ordered his subordinate to conduct his business in accordance with the new regulations.[20]

In this manner, the treaty system empowered Bangkok by allowing it to use the threat of foreign interference as leverage against its vassals. The British insistence on extraterritorial privileges for Burmese traders resulted in the enforcement of the Bowring Treaty in Chiang-Mai and a net loss of autonomy for Lan Na. Whereas client states such as Kedah had once been able to negotiate their own trade agreements and foreign relations, the unique requirements of the Bowring Treaty resulted in a more centralized approach to vassal-overlord relations. Foreign policy and trade pacts would now be dictated by Bangkok. Local sovereigns could either acquiesce or risk replacement. This change of policy demonstrates how the influx of British and French imperialism helped facilitate the process of political centralization. Once Britain and Siam stopped competing and began cooperating, they eliminated the bargaining power of vulnerable states and increased the level of their servitude. In this sense, Siam demonstrated its commitment to a treaty system that, although unequal, still offered important advantages.

The unequal treaties also spawned elements of modernization that the monarchy found distasteful. For example, extraterritoriality created conditions that led to limited press freedoms in Siam. Although Siamese monarchs are widely believed to have patronized the newspaper trade in order to educate their subjects, Copeland has argued that the press and monarchy had a very antagonistic relationship. In 1844, when an American missionary named Dan Bradley established Bangkok's first vernacular newspaper, Rama III openly opposed the endeavor, causing it to fail within its first year.[21] The monarchy, accustomed to a monopoly on the distribution of printed materials, understood the potential of newspapers to open up public discourse beyond its control. In the Bowring negotiations, however, Mongkut agreed not to place restrictions on foreign commercial activities in Siam, and this included foreign-owned publishers. Extraterritoriality ensured that the court's only recourse against newspapers critical of its policies was to bring libel proceedings against the publication in the consular courts and construct a case based on Western principles of journalistic propriety.[22] As a result of this immunity, foreign newspapers became a reliable medium for Siamese persons wishing to disseminate opinions or information critical of the monarchy. The press proved an annoyance to the throne until the end of absolute monarchy in 1932. Neither Chulalongkorn nor Vajiravudh managed to successfully use newspapers as a weapon against the extraterritorial privileges that made public dissent possible.

EXTRATERRITORIALITY AS A THREAT TO SOVEREIGNTY (1893–1907)

In the three decades following Bowring's visit to Bangkok, the conditions of the unequal treaties provided only minor annoyances, along with important benefits, for the Siamese elite. There was no pressing need to abolish or even revise the agreements until the Franco-Siamese crisis of 1893. Siam's defeat at Pak Nam humiliated its rulers by exposing the futility of their efforts to achieve parity with the West. Following its victory, France imposed a new system of extraterritorial regulations intended to grow French influence in Siam and challenge the state's jurisdiction over its subjects. It was during this period that the protégé system became a serious obstacle to effective governance, forcing Bangkok to develop a strategy for abolishing the unequal treaties.

Commenting on the 1893 agreement that ended hostilities between France and Siam, Lord Roseberry noted that it was designed by France to "keep the wound open."[23] In the hopes of eventually annexing the rest of Siam, the French colonial lobby sought opportunities for future intervention in Siamese domestic affairs. France's strategy for provoking future quarrels with Bangkok rested on expanding extraterritoriality. The French inserted Article IV into the convention, which stated, "The Siamese government must place at the disposal of the French Minister at Bangkok or of the French frontier authorities all French, Annamese and Lao subjects from the left (east) bank, and Cambodians detained for any reason whatsoever. It will not obstruct the return to the left bank of any of the former inhabitants of the region."[24]

This article reversed the terms of the Franco-Siamese treaty of 1867, which stated that local police and courts could exercise jurisdiction over any non-European detainees in either Cambodia or Siam. Thus, the 1893 convention represented an extension of extraterritoriality within Siam by granting protégé status to all residents of French Indochina, regardless of ethnicity. Henceforth, French authorities issued protégé certificates to Khmer,

Vietnamese, or Lao persons that guaranteed them French protection in the event of arrest by Siamese authorities. The French hoped to use extraterritoriality to increase their relatively weak presence in Siam and thereby counter British influence. This involved both encouraging the migration of residents of French Indochina into Siam and granting protégé status to non-Siamese persons already inside the kingdom. Alberta Defrance, the French minister at Bangkok, summed up the strategy as follows:

> We cannot claim to have any influence in this country beyond that of getting the treaty (of 1893) put into effect and protecting those who are already French nationals, and above all those who will become future nationals, namely all those people made to migrate in the past from Annam, Cambodia, and the (east) bank. Protecting them involves rescuing them from the kind of slavery in which they are now held by the princes and employees of the government; it implies defending them from the harassment to which they are vulnerable. This entails making a nuisance of ourselves and running counter to the Siamese government. There is no way of escaping this; we have no other means of action in Siam. Put succinctly, Britain controls the government of Siam and its officials. We depend on popular support against the government and against officialdom.[25]

By exploiting the ambiguities of Article IV, the French planned an invasion of Siamese sovereignty by supporting protégé registration on a mass scale. After registering with the French Legation, Indochinese persons would be immune from prosecution under Siamese law. Defrance also increased the number of nationalities that could be granted French protection. Having already assumed responsibility for other European nationalities in Siam, the French Legation viewed the 45,000 Chinese residents of Siam as a potential treasure trove of applicants. Also, the Siamese army was staffed by many Khmer and Lao soldiers brought forcibly from the left bank. Their registration as French protégés might disrupt Siam's military capabilities. Defrance's ultimate goal was to use the enlarged system of extraterritoriality as leverage with the Siamese government. The enlarged administrative apparatus necessary to handle the planned registration of 26,000 *ressortissants* required inflated registration fees and an additional subsidy from the Indochina government in order to defray the costs.[26]

From 1896 to 1907, the issue of protégés became a serious irritant for the Siamese government. As Defrance had intended, the controversy over which nationalities qualified for French protection mired the Siamese foreign office in almost daily disputes with the French Legation. Despite Bangkok's protests, French officials continued to sell letters of protection at random. In 1897, Siamese officials reported that a black market for these letters had developed along the upper reaches of the Mekong. Packets of blank forms were transported up the Mekong, then sold and resold. The highest bidder then signed his own name on the form and instantly acquired immunity from Siamese jurisdiction.[27] Bands of criminals allegedly carried both a French flag and letters of protection with them while engaged in all manner of illicit activities. France's extraterritorial policy also produced the desired effect on the Siamese military. The British minister in Siam observed, "Cases have occurred in which men actually serving in the Siamese army have got letters of protection and then committed acts of insubordination. What government is possible as long as such a state of things is tolerated?"[28]

France was not the only country to abuse the advantages of extraterritoriality. Clauses within the unequal treaty system dictated that any privilege conceded to one nation was automatically conferred on all nations. The French were by far the greatest offenders in this regard, but Britain and the United States also profited from the practice of selling letters of protection.

Early Siamese efforts to revise the system met with failure. In 1902, Siam signed an agreement with France that would have scaled back the immunity of Chinese and other French protégés from Siamese jurisdiction, but back in Paris it was rejected by a French colonial lobby that still harbored aspirations of annexing Siam into French Indochina. By 1904, however, the signing of the Entente Cordiale and the growing sense of rapprochement between France and Britain ended French hopes of acquiring Siam. Extraterritoriality lost its appeal as a system of political intimidation, and France considered surrendering its protector status in exchange for territorial considerations. That same year, France agreed to far stricter regulations concerning its system of diplomatic protection. It also pledged to withdraw from Chantaburi in exchange for Siam ceding the remainder of Champassak and territories opposite Luang Prabang to France.[29] In the 1907 treaty, France agreed to void the immunity of "French Asiatics" in return for control of Battambang, Siem Reap, and Sisophon provinces. Protégés who registered before the 1907 treaty would continue to receive French protection, but persons registering after that point would now be subject to the laws of Siam. Britain was even more demanding. In 1909, Siam transferred political authority over the Malay states of Kedah, Perlis, Trengganu, and Kelantan to Britain.

In return, Britain consented to reassign the consular jurisdiction over all British subjects to Siamese local courts, but only upon Bangkok's completion and implementation of the new modernized law codes.[30]

Thus, the critical loss of sovereignty mentioned by Nathabanja did not become a serious problem until after 1893. Although the Bowring Treaty, with its concessions on extraterritoriality, opened the door to European interference, it was only after the Franco-Siamese crisis that the French began abusing the protégé system in a way that challenged Bangkok's ability to govern its kingdom. Siam's 1907 treaty with France and 1909 treaty with Britain marked a significant milestone in the history of the unequal treaties. Most importantly, the agreements signaled an end to the practice of indiscriminately registering non-Siamese persons as protégés in order to exempt them from Siamese laws, taxation, and military service. It therefore constituted a significant step towards asserting a greater level of royal authority over the country and its legal system.

THE MOMENT OF "REDEMPTION"

The settlements of 1907 and 1909 removed the most threatening aspects of the unequal treaties, but other clauses remained in place. Siam's government still did not have the power to determine its own import tariffs or regulate trade with the great powers. Nor was its judicial system completely autonomous. Western legal advisors, paid by the monarchy, still supervised the international courts staffed by Western-trained Siamese judges. These conditions created the appearance of a colonial apparatus, which injured the pride of the monarchy. As Siam entered the twentieth century, the Bangkok elite worked to achieve a fully independent status within the international community.

In 1919, Siamese delegates traveled to the peace negotiations at Versailles to renegotiate unequal treaties with France, Britain, and the United States.[31] The delegates based their request for a revision of existing agreements on two principles. First, Siam had fulfilled its obligations to modernize key aspects of its bureaucracy and judicial system and had outgrown the need for supervision as mandated in the treaties, which was becoming burdensome. The legal anomalies of extraterritoriality prevented the establishment of a uniform body of consular law, while the recent enactment of a new Siamese penal code proved that legal reform was progressing smoothly.[32] Also, the negotiators hoped to use Siam's commitment to the Allies during World War I as leverage in the discussions.[33] The country had declared war on Germany, seized German assets, and sent an expeditionary force to fight in France. All of these actions demonstrated that Siam "had acted as an independent state in time of war and that it was reasonable and equitable that Siam should possess the full sovereign rights of an independent state."[34]

The effort was a complete failure. Preoccupied with the task of restructuring Europe and dividing empires in Africa and Asia, neither Britain nor France showed interest in Siam's requests. None of the Allies expressed an appreciation for Siam's contributions to the war effort, nor did they acknowledge Siam's claims of modernization. Even the United States refused to consider a new treaty arrangement, stating that the matter was unrelated to the peace process. The American ambassador advised Prince Charoon to send a separate delegation to Washington at some future date.[35]

Siam would have to wait until 1925 for revised agreements with the United States and France. Britain would follow suit the next year. By the end of 1926, all ten European powers with unequal treaty privileges had signed revised agreements. After another five-year grace period, all foreign residents would fall under the jurisdiction of Siamese courts, and the government assumed complete tariff autonomy. The monarchy celebrated this development as the moment when Siam freed itself from the humiliation of the unequal treaties. This achievement was so important that the People's Party attempted to take credit for it a decade later. The military regime that deposed the absolute monarchy claimed that certain vestiges of the old treaties remained in effect. Britain, for example, had stipulated a cap on Siamese steel, machinery, and cotton exports scheduled to expire in ten years. Even though the cap would have terminated in 1936, Foreign Minister Pridi Banomyong took action in 1935, canceling all agreements with Western nations and submitting new drafts to be signed. Upon the conclusion of these latest series of treaties in 1936, the new government declared that it had finally obtained total independence for Siam.[36]

CONCLUSION

The campaign to abolish the unequal treaties established a narrative that became very influential in the creation of National Humiliation discourse. The fight against extraterritoriality raised questions as to whether the country was completely independent; it rewrote Siam's history as a period of loss followed by redemption. Siamese patriots imagined the nation-state as eternal in nature, implying that modern notions of jurisdictions and sovereignty existed in premodern Siam before becoming casualties of Western intervention. Like Wichit's image of the *lost territories,* this narrative depicted the concept of sovereignty as an archaeologist might describe an ancient artifact: an item that had always existed but had just recently been restored to the nation.[37] In reality, efforts to revise the old treaty system transformed the Siamese elite's understanding of autonomy by imposing on them a Western ideological framework. It was a process of creation, not restoration.

Royalists and military apologists might squabble over the precise moment when Siam's sovereignty was restored; perhaps it would be more enlightening to ask when that sovereignty had been lost in the first place. Without blaming Mongkut for his decision to ratify the pact, legal scholars such as Nathabanja pointed to the Bowring Treaty as the critical juncture when Siam signed away several crucial aspects of its independence. As this chapter has argued, however, Nathabanja's discourse of compromised autonomy and the dangers of foreign intervention were reactions to the Franco-Siamese crisis. It was only after 1893 that France's protégé system made extraterritoriality such a pressing concern that Chulalongkorn elected to cede more territory in order to abolish it. By the 1920s, the campaign to eliminate all remaining vestiges of the unequal treaties appropriated the funerary language associated with the Franco-Siamese crisis: loss of honor and prestige, loss of sovereignty, loss of territory.

How did the Thai public react to the abolition of the unequal treaties? In the 1920s, most peasants were illiterate, there was no middle class aside from Chinese merchants, and even economic elites rarely took an interest in the government's foreign policy.[38] It is likely that ordinary people in Siam knew very little about the Bowring Treaty, the 1893 crisis, or the intricacies of extraterritoriality. Nor did the government see any reason to inform the people regarding these matters. The embryonic narrative that would become Siam's *chosen trauma* was therefore limited to the diplomatic community. In the 1930s, that would change. The military junta that assumed power after 1932 would go to great lengths to convince the Thai people that their country had been abused and dishonored by European imperialists. Whereas royal diplomats negotiated with Europeans to restore Siam's sovereignty, their military successors would resort to force of arms to restore its territory.

2 The Birth of National Humiliation Discourse

Today the date of May 9, 1941, no longer occupies a special place within the pantheon of important Thai historical events. Those history books that mention it usually do so to foreshadow the more important Thai alliance with Japan. At the time, however, the signing of the Tokyo Peace Accord ending the war with French Indochina was celebrated as the greatest triumph of Thailand's modern era. The war was a direct consequence of Phibun's efforts to popularize moments of injustice and defeat in Thailand's past. In the 1930s, Wichit meticulously defined a historical narrative on the *lost territories,* which claimed that the technologically superior West had bullied Thailand over the past half century and partitioned the peninsula. Through speeches, maps, and publications, the government communicated this sense of national humiliation to the people of Thailand. As a result, the border negotiations with French Indochina became a rare foreign policy issue that aroused public interest. Using National Humiliation discourse, the state persuaded large segments of the population that France had wronged Thailand in the past and that the border negotiations represented an attempt to avenge those wrongs. As 1940 drew to a close, growing support for a confrontation with French Indochina gave Bangkok a pretext for military escalation. Thailand's supposed victory in this conflict, in the form of the "return" of the four provinces, provided Phibun's military regime with a strong sense of political legitimacy.

THE PATH TO WAR

The causes of the 1941 conflict between Thailand and French Indochina—and especially Phibun's role in the dispute—have been the subjects of considerable debate among historians. In the immediate aftermath, many Western observers dismissed the conflict as the direct result of Thai opportunism. Scholars blamed Phibun Songkhram for the hostilities, describing him as a Japanese pawn who manufactured irredentist sentiment and exploited France's defeat in Europe, all in the pursuit of building a Greater Thailand.[1] In the 1960s, however, both the French and Thai governments released new information regarding the dispute, which softened Thailand's image as a ruthless aggressor nation. Using this new information, E. Thadeus Flood demonstrated that the imprecise border between Thailand and French Indochina had been an issue for decades before hostilities broke out between the two powers.[2] More recent studies explain Phibun's actions in 1940 within the context of ongoing diplomacy. As Kobkua argued, the irredentist drive to renegotiate Thailand's boundaries did not originate with the field marshal himself. Instead that dream constituted a "dormant sentiment hidden in the heart of every Thai leader since the loss of certain territories to France between the years 1893 and 1907."[3] These aspirations were confirmed by a 1941 newspaper interview with former King Prajadhipok, in which he rejected the popular perception that Japan had secretly instigated Thailand's quarrel with French Indochina. Prajadhipok, no supporter of Phibun or the military regime, confirmed that the northeastern border had been a perpetual foreign policy concern under the monarchy.[4]

The Thai government attempted to address the border issue on at least two occasions before Phibun began his irredentist campaign. Bangkok's main concern involved the 1904 treaty, which ceded two enclaves from the left bank of the Mekong River to France—one opposite Luang Prabang and the other across from Pakse in modern Laos. After this transfer, the river was no longer a continuous border between Thailand and French Indochina. In addition, the French interpreted the 1893 treaty to mean that the entire river, including any islands, constituted Indochinese territory. The irregular nature of this international boundary caused a series of diplomatic headaches for the Thai, further souring their relations with France.[5] Following World War I, the Thai worked to persuade France to sign a new treaty regarding the northeastern boundary. The 1926 Convention made modest alterations to the border, changing the demarcation line from the Thai riverbank to the deepwater channel of the Mekong. The revision was a step forward (from the Thai perspective), but it left Bangkok disappointed for two reasons. France stipulated an exception to the deepwater channel boundary rule, claiming that any river islands remained the exclusive property of French Indochina. Second, the agreement failed to establish the Mekong River as the official Thai–French Indochina border running from Burma to Cambodia, so the two left-bank enclaves ceded in 1904 remained French territory.[6] In 1936, the People's Party government attempted to revisit the border arrangement as part of its renegotiation of foreign treaties but could not convince French Indochina to alter the status quo.[7]

The border issue resurfaced in 1939 due to France's weakening position in both Europe and Asia. Anticipating conflict with Germany, the French were eager to safeguard their colonial possessions. To that end, the Quai d'Orsay proposed a mutual nonaggression pact with Thailand in August 1939. Sensing France's desperation, Phibun attempted to use the nonaggression pact as leverage to revisit the border with French Indochina. The Thai government informed French officials it would gladly sign a nonaggression treaty, if the issue of boundary demarcation was also part of the negotiations. According to Direk's account, the French government agreed in principle and planned to send a special diplomatic mission to Thailand to work out the details.[8] Armed with this assurance, the Thai government signed the Franco-Thai nonaggression pact in Bangkok on June 12, 1940. According to Flood, the treaty included a secret clause whereby France agreed to make the deepwater channel the boundary for the entirety of the Mekong and return to Thailand the two sections of territory opposite Luang Prabang and Pakse.[9] The Thai government was encouraged by the prospect of a peaceful border settlement, because it symbolized France's willingness to negotiate with Thailand as an equal rather than a semicolonized subordinate. The Third Republic's surrender to Germany on June 22 only increased Thai sympathy for France. Two days later, as part of his National Day radio address, Phibun encouraged his fellow citizens to put aside historical resentments (which his government had intentionally inflamed) and look towards a bright new era of Franco-Thai relations: "In view of recent events I have received many enquiries from those of you who take an interest in our neighbor, Indochina. I beg you, my dear brother-citizens, to forget that past and think of it as only a bad dream. In this way you will be able to sympathize with the fate of France, our friend, and extend her your understanding."[10]

This improvement in Franco-Thai relations was short-lived. The new Vichy government was determined to avoid the appearance of weakness regarding French possessions in Africa and Asia, and it refused to honor secret promises made by the Third Republic. This attitude was strongly supported by the colonial government in Hanoi. Phibun became increasingly suspicious as France pressured Bangkok to ratify the nonaggression pact even as it stalled on the question of boundary readjustment.[11] For Thailand, the two issues were inseparably linked. Phibun feared that once the treaty was signed, France's incentive to redraw the border would disappear along with Thailand's hopes for regaining any territory. In August, France notified the Thai government that it had consented to allow Japan to station troops in French Indochina and use its naval bases. This revelation brought a new sense of urgency to the discussions. If Japan moved to occupy all of Indochina, it would crush Bangkok's dream of making the Mekong its northeastern boundary. Phibun's government raised the possibility of growing Japanese influence in Southeast Asia to stoke fears about national security and increase hostility towards France.

On September 12, the Thai government made its last diplomatic effort to solve the impasse, agreeing to ratify the pact on the condition that France would honor the proposals in the aforementioned secret exchange of letters. The first two clauses required the establishment of the deepwater channel as the international border and the transfer of left-bank territory near Pak Se and Luang Prabang to Thai sovereignty. In addition, the Thai government made a third request: "His Majesty's Government would also be grateful if the French government would be so good as to give them a letter of assurance to the effect that in the event of a change from French sovereignty, France will return to Thailand the territories of Laos and Cambodia."[12]

France's immediate rejection of this final proposal placed the Thai government in a difficult position. Either the country would quietly discard its policy on the Indochina boundary, or else it must begin to consider the use of force. By this time, the border issue had attracted so much public interest that Phibun could not abandon it without seriously damaging his credibility. He decided to use the media to ratchet up the pressure on French Indochina. In mid-September, Bangkok newspapers published editorials advocating the justness of the nation's cause.[13] By early October, university students marched in the streets of Bangkok demanding the return of the *lost territories,* even if it meant war with France. As the country began sliding towards military confrontation, Phibun contacted several foreign governments regarding their opinions of Thailand's claims. British and American officials insisted on maintaining the prewar status quo.[14] The only great power sympathetic to Thailand's claims was Japan. Once Phibun committed himself to aggressively pursuing an irredentist agenda, he also brought the country closer to the Japanese.

Later that month, the prime minister gave a national radio address that explained the border conflict to the people of Thailand using National Humiliation imagery. He insisted that Thailand's claims were not threats of aggression; they represented an opportunity for France to atone for its past acts of belligerence. Phibun called on the nation to remain patient and calm, promising that if all citizens heeded the government's instructions, the country would eventually obtain a proper adjustment of the frontier.[15] The speech helped mobilize the nation behind the prime minister and sent a clear signal to French authorities in Hanoi that Thailand was fully prepared to achieve its objectives through military action. Over the next month there were numerous reports of airspace violations on both sides as ground troops mobilized along the borders. On November 28, French planes responded to Thai aerial incursions by bombing the northeastern city of Nakorn Phanom, injuring six civilians. Bangkok newspapers fueled nationalist outrage by portraying the bombing as the beginning of another French attempt to invade and colonize Thailand. Throughout the next month there were frequent clashes, as both Thai and French troops conducted raiding parties along the frontier. Finally, on January 5, 1941, the Thai army invaded French Indochina and within two weeks occupied portions of the Luang Prabang, Sisophon, and Siem Reap districts.

Phibun was not the first Thai leader to raise the issue of border negotiations with French Indochina. His real contribution was to bring the border dispute into the realm of popular discussion. The frontier situation had been a source of elite embarrassment since 1893; now with the state's new irredentist policy, the territories became a source of humiliation for the entire nation. It was this new narrative on victimization that helped push the country towards war. Likewise, the Japanese did not instigate the Indochina border conflict, but the conflict did help move Thailand away from its stated policy of neutrality towards Japan's sphere of influence.[16] Japan became directly involved in the Franco-Thai confrontation only after Phibun had already committed the nation to a military solution, which required Tokyo's consent. Flood described the conflict as "an important milestone in the long road that finally brought the two Asian powers together against the West."[17] It is important to note, however, that Thailand's invasion of French Indochina was not the result of Japanese prodding. It was born out of the military regime's search for political legitimacy.

CONSTRUCTING A *CHOSEN TRAUMA*

In order to generate support for Thai irredentism, the government began transitioning towards a new narrative regarding the 1893 Franco-Siamese crisis, one that portrayed Siam as the victim rather than the victor. Prior to the

1932 military coup, the victor narrative had been useful in boosting Thai confidence by congratulating the nation for maintaining its independence from Western imperialism. After taking power, the military elite realized that a new historical memory of the crisis was needed to erase the royal legacy and provide the new regime with political legitimacy. By portraying Siam as the victim of the Franco-Siamese crisis, the Phibun government hoped to increase animosity towards Western powers while also building support for military rule.

Reshaping public memory required the publication of materials suppressed by the monarchy. Following the actual defeat in 1893, Siamese princes banned discussion of the event for several decades.[18] The spectacle of King Chulalongkorn, Thailand's greatest monarch, frantically rushing back to Bangkok and submitting to the demands of a foreign power under threat of invasion, had severely damaged royal prestige. Any dialogue on these events might be interpreted as an attempt to undermine the institution of the monarchy by blaming it for the country's colossal failure. Furthermore, Siam's leaders worried that public debate of the issue at a time that France was still actively involved in Siamese affairs could provoke further hostilities between the two countries. From 1893 to 1907, French troops occupied Chantaburi and Trat provinces, while French officials worked to destabilize the Siamese government by registering large numbers of its subjects as protégés. The monarchy feared that any criticism regarding past conflict would jeopardize relations with France and possibly provide the French colonial lobby with a pretext for further involvement in Siam. In 1925, Prince Damrong blocked the publication of a Thai official's memoir concerning the French occupation of Chantaburi Province, citing its possible adverse effects on foreign relations.[19]

The military coup of 1932, however, reversed the dynamics of the conversation and made the 1893 crisis a central focus of an emerging discourse on Thai victimization. Siam's new rulers, the People's Party, adopted a much different approach to the loss and began linking it with the perception that the country's level of development still lagged far behind the West. Like their royal predecessors, the new elite were acutely sensitive to Siam's inferior status within the world community, which they had used as justification for overthrowing the monarchy. At the same time, the military clique understood that the economic depression of the 1930s had significantly weakened the Western imperialist apparatus, providing an ideal opportunity to address the remaining inequalities in trade agreements with Europe.[20] The gradual atrophy of France's military muscle also allowed the Thai government to begin publicly criticizing the French and actively cultivating public resentment over

France's mistreatment of Siam in the past.[21] This new attitude represented an important shift in Thai historiography. Royal-Nationalists interpreted the Franco-Siamese crisis as a victory for Siam by emphasizing the king's brilliant strategy of sacrificing a finger to save the hand. The irredentists among the military elite, however, viewed the crisis of 1893 as the low point in the country's history. The humiliating defeat at Pak Nam and consequent surrender of territory meant the army (and, by association, the country) had lost its honor. Despite this emphasis on national shame, irredentist historians did not assign blame to the monarchy, which the People's Party still credited with preserving the kingdom. Instead, the new narrative focused attention on past instances of French imperialist coercion and its costs. In a 1940 speech on the subject, Wichit argued that previous historical accounts had been forced to conceal the truth concerning the 1893 crisis for fear of foreign reprisals.[22] Under the Phibun government, however, scholars used National Humiliation discourse to analyze their history of foreign relations. The regime speculated that once the people understood how France had taken advantage of Siam in the past, they would support its attempts to correct these injustices, starting with a revision of the Indochina border.

Now that the absolute monarchy had been deposed, the Thai state argued that France's 1893 invasion constituted a crime against the Thai nation. The accusation rested on a geographical anachronism, namely that the territory in question had been incorporated into a fully formed Siamese nation-state, and that French invaders had stolen it. Wichit's writings frequently described French colonial officials as a band of pirates, rather than the diplomatic emissaries of a civilized country.[23] In the months prior to the border war with French Indochina, Wichit published several articles attempting to expose how France had repeatedly violated international conventions in its interactions with Siam: "I wish to prove that [France's] action regarding territory from Sib-song Chu Thai to Cambodia was a gross act of cruelty, devoid of moral principles. They at first tried to cheat us, but when they could not do so they commenced to rob us. Not satisfied with robbing our territory, they took our money as well. . . . The more I delved into the records of the past, the more I came across gross cruelty, oppression, and bullying."[24]

National Humiliation rhetoric marginalized the heroism of the king (without denying it) and instead stressed that the Franco-Siamese crisis was an embarrassing defeat at the hands of French barbarians. In this narrative, the Thai state redefined the meaning of heroism—depicting the nation as heroic because it had been the victim of colonial oppression, which now gave it the moral high ground in the current border dispute. One example from the newspaper *Nikorn* described the original Franco-Siamese confrontation over the left bank of the Mekong River as an "invasion." Although the army fought courageously, its weapons were not sharp enough to cut through the net used by France to ensnare the peoples of Southeast Asia. Since Siam was a peaceful country, the army accepted defeat and withdrew from its eastern lands rather than prolong the misery of war. The victorious French military then divided the country into arbitrary administrative districts that separated the Thai peoples from their relatives in French Indochina. According to the article, the sword of France cut deep into the right shoulder of the nation's body, leaving the country with a gaping wound that had yet to heal.[25] In this manner, irredentists such as Wichit reconstructed historical memory as a form of national trauma, something that was universally felt among all Thais at the time, rather than just a source of royal shame. Wichit described how it became popular for Thais to tattoo the word "Trat" on their arms, in remembrance of France's refusal to honor its pledge to withdraw from Siam and its continued occupation of the southeastern province.[26] This fabricated legacy helped the generation of the 1940s imagine a connection to their ancestors and subsequently formed the core of anti-Western sentiments being expressed. Pamphlets titled, "Awake Thai People!" were distributed throughout Bangkok and other cities, reminding readers that "RS 112 is a sad history that is inscribed on the hearts of the entire nation.... This bitter memory will be handed down from generation to generation until it is somehow erased."[27] This sense of victimization could only be erased if justice were done—meaning that France must agree to return the *lost territories* to Thailand.

DEFINING THE *LOST TERRITORIES*

Irredentism is often an exercise in geographical anachronism. Phibun and Wichit argued that certain areas of what are now the nation-states of Laos and Cambodia were once an integral part of a Thai nation-state that existed prior to France's arrival in mainland Southeast Asia. Over time, these lands have been canonized as the *lost territories*. The precise meaning of this term, or its exact geographical boundaries, proved remarkably flexible during the twentieth century.[28] A Thai geography textbook published in 1908 referred only to the "left bank territories of the Mekong" as a region that once belonged to the Siamese kingdom.[29] By the late 1930s, school texts incorporated maps indicating both Laos and Cambodia as part of Thailand's territorial heritage.[30] In his initial negotiations with the French, Phibun requested only the return of the two right-bank enclaves ceded in 1904; yet at the same time the Ministry of Interior printed *lost territory* maps that included the Burmese and Malay states ceded to Britain.[31] Even Wichit's definition of what once belonged to Thailand varied depending on his audience. In October 1940, the minister of fine arts told a group of teachers and students at a military college that Thailand should not content itself with land from Pakse and Luang Prabang but should demand the return of all territory taken by France.[32] Two months later, he slightly modified his expectations: "If I may be allowed to pick out the territories to be returned to Thailand, I should propose only Sipsong Chuthai and Luang Prabang with the establishment of a national border along the Mekong frontier by which France will be requested to cede some islands in the Mekong and a small plot of land opposite Pakse."[33]

This quote illustrates the problem facing the Thai government as it formulated its irredentist demands. The government had difficulty identifying the territories it hoped to recover because it was still in the process of constructing, or imagining, the extent and nature of its loss. The *lost territories* were not a location. They functioned as a symbol, a monument commemorating the idea of a National Humiliation. Since the meaning of the symbol proved remarkably flexible, it could also be continually reinterpreted and used by later generations to meet contemporary needs.

The *lost territories* facilitated the transition from the Royal-Nationalist narrative of victors to the National Humiliation story of victims. This shift provided the Phibun regime with a political issue that unified the country behind his leadership—irredentism. As a respected intellectual who served both the monarchy and the succeeding military regimes, Wichit Wathakan played an important role in defining the loss and pushing irredentism to the forefront of the nationalist agenda. His work, *Prawatisat sakon* (A Universal History), was one of the first publications to directly acknowledge Siam's defeat and argue that it should be integrated as part of Siam's national history.[34] The twelve-volume treatise chronicled France's expansion at Thai expense, dividing the nation's loss of territory into five specific incidents. First, the eastern section of Cambodia ceded in 1867, followed by the cession of Sibsong Chuthai in 1888, the left-bank region in 1893, the loss of the right-bank territories in 1904, and finally *monthon burapha* (the eastern territories) in 1907. This chronology was republished as a separate volume in 1940, complete with maps.[35] Sections also appeared in Bangkok's English-language newspapers under the heading, "Thailand's Case." In the introduction of the

English version, the author explained that the purpose of his essay was to help the world understand the bitterness Thais felt towards the French by explaining the historical background of the current border dispute.[36] Its real purpose was to manufacture resentment towards France, not to explain it. Wichit used his skills as an author, songwriter, and playwright to communicate this sense of victimization and the importance of regaining the *lost territories.* He composed a play titled *The Five Periods Thailand Lost Territory to France,* which was performed at fundraisers with Wichit himself providing an introduction.[37] His popular song "Cross the Mekong" included the lyrics, "the two banks of the Mekong will be like one," implying that French Laos would soon be absorbed by Thailand.[38]

Thongchai has argued that cartographic depictions, such as the maps featured in *Thailand's Case,* sometimes invent geobodies that never existed and project them into the past.[39] Wichit's historiography provides an important example of this phenomenon. His work assumed that Siam had been a nation-state in 1893, and that the Chakri dynasty exercised a modern sense of sovereignty over the Lao and Khmer territories in question. In actuality, France and Siam were locked in competition for control over those areas, a competition that Siam lost.

The ability of modern maps to give form to imagined premodern polities serves to codify the loss, helping each generation of Thais instill a sense of victimization in its descendants. It is also important to note how Wichit employed chronology to quantify Thai suffering, identifying five examples of Franco-Thai diplomatic interaction and grouping them together under the category of "territorial loss." This sequential model pinpoints the negotiations over Cambodia in 1867 and the Sib Song Chuthai in 1888 as examples of amputation that preceded the Franco-Siamese crisis. It is doubtful, however, that the original participants perceived those events in a similar manner. In the case of Cambodia, the Thai monarchy agreed only to recognize the establishment of a French protectorate, and this in return for France's pledge never to fully annex the region. In 1888, the Thai military commander Chaomuen Wai Woranat withdrew his forces from northern Laos, leaving the French in possession of the Sipsong Chuthai region.[40] Neither incident involved military engagement. Did the Thai elite view themselves as ceding these regions to France, or did they interpret these areas in terms of shared or questionable sovereignty? Clearly these two events did not constitute the same type of defeat Siam experienced years later. By grouping them within the larger narrative of "How Thailand lost its territories to France," Wichit attempted to enlarge the sense of humiliation associated with 1893 and apply

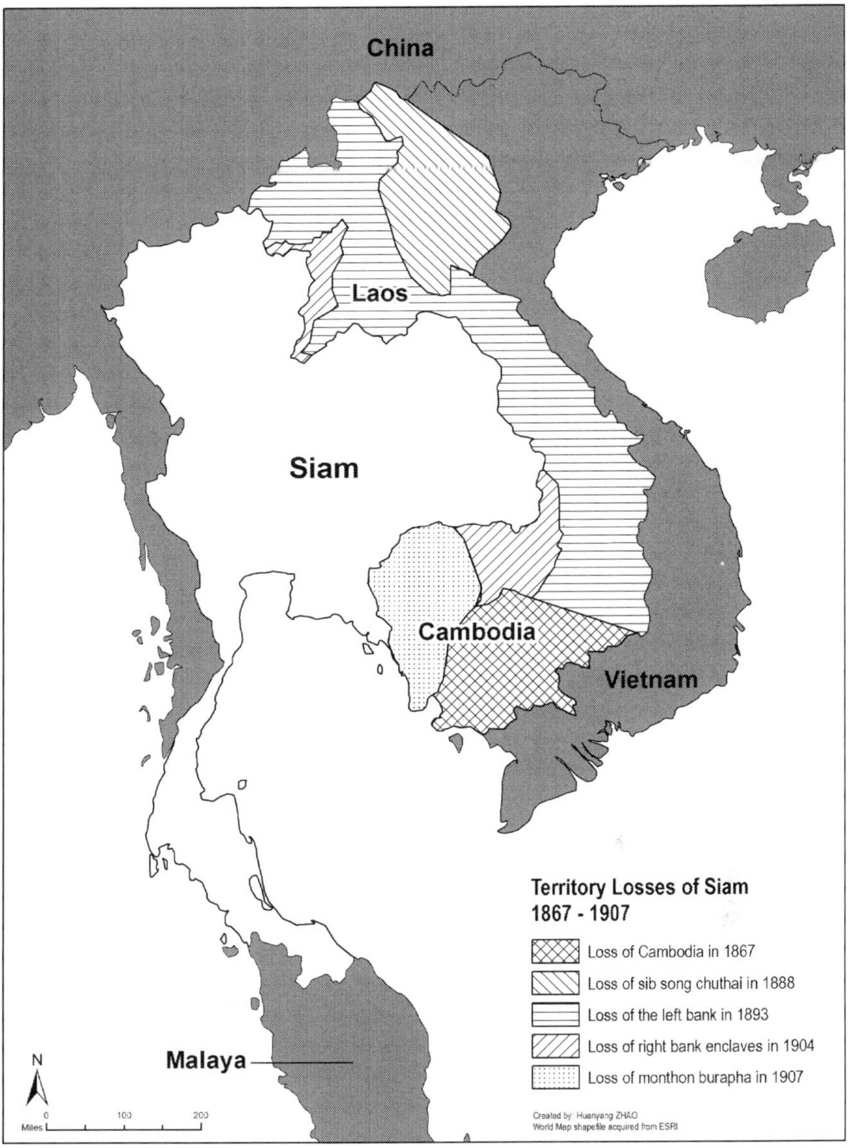

Figure 1. A reproduction of an irredentist map circulated by the Thai government in 1940. (Created by Huanyang Zhao)

it retroactively to previous episodes of Franco-Thai interaction. As a result, the wound inflicted by France appears to protrude even deeper into the past.

THE "LEFT-BANK THAIS"

An important component of National Humiliation ideology was its insistence that the Lao and Khmer were not separate ethnic identities but constituted subgenres of a greater Thai race. Prior to the twentieth century, the Kingdom of Siam was overtly stratified according to racial characteristics. The Siamese elite distinguished themselves from the Lao of the Mekong River valley. Towards the end of Chulalongkorn's reign, the monarchy began to appropriate Western anthropological classifications to show themselves as more civilized than the rural peoples of the northeast.[41] As late as the 1920s, school textbooks still specified how the Lao in the region of Laos were different from the Thai in Siam.[42] The next decade, however, witnessed an attempt at racial homogenization that would erase ethnic and cultural differences and stress links between the Thai, Lao, and Khmer races. Beginning with the book, *The Tai Race,* written by an American missionary, scholars began speculating about the existence of an ancient race of which the Siamese and the Lao were modern descendants.[43] Building on this premise, Wichit Wathakan imagined the Thai race as being divided into two branches: the "greater Thai" and the "minor Thai." His 1933 book, *Siam and Suwannaphum,* classified the Shan of northern Burma as part of the first category, while the Siamese and Lao belonged in the second category. According to his theory, the word "Lao" was actually a misnomer that resulted from the imposition of French rule over the left bank of the Mekong. In reality, he argued, the Lao had just as much Thai blood as the Siamese. Wichit's play *Ratchamanu* adopted a similar theme by attempting to portray the Thai and Khmer as members of the same race, with the Thai acting in the role of the elder brother.[44]

These racial theories provided fodder for the irredentist movement in Thailand just as similar theories had done in Europe. In 1939, Chalerm Kasaiyakananda published a piece on Thai nationality in *Yudhakos,* the monthly journal of the Thai military.[45] In the article, Chalerm criticized the country's education system and complained that his generation had been taught that there were many races in Thailand. This idea, he argued, was not only inaccurate but also dangerous, since the recent demise of Czechoslovakia was caused by its divided nationalities. There should be no more talk of ethnic plurality, Chalerm continued, because the current constitution defined Thailand as one and indivisible. The government's decision to change the country's English name to Thailand in 1939 reflected the illusion that the country was ethnically homogenous. It also promoted connections between Bangkok and related ethnic groups in neighboring countries. Other writers applauded the name change, as it affirmed their view of the country as the center of all the branches of a larger Thai race, encompassing peoples in Burma, French Indochina, and Southern China.[46] At the end of 1940, while the Bangkok media promoted rumors regarding the impending collapse of French Indochina, nationalists envisioned the creation of a new "Golden Peninsula," where the various races of mainland Southeast Asia would unite under Phibun's leadership.[47]

By October 1940, the Thai state regularly referred to the Lao as "left-bank Thais" in its official communications. The new terminology was part of an effort to promote Thai expansion. The government encouraged the people of Thailand to empathize with their "relatives" living under French rule. In a radio broadcast, Phibun explained that people who still believed the Lao, Khmer, and Thai to be separate races were mistaken. The Lao and Khmer were Thais deprived of their independence when they fell under foreign rule but who still maintained many similarities to the Thai in religion, culture, and tradition despite the effects of French oppression: "The Thai people over there also believe in Buddhism while the French believe in the Catholic religion; the Thai eat rice, but the French eat bread; the Thai eat curry and *namprik,* the French eat beef-steak; the Thai reside in up-country districts, the French reside in the city; the Thais are of yellowish complexion, the French white; the Thai cannot possess radio receiving sets, the French can; the Thai can not possess even knives or firearms to protect their property, the French can and use them."[48]

According to Phibun, the only real difference between Thai citizens and left-bank Thais was the freedom provided Thailand's citizens under the Constitution. Yet he remained confident that once the border dispute had been settled, these "relatives" would be returned to Thailand's jurisdiction and enjoy the protection of Thai sovereignty.[49]

The suffering of the left-bank Thais living under French rule became an important irredentist theme in the months leading up to the 1940 border war. The suffering of Thai relatives in French Indochina became part of the overall legacy of loss and created connections with the Thais in Thailand. Wichit described his concern for Thailand's ethnic relatives and related his experience of looking at the Mekong and seeing a "river of tears" shed by those living on the other side.[50] For several months, Bangkok newspapers carried stories on the "horrible" conditions in French Indochina and suggested that the colonial state was on the verge of collapse following the arrival of Japanese troops. Cross-border skirmishes along the Mekong between French and Thai troops caused Indochinese merchants in nearby towns to close down their shops. Thai correspondents alleged widespread food shortages in Cochin China, owing in part to the decline of rice shipments from Bangkok to Saigon.[51] Thai newspapers also reported that growing discontent with the colonial regime had forced the French to disarm colonial soldiers to prevent them from either rising up against their officers or taking their rifles with them as they deserted to join the Thai army.[52] In an effort to stir up emotions on both sides of the border, Radio Thailand broadcast paragraphs from a French publication, *Indochine S.O.S.,* a highly critical account of the methods used by the French colonial secret police.[53] The author, Andrée Viollis, claimed to have observed French officials causing starvation, withholding drinking water, and caning the soles of the feet of Indochinese suspects. French police forced suspects to drink kerosene, squeezed their bodies with wood presses, or used pins to prick under the fingernails. Interrogators inserted coils into the penises of captives before violently pulling them out. Women were tied to the ground, their legs forced open and red ants released into their vaginas. Worst of all, the broadcast mentioned examples of Senegalese and Arab soldiers raping and murdering local women.[54]

This accusation of violence against women was very effective at increasing hatred of France. Newspaper editorials claimed it was common practice for a French administrator to take a native girl as a mistress, only to later abandon the woman and her offspring once his term of service expired.[55] The large number of African troops in the French colonial militias was also used to unnerve the Thai populace, appropriating the stereotype of the "black barbarians" who were likely to run amok in the event of an invasion. A political cartoon from a Thai newspaper exploited popular conceptions of the French as sexual predators. In it, a messenger arrives on horseback to announce that the French army, including *khaek dam* (Black Africans), is approaching the village. The chief then tells his daughter to hide herself. When the French officer arrives, accompanied by his African adjutant, he orders the villagers to provide his troops with female companionship.[56] These images demonstrated the plight of the Lao and Khmers to Thai audiences, and they also allowed nationalists to proclaim the superiority of Eastern morality over Western depravity.[57]

Thai propaganda attempted to use religion as a wedge between French and Thai peoples by claiming that the French restricted the practice of Buddhism and encouraged Catholicism. Newspapers carried stories of colonial officials transforming monasteries into prisons or police stations and then melting down the statues of Buddha for use as copper wire.[58] Buddhist monks were forced to pay the capitation tax and salute any French soldiers they encountered on the street.[59] With Thai nationalism on the rise in the late 1930s and early 1940s, French police often suspected monks of being part of a Thai spy network that had infiltrated the colony. During one incident in Cambodia, French police arrested several monks on suspicion of having provided intelligence to the Thai military. In the process, one of the monks was shot in the left eye socket. After interrogation, officials found no evidence of conspiracy and allowed the monks to return to their monastery.[60] The harsh treatment of religious clergy fueled resentment against France and lent credence to Thai accusations that the European colonizers wanted to destroy Buddhism.

Within this new environment of Buddhism under siege, the government transformed religious buildings into models of pan-Thai unity. One example was Wat Phra That Phanom in the northeastern Nakorn Phanom Province. This temple had functioned as an important spiritual center for peoples of the Vientiane cultural region for hundreds of years before the Mekong River became an international boundary. During the town's yearly festival, people from the left bank and several other provinces in Thailand would travel to Nakorn Phanom to worship at the site.[61] In October 1940, Wichit visited Phra That Phanom and quickly recognized its potential as a symbol of the close cultural interactions that transcended political borders. On his return to Bangkok, he persuaded the government to spend 20,000 baht on renovating the temple and gilding the main Buddha statue.[62] The juxtaposition was striking. At a time when Bangkok newspapers were filled with reports of French officials looting and ransacking monasteries in French Indochina, the Thai government was establishing itself as a protector of the religious ties that united the left and right banks of the Mekong.[63]

Wichit's visit to Nakorn Phanom was part of a larger propaganda campaign to convince the Lao and Khmer peoples of Indochina that their interests coincided with those of Thailand. As early as 1938, foreign journalists reported on the activities of Thai agents in Laos, including an increase in the availability of anti-French pamphlets.[64] In the final months of 1940, Radio Thailand boosted its broadcast signal to reach a wider audience in French Indochina. The Thai air force flew multiple sorties over Indochinese air space in order to drop handbills written in Lao, Khmer, and even Vietnamese, explaining Bangkok's intentions to the people below. Josiah Crosby of the British Legation in Bangkok reported to his superiors that Thai propaganda agents were hard at work promoting the pan-Thai agenda throughout Laos and as far north as the Sipsong Panna region of southern China.[65] Propaganda aimed at the left-bank Thais incorporated two major themes. First, Bangkok wanted to convince the Lao and Khmer that they had once been united with the Thai, but that the 1893 crisis resulted in a racial partition. Second, the campaign announced that Thailand was preparing to avenge that humiliation and reunite with its brethren languishing in colonial bondage.

The Thai state claimed that its propaganda campaign in French Indochina was an effort to educate its neighbors concerning their own history. Newspapers, radio broadcasts, and handbills all repeated the theory that the region's troubles could be traced back to the interference of Auguste Pavie.[66] The peninsula had been racially and politically unified before the military intervention of the French, who fabricated false boundaries and even false names signifying different branches of the same race. These pamphlets used language suggesting that the author was not from Thailand but a local individual who had come to realize the truth, as the following example indicates:

IMPORTANT EVENTS FOR THE THAI BLOOD

> The moment is coming when we are going to find ourselves united to form one bloc as before.
>
> We should all recognize and understand the history of our race, for the expression "Lao" certainly did not come from us. It is the name the foreigners gave us. Not having understood this fact, we have continued to call our race *Laotienne* as they have done. The same mistake was made concerning Thailand, to which the foreigners gave the name Siam. Today that name no longer exists, having been replaced by a Thai name that better corresponds to our race.
>
> The Thai Blood belong to a race already four thousand years old. We are, each of us, of Thai blood and we have formed the same country since antiquity. We became separated one from another hardly forty-seven years ago, by the French barbarian pirates who named those of us on the right bank "Thai," and those of us on the left bank "Lao." In actuality, all the individuals on both banks, regardless of the villages and groups to which they belong, speak the same language and say, "We are related and have the same blood in our veins."[67]

The assertion that the two peoples had been separated for only forty-seven years was part of the Thai state's attempt to draw the Lao into their recently constructed tent of victimhood. Other forms of propaganda contained the chronology of France's aggression. The Thai government produced a *Book of Songs* that it distributed to traditional Isan singers throughout the border regions. The book was designed to "familiarize [the singer] with the history of successive territories seceded to France."[68] Each verse described a separate incident in which Thailand had been forced to give up territory to France. Bangkok proved very adept at exploiting cultural links for propaganda purposes, as evidenced by Phibun's decision to send *mo lam* singers to Laos in 1940.[69]

After explaining how people on both sides of the Mekong had been injured by the tragedy of 1893, Thai propaganda sought to persuade the Lao and Khmer that they could avenge the loss by working together. In his October 1940 nationwide radio address, Phibun posed what he saw as the central question of the Franco-Thai dispute: "When will the French go away and when will our Thai brethren and the Annamese be free?"[70] There was strong sentiment within Thailand that the French had "profited off the backs of Thais" for long enough, and it was time for them to return to their own country.[71] The Thai state wanted the people of Indochina to know that neither Laos nor Cambodia was Thailand's enemy in this conflict; only those who actively supported the colonial apparatus would be targets. During the war, Thai planes dropped leaflets over Laos and Cambodia warning residents to avoid French office buildings and military installations, as these would be the primary targets of future bombing raids.[72] Many of these same tracts asked readers to join with the Thai against their common enemy. One pamphlet confiscated by French police contained the following invitation, supposedly written by the Governor of Ubon Province: "I also invite you—Thai, Annamite, Kha, and Cambodian brothers and sisters—to rise up and arm yourselves with rifles to chase the enemy from our country, the French who have drunk our blood for so many years already. Therefore, let us unite to chase out the French race along with their troops who are the most cruel and inhumane of men."[73]

In a December 1940 newspaper article, Wichit asserted that Indochinese peoples were already working to help the Thai against the French. Some began cutting telephone lines and refusing to pay the capitation tax.[74] Others demonstrated their faith in Thailand by emigrating. Media coverage of the dispute featured ongoing reports on the constant stream of migrants across the border into Thailand, including the efforts of local government to accommodate the newly arrived refugees.[75] The state saw this influx of migrants as another opportunity to establish itself as a patron of all Thai peoples. It granted immediate citizenship to immigrants from all regions of Laos and Cambodia and worked to raise funds to provide for newly arrived refugees.[76] A group of private citizens who had been born in 1893 contacted Phra Pathum Thewaphiban, the director general of the Ministry of Interior, also born that year, to request that he compile a list of potential donors. Donations received from these wealthy individuals were used to support families crossing into Thailand. This organization adopted the name "47" and asked all patrons to contribute amounts with the terminal figure 47, signifying the number of years that France had occupied the left bank.[77]

National Humiliation discourse provided the Thai state with a useful tool for disguising its expansionism as a policy of liberation. Irredentists did not view their twin goals of freeing the peoples of Indochina and annexing those territories as contradictory. As we have already discussed, Phibun's government rejected the notion that Laos or Cambodia were legitimate national spaces separate from Thailand, just as it refused to acknowledge the Lao or Khmer identities as being culturally distinct from Thai identity. Bangkok viewed these people as Thais living in a part of Thailand that had been occupied by the French for forty-seven years. Wichit himself described the situation in similar terms, claiming that although "the body of Thailand was safe, its arms and legs were bound and abused."[78] From another perspective, the insistence on freeing "our Thai brethren" was a discourse on self-liberation. It provided a language capable of expressing the trauma of 1893 without completely repudiating Royal-Nationalist historiography.

WE HAVE WAITED LONG ENOUGH

In all of its public statements, the Thai state vowed that it would go to any lengths to regain the *lost territories*. Within Phibun's cabinet, however, there was serious disagreement over how to respond to the Vichy government's refusal to revise the boundary lines. While the prime minister remained convinced that war was the only possible means of obtaining the country's objectives, Pridi argued that the government should opt for a more peaceful solution by bringing the matter before the International Court of Justice.[79] The idea of submitting Thailand's grievances before a judiciary body, which could take years, failed to satisfy a public that craved immediate action. Following Phibun's radio address in October 1940, popular support for military intervention grew steadily. Each week the newspapers reported a new violation of Thai airspace by French planes or the exchange of gunfire across the Mekong River. As the public became increasingly impatient, media outlets began to question the government's resolve: "The people really wish to know why we are still waiting, and are inclined to the belief that this only affords a chance for the other party to be better prepared every day. We have waited long enough, and we realize that such waiting, based on peaceful methods will result in still more waiting without end. Hence we all wish to know how long we should have to wait and what is it that we are waiting for. Who can enlighten us?"[80]

Implicit in the phrase "We have waited long enough" is the notion that Thailand had been attempting peaceful negotiations for the past five decades, but now the time for diplomacy was over. In late November, the newspaper *Thai rashdra* conducted a public poll on how the government should resolve the situation with French Indochina. It reported receiving 3,300 responses, each one in favor of declaring war.[81] Pridi's appeal for restraint was doomed from the beginning, largely because Phibun's own supporters felt a peaceful solution would be far less satisfying. The Thai military viewed the humiliation of 1893 as born out of conflict; it could only be undone through conflict.

The army saw violence as unavoidable because France refused to admit its own diminished status as a defeated nation. Even with Germany occupying Paris and Japanese troops in Hanoi, French officials maintained their condescending attitude towards Bangkok. "We have requested the return of our territories," wrote one journalist, "but instead of negotiating France shows us only contempt."[82] British ambassador to Thailand Sir Josiah Crosby agreed with this assessment. Reporting on the deterioration of Franco-Thai relations, he remarked that the changing political climate in Asia had no effect on the "1893 mindset," which was still prevalent among French colonial officials.[83] The Bangkok media felt slighted when administrators in Saigon did not appear to take the Thai military seriously. "France once bullied us with only three warships," remembered a journalist. "They must think we can still be easily defeated."[84] Thai nationalists, on the other hand, were acutely aware of how the fortunes of the two nations had changed over the past fifty years. They saw Thailand as a rising Asian power that would help fill the vacuum of power created by the implosion of Western imperialism. The most strident voices within the irredentist movement insisted that it was now Thailand's turn to humiliate France. Pamphlets began to circulate demanding that the French return all the territory they had taken, pay 47 million baht in reparations (a million baht for each year of occupation), and apologize for "treading on Thailand since the beginning."[85]

Several voices in the Thai media insisted that the nation could not exorcise the ghost of defeat except through military victory. In his October speech, Phibun spoke of Naresuan and Taksin, two heroes who had expanded the nation's territory through their great courage. He called on the people, saying they must demonstrate the strength and wisdom of their ancestors for Thailand to achieve its goals.[86] Newspapers echoed his sentiments, arguing that the country must fight to restore its honor and force the French to pay for their misdeeds. In a piece titled "It's Our Time Now," one writer recounted how France had continually abused the Thai before concluding, "Nothing less than washing our feet with French blood could make us forget our fury." A military victory would bring honor to current soldiers and those who fought in the past. The author considered such a victory to be a debt owed to the ancestors. "We know," he wrote, "the spirits of those who lost their lives during RS 112 would be proud that their descendants are finally taking revenge on the enemy."[87] Finally, a military victory over France would prove to the world that the country had made great strides in the past decades. In the past, Thailand had been defeated due to lack of armaments, but it was no longer the same country as in 1893. Thai nationalists repeatedly used the analogy of the country as a child that had now grown into an adult: "It has been the constant dream of all of us that one day we shall recover our lost territory, but the reason we would not give utterance to such a thought was because our fist was quite small. . . . Now we are sufficiently grown up to cry out for the recovery of our territory, a territory taken away from us without sufficient cause."[88]

Since the 1932 coup that deposed the absolute monarchy, the government sought out every possible opportunity to emphasize the importance of the army and display the growing military might of the nation. On New Year's Day 1941, the air force put together an aerial show over Bangkok that greatly impressed the citizens below. These demonstrations of strength increased the people's confidence in the military and in their prime minister. Thailand's ability to incorporate Western technology was often the subject of propaganda leaflets handed out both at home and in French Indochina. The aforementioned *Book of Songs* contained the following stanzas:

> Thailand now has money, arms, and gold for war
> The Thai have everything they need for a capable army
> Machines, motors, plane, automobiles

We have everything they have.
The Thais are well prepared
With various weapons, cannons, and machine guns
All being transported by train and by automobile towards the frontier
In anticipation of the French invasion.[89]

In addition to improving its military technology, the Thai state wanted to change the nation's attitude. Whereas past generations stood in awe of the supposedly superior capabilities of the *farang*, Phibun hoped to instill in the younger generation a belief that Thailand could defeat the French. At the dawn of the New Year, Bangkok newspapers described 1941 as a year of hope, a moment Thai peoples had been anticipating for seventy years.[90] Proponents of National Humiliation maintained that defeating France and restoring the *lost territories* would erase the shame of 1893 and demonstrate the level of progress Thailand had achieved under a constitutional form of government.

MASS DEMONSTRATIONS

Thailand's border war with French Indochina illustrates the usefulness of National Humiliation discourse in mobilizing popular support for the state's agenda. Throughout their irredentist campaign, Phibun and Wichit transformed the border negotiations, once a minor diplomatic concern, into a national crisis. By the end of 1940, the government had large segments of the country clamoring for war. Print media and records from the Ministry of Interior reveal that thousands of people actively participated in the government's efforts to acquire the *lost territories*. They did so believing that such a campaign would help restore the nation's honor. Students and workers organized marches, individuals mailed in donations, civil servants contributed a portion of their monthly salary, women's organizations established auctions and fundraisers, and countless people volunteered for service or publicly pledged themselves to the government's cause. Prior to Phibun's October 1940 speech, the government had gradually been preparing the people for conflict; following this speech, the media and the people began pushing the government towards war.

The pro-war demonstrations began with a procession of university students that included the Yuvachon, a paramilitary organization modeled after Germany's Hitler Youth. On October 4, more than 10,000 young men assembled at Sanam Luang for their annual meeting. In his keynote address, Yuvachon director Prayun Phahonmontri explained the government's policy regarding the *lost territories* and the justness of the cause. He told his audience that the country had been asleep for decades, but now that it had awakened, all citizens must prepare to sacrifice everything for the benefit of the nation.[91] A few days later a group of Yuvachon marched to Colonel Prayun's office to contribute monies towards the government's *lost territories* fund. The growing momentum of the irredentist movement was a concern to Pridi Banomyong, who held his own assembly at the University of Political and Moral Sciences (now Thammasat University), where he attempted to convince university students to cancel a planned demonstration. As rector, Pridi warned students that these types of popular rallies would jeopardize the negotiations process by needlessly antagonizing the other side.[92] The students did not heed his warning. On October 8, approximately 3,000 students assembled at the university to begin their procession in support of taking the *lost territories*. Marchers carried placards bearing the following slogans: "Thais are willing to die to get our land back." "We must fight if they will not give it back." "If words do not work, we must use bullets." "No more hesitation, they stole Pakse, it belongs to us."[93]

The students first stopped at the temple of the Emerald Buddha in the Grand Palace, where they knelt down and pledged their lives to the service of the government, then continued on to the Ministry of Defense. There they listened to a brief speech by Phibun, who thanked them for their support and accepted a monetary donation.[94] This pattern was repeated a week later by 5,000 trishaw drivers, who also visited the Emerald Buddha and offered to give a day's salary to the cause. On October 15, the students of Chulalongkorn University conducted a torchlight procession through the streets of Bangkok. Their route included stops at Hua Lamphong train station, the Emerald Buddha, the equestrian statue of Chulalongkorn in front of the Ananta Samakhom throne hall, and finally the prime minister's residence at Suan Kulap Palace.[95]

Among their many signs and posters, the students in the torchlight procession also carried a paper coffin commemorating the recent death of Chantha Sintharako. Three weeks earlier, French police had shot and killed Chantha in Vientiane after discovering that the Thai merchant had no entry permit.[96] French authorities claimed the police acted in self-defense, but the Foreign Ministry in Bangkok demanded an inquiry. As part of the investigation, the government of Thailand sent a doctor to Nong Khai to perform an autopsy on the body.[97] Over the next few months, the Thai merchant became a symbol of French colonial brutality towards people on both sides of the river. Handbills circulated throughout Bangkok claiming to be the voice of Chanta's ghost calling the Thai people to avenge his death. The students considered him to be the first casualty of the Franco-Thai conflict.

The original march by students at the University of Political and Moral Sciences established a pattern that was repeated over the next two months by students, civil servants, and citizens all across Thailand. The first destination on the demonstrators' route was always some form of sacred space, generally the town's most important Buddhist temple. Marchers assembled in front of a statue of the Buddha to swear allegiance to the government. In most cases, the ceremony took on the form of a religious ordinance illustrating the strong ties between church and state in Thailand. In Yala Province, the entire assembly knelt before the Buddha as the Phra Rathikitwichan, a Buddhist monk, read the following oath:

> As a resident of Yala, whose flesh, blood, and heart belong to Thailand, I pledge the following in front of the Phra Phuthasihing in memory of my Thai ancestors and my fellow Thais.
>
> 1) I will sacrifice my life, possessions, and happiness as necessary for the nation.
> 2) I will refrain from causing any division within the Thai nation, and will let go of any anger and resentment from personal issues.
> 3) I am the enemy of all who would harm the Thai nation and I pledge to fight those enemies with courage.
> 4) I will obey and follow the instructions of my community and civic leaders.
> 5) I will do my best to be of service to my community and to serve my fellow countrymen as needed.[98]

The marchers then continued on to a gathering in front of the county or provincial building, where they presented a government official with a sum of money to contribute towards the *lost territories* fund. Finally, demonstrators gathered for a speech by the provincial governor. These speeches helped communicate the idea of *chosen trauma* to the average person. Each oration varied as to content but generally followed important talking points regarding the prime minister's policy on the border dispute, an explanation of when and how Thailand lost its territories, and an exhortation for each individual to join in supporting the government. The governor of Pathum Thani Province lectured his constituents at length, giving a brief history of colonialism in Asia and an explanation of how the Lao and Khmer people had much in common with the Thai.[99] The media reported these gatherings as spontaneous demonstrations, but they were organized in advance by government officials. Local leaders documented the number of people in attendance and the amount of the donations and reported this information to the provincial leaders, who forwarded it to the Ministry of Interior. From October through December 1940, many provinces hosted rallies attended by thousands of people, although eager district or provincial officials may have exaggerated these numbers to prove their patriotism to Bangkok.

These types of agitation were government organized, but a number of private individuals or organizations responded to the growing momentum of the irredentist movement. The Ministry of Interior records are filled with letters from ordinary citizens inspired to do their part for the nation after learning the "true history" of the *lost territories*. Since poorer households often did not have cash on hand, they donated whatever goods they had available. A farmer from Ang Thong Province pledged his two cows to the government, and a couple from Pathum Thani contacted the government about donating family heirlooms.[100] Students in Nakorn Phanom wanted to commemorate the tragedy of 1893 by pooling their lunch money into a fund intended to purchase a machine gun for the army.[101] The movement to recover the *lost territories* also received support from unexpected sources. Groups that had been marginalized and attacked following Phibun's ascension to power in 1938, including Chinese merchants and the Roman Catholic Church, now sought to demonstrate their patriotism by donating money or marching along with the pro-government demonstrations.[102] Islamic leaders, who elected not to participate in the public processions due to embedded Buddhist rituals, found other ways to be patriotic. Ai Batu, an imam in Narathiwat Province, encouraged the Muslims in his district to gather for an Islamic prayer ritual to bless the nation.[103] Phibun's foreign policy agenda even received backing from the Royal Palace Bureau, which instructed all its associates to contribute one-tenth of their royal annual salary to the Ministry of Defense for the purchase of arms. Considering the level of animosity that existed between the monarchy and the government, this royal donation demonstrates how important the symbol of the *lost territories* had become in creating a sense of national unity.[104]

THE CHILD IS NOW AN ADULT

For three weeks in January 1941, Thailand and French Indochina fought an undeclared war along the Mekong River. The Thai army went on the offensive first, occupying much of the disputed frontier territory and forcing French troops to withdraw. The navy, however, suffered a disastrous defeat in the Gulf of Thailand, which left Bangkok vulnerable to a possible naval blockade. In response, Phibun requested that the Japanese broker a ceasefire between the two parties and mediate negotiations for a permanent truce. The Thai public, which was not informed of the naval defeat, eagerly awaited a settlement. Thai expectation had been modest at the beginning but increased exponentially after weeks of articles on military victories in the Bangkok press. Newspapermen in particular saw no reason for Thailand to compromise now that they had the upper hand, especially since they accused France of starting the war by bombing Nakorn Phanom.[105] Journalists warned that France could not be trusted to negotiate fairly, given that all previous treaties between the two nations had been such one-sided affairs. They reasoned that Thailand had all the leverage going into peace talks and should keep fighting until France acquiesced to all of its demands.

Three-way diplomatic talks dragged on for almost four months, until all sides agreed to sign the Tokyo Peace Accord on May 9, 1941. Under the terms of the agreement, Thailand regained most of the land it had ceded to France in 1904 and 1907—namely the right-bank enclaves near Luang Prabang and Champassak and the majority of Battambang, Sisophon, and Siem Reap provinces in western Cambodia.[106] The treaty also recognized the deepwater channel of the Mekong as the international boundary between the two countries. In return, Thailand committed to grant French citizens in the returned territories the same rights as Thai citizens and to pay France 4 million baht in compensation for railroads and other infrastructure constructed during the past thirty-four years.[107] The Thai delegation was deeply disappointed with the result. The territorial concessions fell short of the delegation's initial request to obtain all of Laos and Cambodia, and the forced payment of reparations created the impression that this was a business transaction rather than a military triumph. These two issues provoked intense questioning of the prime minister during the debate over ratification in the National Assembly. Detractors pointed out that the 70,000 square kilometers of territory Thailand received was but a small fraction of the more than 400,000 it had lost over the years. How could the government claim victory, they demanded, when it now owed France such a large sum of money? There were also questions concerning the economic viability of the new provinces. Were they self-sustaining or would they have to be supported by diverting funds away from the rest of the country?[108] Phibun was able to brush aside these questions because he understood the value of the *lost territories* to be symbolic rather than practical. As Wichit had observed, "The land we've asked for might be little more than jungle, but it's our jungle and we want it back."[109]

Despite the disappointing details of the Tokyo Peace Accord, it represented the first significant expansion of Thailand's boundaries since the founding of the Chakri dynasty. The Thai press lauded the treaty as the country's greatest foreign policy achievement in recent memory. Newspapers reported the details of the agreement, including the amount of reparations required of Thailand. The fact that Thailand had fallen well short of its original demands embittered top officials but did not diminish public enthusiasm. As head of the Thai delegation to Tokyo, Prince Wan was met by hundreds of supporters when he arrived at Bangkok's Don Muang Airport.[110] Bangkok was humming with talk of new provinces and new citizens, but most of the media commentary focused on the treaty as a statement to the rest of the world. Thailand's success in retrieving a portion of its *lost territory* was an important step in nullifying the humiliating legacy of 1893 and redeeming its national honor. An editorial in *Nikorn* illustrated Thailand's desire to show the world how civilized their country had become: "This success has not only redrawn the map of Thailand, it has redrawn the map of our hearts and minds. That is to say, it has made us realize that our beloved nation of Thailand has increased in honor, and caused the world to recognize that we are not the same country that we were forty years ago. Quite the opposite, other nations are now praising us."[111]

Progress was also the theme of the National Day celebration on June 24, 1941. Several parade floats depicted Thailand's rapid pace of development since the change in government, while others were designed to remind people of the country's rise as a military power.[112]

The Franco-Thai conflict marked the zenith of Phibun Songkhram's power and influence. The victory over France provided the prime minister with a generous supply of political capital to be utilized during the coming year. Newspapers compared him with Taksin the Great, the last monarch to successfully add territory to the kingdom.[113] In the National Assembly, there was a movement to name one of the four new provinces after the field marshal.[114] An assemblyman from Buriram Province explained that his constituents considered Phibun to be a man of great merit, one who had been born to bring the lost provinces back to Thailand. Others compared him to Chulalongkorn, saying that Phibun had freed thousands of people from slavery under the French. After careful debate, the National Assembly determined it would follow the will of the people by changing the name of Sisophon to Phibun Songkhram Province. No other Thai citizen, before or since, has received such an honor.

3

National Humiliation and Anti-Catholicism

In the summer of 1942, Bishop Pasotti of the Ratchaburi Diocese wrote a letter to the Ministry of Interior protesting the deteriorating status of the Catholic Church in Thailand. Since the beginning of the border conflict with French Indochina in late 1940, the Church's standing had been jeopardized by its close association with France. Thai Catholics had been labeled as "fifth column" and subject to all manner of persecution. French citizens, including clergy, had been ordered to leave the country. Those priests who returned were restricted from administering to their former parishes. Provincial and municipal leaders banned all church services and pressured Catholics to return to the national religion of Buddhism. Thai mobs attacked local priests and looted Catholic churches. Government officials closed down churches, schools, and dormitories, which were converted into public schools, offices, or even Buddhist monasteries. When the Church replaced French priests deported by the government with Italian clergy, they too were threatened, both by mobs and local government. Pasotti pleaded with the ministry to help protect Salesian priests and restore Catholic property to its rightful owners. "Such an uncivil state of affairs," he wrote, "is not in keeping with the spirit of the alliance between our two countries, Italy and Thailand, who are at this moment fighting together for a common purpose."[1]

If Bishop Pasotti truly believed that Thailand and Italy shared a common goal, then he grossly misread the mood of the Thai government. Phibun's military regime viewed 1941 as a year of destiny. The border conflict with French Indochina was to be the beginning of a larger effort to create a new Thailand that would be free of foreign dominance. Thailand's victory in that struggle signaled the emergence of a new era in which all the perceived injustice and humiliation it had suffered at the hands of European imperialism would finally be avenged. For this reason, many Thais embraced Japan's vision of a Greater East Asia where a rejuvenated Thailand would play an important role.

On the domestic front, Prime Minister Phibun Songkhram attempted to reduce the influence of Chinese middlemen and European corporations over the Thai economy. In this atmosphere of extreme nationalism, the state placed limitations on institutions with perceived connections to Western imperialism, and religious organizations were no exception. Among the government's targets, the Catholic Church received special attention due to its history of intervention in Thai governance dating back to the reign of Chulalongkorn. By the 1940s the Church had enjoyed four decades of peaceful coexistence with the government; but the Thai elite did not forget its history of defiance towards state authority. The state presented its anti-Catholic campaign in the context of national humiliation, as an opportunity to destroy an important symbol of the old colonial order in Southeast Asia.

The Thai state's persecution of Catholicism during World War II constitutes a sensitive issue, making sources difficult to obtain. The Phibun government was intentionally secretive regarding its religious agenda. Ministry of Interior records confirming anti-Catholic policies exist, but their language regarding the origins and exact nature of this policy is vague. Eyewitness accounts from Catholic participants are much clearer regarding the course of events, but they involve questions of objectivity in addition to being carefully guarded by Church stewards. Admittedly, the scarcity of documentation has created obstacles to the construction of a usable narrative detailing religious persecution.[2]

This is one reason that historians have paid far less attention to Thailand's wartime domestic issues and focused on the country's foreign policy, particularly its relationship with Japan. As Flood observed, few areas of Thai history were targets of as much speculation as foreign relations preceding the war in the Pacific.[3] For several decades after World War II, the accepted narrative on wartime conditions in Thailand emphasized the country's survival from both Japanese and Allied incursions. Thamsook Numnonda's study of this period concluded that Thailand's only goal was to emerge from the war with its independence intact, and at this it succeeded brilliantly.[4] More recent articles have challenged this perspective by demonstrating how Phibun's expansionist policies during the war did much to jeopardize Bangkok's postwar standing within the international community. Eiji Murashima's investigation into Thailand's 1942 campaign in Burma argued it was Thai leaders who pressured Japan to allow it to conduct military operations in the Shan states, not the reverse.

Disregarding the country's precarious status, Phibun saw the war as an opportunity to restore all of Thailand's *lost territories,* which had been the dream of Thai rulers since Chulalongkorn.[5] He intended to construct a Greater Thailand that would encompass all areas inhabited by the Thai race. It was only after the dismal failure of this offensive that Phibun began to reconsider his declaration of war on the Allies and disavow his plans to make Thailand into a great power.[6] E. Bruce Reynolds has examined Phibun's domestic and foreign agendas and characterized his policies as "fascist." From 1938 to 1944, Bangkok emulated political models in Italy and Germany by forming militant youth groups, persecuting ethnic and religious minorities, and promoting an irredentist agenda aimed at recovering territories in French Indochina.[7]

This chapter builds on the work of Reynolds and Murashima by arguing that the Thai state rationalized its extreme nationalism as an attempt to confront its own history of victimization. Phibun's persecution of Catholicism had roots in the late-nineteenth-century confrontation between the Church and the Thai state, when priests and missionaries used their influence over converts to protect them from the demands of Thai feudalism. Clerical interference defied the nobility and frustrated Thai rulers, who explored ways to limit the Church's power without antagonizing its French imperialist patrons. Fifty years later, Phibun opted for an aggressive solution to what had been a long-standing grievance of the Thai government. Growing public antipathy towards Catholics reflected the state's success at manufacturing a history of victimhood in order to redefine national identity. Leadership articulated new boundaries of identification in which the values "Catholic" and "Thai" became mutually exclusive.

Catholicism was a soft target that helped the government to intensify anticolonial sentiment among the Thai populace. Michael Murdock's work on early Chinese nationalism demonstrates how confronting imperialism in the theoretical sense proved unsustainable, while attacking powerful institutions, such as a military presence, can provoke a fatal backlash. For this reason Christian churches often proved to be an ideal objective for focusing public attention on the presence of foreignness within a country.[8] In the Thai case, Catholics were the perfect symbol of imperialism. The Church was depicted as the antithesis of national identity because of its association with France, its history of political intervention, and the fact that a large percentage of converts were ethnic minorities. Finally, the anti-Catholic movement provides further evidence of the effect of National Humiliation discourse on both foreign and domestic policy during the 1940s. Just as Phibun's aspirations of external expansion resulted in attacks on French Indochina, his goal of a homogenous populace led to religious persecution. His regime viewed Catholicism as part of the legacy of Western imperialism in Thailand, and it had to be removed.

RAMA V AND THE CATHOLIC QUESTION

Phibun's violence against Catholicism had its roots in the late-nineteenth-century political struggle between missionary and monarchy. Thai rulers dating back to Ayuthaya viewed religious proselytizing efforts as a subtle method of spreading French influence in their kingdom. After the Apostolic Vicariate of Siam was founded in the mid-seventeenth century, the government carefully restricted its reach. As evidenced by the close relationship between Bishop Pallegoix and Mongkut, the relationship between the Church and the monarchy improved over time. In 1878, Chulalongkorn issued a royal edict granting missionary access to the northeast.[9] Even then, the Siamese government was extremely reluctant to grant passports to Catholic clergy for several reasons. France's conquests in Vietnam and expansion westward towards the Mekong threatened Siam's claim to the Lao territories, which were still semiautonomous vassal states. To counter this threat, Siam began gradually tightening its grip over the Lao regions, hoping to bring the northeast under direct Siamese control. Bangkok was concerned that the introduction of Catholic missionary work in this region would complicate its efforts at centralization. Furthermore, Chulalongkorn worried about having French priests in cities such as Sakon Nakhon, Nakhon Phanom, and Ubon due to their strategic importance as military posts along the Mekong River. He feared the clergy were actually spies sent to conduct surveillance activities and provoke a border conflict between Siam and French Indochina.[10]

Despite Chulalongkorn's apprehension, Catholic priests did not act as spies, nor did French colonial authorities ever plan to employ them in such a manner. As J. P. Daughton has demonstrated, Catholic missionaries and colonial officials in French Indochina were often at cross-purposes. Republican administrators brought their anticlerical attitudes with them to Indochina, while clergy seldom hesitated to pursue their ecclesiastical goals in a manner detrimental to the empire. "Far from being eager servants of empire," Daughton writes, "missionaries remained acutely suspicious of colonial authority."[11] This mistrust of secular authority caused priests to safeguard their own autonomy and work to increase the mission's influence over local communities. Missionaries worked to build Catholic communities independent of Siamese jurisdiction, which naturally brought the Church into conflict with local rulers. Catholic clerics complicated relations between Bangkok and vassal states by disregarding Siamese law and acting as intermediaries between the government and the people.

Beginning in the 1880s, French Catholic priests utilized their extraterritorial status to build powerful patron-client relationships with minority communities in the northeast. The Siamese nobility hesitated to confront priests for fear of provoking an international incident that might jeopardize Franco-Siamese relations. Because they existed outside of Siamese jurisdiction, missionaries could act as advocates for the Vietnamese, Lao, and hill tribe races that occupied the margins of society. In order to gain the people's trust, the Church used the same methods as the French consulate. Priests presented their gospel using a language of justice and equality, telling minorities that local rulers oppressed them and offering to use Church influence to protect them from Siamese cruelty.[12] The Vietnamese in Siam began to equate conversion to Catholicism with limited protection from taxes, corvée labor, and debt bondage. As conversions increased, the clergy assumed civic and judicial authority within Catholic communities in addition to their ecclesiastical roles. In one example from Nakhon Phanom, a priest directed all seventy-five families from one village to move their houses to the banks of the Mekong, thereby establishing a new village under his leadership. The Church intended these communities to operate outside the Siamese system of governance. Priests forbade their followers from drinking the water of allegiance (a Buddhist ritual) if they became civil servants.[13] Missionaries arbitrated legal disputes between fellow Catholics instead of directing them to consult the Siamese magistrates. Since these communities were self-governing and composed of ethnic minorities, questions naturally arose concerning their loyalties. In 1884, Chulalongkorn was shocked when he passed through a Catholic community in Lop Buri and saw the French flag flying over one of the homes. Siamese nobles in the Lao territories were considerably alarmed by this disregard for governance and law, but they dared not actively oppose the priests before receiving instruction from Bangkok.[14]

As protectors of their communities, priests caused enormous headaches for Siamese ministers by insisting that their parishioners be exempt from both taxation and corvée labor. They claimed that the corrupt and antiquated system of revenue collection in the northeast allowed tax collectors to exploit ethnic minorities. To correct this injustice, Catholic priests presented three separate types of reform. First, the northeast provinces should follow the procedures already established in Bangkok. Second, the amount of taxes collected from Catholics should be substantially reduced. Third, the priests themselves should be allowed to act as tax collectors for all Catholic villagers. This attitude of defiance spread to Vietnamese Catholics, who refused to perform labor for the local magistrate unless they were paid and then registered with their priest as a protégé.[15] This presented a dilemma for Siamese authorities. Enforcing the current quota could lead to a confrontation with the Church, in which case the clergy might request French colonial intervention. Yet exempting Catholics from civic obligations would damage their credibility with the rest of the population. Any modification of the tax rate in favor of minorities would be an admission that the power and influence of Catholic priests superseded that of the king's ministers.

French missionaries also clashed with the Siamese establishment over the issue of debt bondage, which had been abolished in Bangkok but was still practiced in the northeastern regions. Indentured servants provided much of the manpower required by the Siamese nobility. Catholic priests viewed debt bondage as a form of slavery and denounced it as an antiquated and barbaric practice used by the Siamese to further exploit the Vietnamese, Lao, and hill tribe minorities. Clergy petitioned Chulalongkorn to ban debt bondage in the northeastern Lao territories and sheltered those attempting to escape. Many priests allowed runaways to hide in their homes or on Church property.[16] Caught between the nobility and the Church, Chulalongkorn opted to pacify the clergy and avoid conflict with France.

These incidents reinforced opinions within Chulalongkorn's government that Catholic priests were imperialist agents attempting to provoke Siam into open conflict with France. The king in particular was deeply concerned that the clergy's abolitionist activism would undermine both his relationship with the nobility and the sovereignty of the entire kingdom. Siam had carefully observed the French conquest of Vietnam and noted how disagreements between missionaries and the imperial court at Huế had provided France with a pretext for armed intervention. Chulalongkorn became convinced that France would also exploit any conflict with the Church in Siam to expand its own influence westward towards the Mekong River.[17] During the 1880s, France and Siam both hoped to extend state control over the region of Laos, and Chulalongkorn believed his modernizing reforms would give his kingdom the edge. The king was also constructing an image of a modern civilized Siam. The Catholic Church's accusations that the Siamese still practiced slavery in the northeast threatened to undo his efforts. By focusing attention on the institution of debt bondage, the Church weakened the king's argument that Siam was already a civilized country that did not need European administration.

While the monarchy and nobility deliberated over how to manage the challenge of Catholicism, violence in Nakhon Phanom Province led local authorities to take matters into their own hands. In 1885, a crowd of Catholic converts stormed Wat Kaeng Mueang in a fit of religious fervor and destroyed the Buddhist temple's sacred statues and relics. The Siamese minister's retribution proved surprisingly swift and brutal. He ordered the destruction of several homes owned by the Church and inhabited by converts. Catholic civil servants were arrested and flogged. Other converts were threatened or blackmailed until they promised to leave the foreign religion. French priests did not escape reprisal. Local merchants organized a boycott that prevented priests from purchasing food except at exorbitant prices.[18] Fearing the backlash in Nakhon Phanom would spread, Father Alexis traveled to Bangkok to counsel with Chulalongkorn. Both parties wanted to end the disturbances as quickly as possible. Eventually the Siamese government and Catholic Church adopted a strategy of compromise and mutual adaptation. The clergy agreed not to interfere with the collection of taxes, corvée labor, or the water of allegiance ritual within Catholic communities.[19] The Siamese elite realized that the exploitation of Vietnamese and other minorities drove these groups into the protection of Catholic priests and that conflict between state and clergy only empowered the priests in the eyes of the Christian community. Chulalongkorn used the example of Catholic abolitionist activism to convince his nobles that phasing out debt bondage was necessary to protect the country's sovereignty, since European powers could use it as an excuse to intervene in Siam. Once again, solving the problem of extraterritoriality served to advance Bangkok's power over the northeast and weaken local authority. In return for the Church's agreement, the government allowed priests to perform the water of allegiance ritual in a Church for all Catholic civic officials.

The conflict between nobility and clergy helps explain why the Siamese government had been so reluctant to allow missionaries into the Lao territories from the beginning. Because the northeast was still administered by the nobility and not under the direct control of Bangkok, social customs and legal conditions differed greatly from those in the capital. When Catholic priests perceived an absence of "civilized" governance in the territory, they exercised that authority for themselves. Priests assumed the role of intermediaries between the people and the government to strengthen Christian communities and protect them from exploitation. The Siamese imagined the

French colonial authorities and the Catholic Church as partners in a conspiracy that threatened the kingdom's security. In actuality, the French consul-general Jules Harmand viewed the Church's activities in the northeast, especially its combative relationship with the local government, as a detriment to French influence in Siam: "The Siamese government is truly tired and annoyed at the mass of complaints made every day by the missionaries either directly to them or through the French consulate. Three quarters of our voluminous correspondence with the [Siamese] ministers is composed of letters and notes relating to their contestations. With Your Excellency's permission I would, within the bounds of justice, like to control this habit. For the irritation caused to the Siamese government by this practice might at any time compromise our political action and change the favorable attitude which it normally tries to show towards France."[20]

Far from instructing priests to provoke conflict with Siamese ministers, the colonial government wanted to restrain the Church's activities for the sake of improving Franco-Siamese relations. Church leaders in Indochina constantly complained about the colonial state's failure to support the Catholic missions: "It is most regrettable that the French government cannot understand how important and useful its moral support would be for missionaries. . . . Such criticisms, which state publicly that the priest should confine himself to Church matters alone, have prompted attempts to deprive him of all influence. In consequence he has lost all prestige, and with it all remaining social respect. Without such prestige the missionary has no further social authority in present circumstances, and his words remain without effect on the poor pagans in whose eyes he has been downgraded."[21]

Thus, prior to 1893 it was the Church that relied on the political backing of the French consulate to support its religious mission, rather than the consulate making use of the clergy to extend French political influence. This evidence suggests that although clergy such as Bishop Jean-Louis Vey of Bangkok encouraged the French colonization of Siam, the Catholic priesthood was not an integral part of French colonial planning. After the Franco-Siamese crisis of 1893, however, this changed. The Church became a more important part of France's strategy for Siam as the colonial state developed a new interest in religious and ethnic minorities. Consul General Auguste Pavie recommended that all Asiatic Catholics be registered as French protégés so that France could capitalize politically from the growth of the Bangkok mission. In 1894, the French parliamentary commission awarded the Vicariate of Siam 250,000 francs to promote missionary work. Pavie believed the Church could help counter British influence while advancing French interests in Siam.[22]

These clashes created a troubled legacy of Church-state relations. The close correlation between Catholic baptism and protégé registration linked conversion with citizenship status. France's abuse of extraterritorial privileges after 1893 caused Siamese rulers to view an individual's entry into the Catholic Church as a selection of France over Siam. In the 1930s and 1940s, when concepts such as nation, citizen, and boundaries became sacred matters, irredentists used this narrative to question the patriotism of Catholic Thais. Also, the clergy's attempt to intercede in political and judicial affairs associated the Church with French imperialism in the eyes of Siam's ruling classes. Priestly resistance to Siamese law diminished the nobility in the eyes of the people and caused them to look to the clergy and consequently to France, for protection and leadership. Chulalongkorn was wary of the Catholic Church because he believed that its missionaries were backed by the resources of French Indochina.

Interior Ministry records from the 1940s demonstrate that Phibun's regime still resented how the Catholic Church had embarrassed and defied Siamese rulers in the past. After Germany's occupation of France in 1940, the Thai government realized it could now settle a score with the Catholic Church without serious ramifications. Proposed strategies included limiting the amount of land that foreigners could own or preventing foreigners from purchasing land altogether. The Ministry of Interior also considered enacting laws to restrict the number of foreigners who could enter the country to teach religion or perform humanitarian service.[23] At the year's end, when border negotiations broke down, Phibun was determined to use this opportunity to avenge past losses to imperialism. He intended to break the power of the Catholic Church as a means of removing French influence and restoring national pride.

DEFINING CATHOLICS AS NON-THAI

In December 1940, as Thai troops prepared to invade parts of Indochina and capture the *lost territories,* the Phibun regime prepared to move against the French. The principal target inside Thailand was the Catholic Church. The government used National Humiliation discourse to characterize Catholicism as a foreign ideology that threatened to destroy traditional Thai values. Propagandists associated Catholics with French imperialists, describing converts as people who had forgotten their own identity and heritage. The discourse on "Thainess" formed the main theme of leaflets distributed by a secret organization known only as the Thai Blood Party. It also became a frequent subject of government correspondence and speeches by civic officials and schoolteachers. A priest stationed in Sakon Nakhon Province wrote to his superiors, "The local authorities, starting from the [district leaders] down to the least of the teachers in their public speeches, do nothing but backbite and curse the Catholic religion and all the priests."[24] The government began disseminating the idea that Catholicism was "un-Thai" during the early months of the Franco-Thai conflict in 1940. By 1942, it was the government's official position on the Church.

The Thai Blood Party quickly became an important player in the campaign to redefine Thai identity and build nationalism. Very little is known about this secret organization aside from the nationalist agenda found in its literature. The party probably derived its name from Wichit Wathakan's historical drama titled *Luead Thai* (Thai Blood), and some suspect that Wichit himself was the party's founder. Whatever its origins, this group became very active in stirring up public support for war with French Indochina. Thai Blood propaganda emphasized that the Thai, Lao, and Khmer were actually members of the same race, and that Thailand had gone to war with Indochina to drive out the French colonial oppressors and bring democracy to their Lao and Khmer brethren. The nation had to be completely united and vigilant in protecting itself from the enemy within, or this objective could not be achieved. According to the Thai Blood, the Catholics jeopardized this ultimate goal by threatening the nation's unity.

Thai Blood literature presented religion as an essential part of national identity in order to marginalize Catholics. Whereas Buddhism had always been an integral component of Thainess as defined by the ruling elite, Catholicism was represented as a definitively French religion. In a country without separation between church and state, nationalists reasoned that an individual's religious devotion to a French church would naturally translate into political loyalty to France. By forsaking Buddhism, Catholics not only turned their back on their own people, they willingly associated themselves with Thailand's historical enemy. As one Thai Blood pamphlet warned, "The Thai Blood Party believes [Catholics] are enemies of the nation and people who worship the doctrines of our enemy. We hold they have forgotten their nation, forgotten their religion, the true religion because they are drunk on the faith of our enemies. . . . These are people who have been taught by our enemies. They are waiting for an opportunity to make us their slaves and completely destroy our nation."[25]

Despite such inflammatory rhetoric, Thai nationalists such as Wichit understood that French Indochina was much too weak to consider an invasion of Thailand. It was this weakness that allowed the Thai state to adopt such an aggressive position regarding the *lost territories.* And yet we cannot dismiss the effectiveness of this type of propaganda at creating an atmosphere of crisis, because it invoked the collective trauma of the Franco-Siamese crisis, which by this time had become a visible scar on the body of the nation. During the border crisis of 1940, irredentists referred back to the loss of territory in 1893 at every opportunity to remind people how France had humiliated their country. Thai Blood literature also preyed on fears that the Church was helping to facilitate French expansion into Thailand. Catholic Thais, they reasoned, had been deceived by a corrosive dogma. Only after Cambodia and Laos were liberated, the French driven out of Southeast Asia, and the Catholic Church eliminated could these misguided souls finally be brought back to Buddhism. Thai Blood pamphlets warned the population, "Do not forget that we Thai have received bitterness for the past many years. But now is our time. The Thai Blood want us to be united as one to help chase out the nation that is our enemy and force him to take his wicked doctrines out of the Golden Peninsula. Then our brethren who have been deceived by these superstitions will return to the paths our ancestors built for us."[26]

Until all this could be achieved, the Thai Blood encouraged people to treat Catholics as they would treat French citizens. One tract titled "An invitation to public opinion" provided very specific instructions. It discouraged Thais from associating with their Catholic neighbors and forbade business dealings. Patriotic citizens should watch Catholics closely, remember their faces, and avoid talking about sensitive information if they were within listening distance. The pamphlet concluded with a warning that anyone who did not follow these guidelines was a traitor to their country.[27] Economic boycotts were very popular during both the war effort and the campaign against Catholics. People avoided Catholic merchants, and Buddhist vendors sometimes refused to sell food to Catholics. Even pedicab drivers participated by refusing to transport Catholics in their vehicles. The Thai Blood successfully organized boycotts, first in Bangkok and later in Chiang Mai, and encouraged other provinces to follow these examples.[28] These boycotts made life particularly difficult for Italian priests living in the Isan. Most merchants refused to sell them food or charged exorbitant prices.

In the public schools, administrators organized assemblies focused on discrediting Catholicism in the minds of their students. Some teachers talked about Christianity as though it were a primary reason for the overall decline of the Western powers. Eventually, the government shut down Catholic schools and transformed them into public schools with a new curriculum. Teachers ordered crosses and other icons to be torn down from the walls and then asked Catholic students why, if the Christian god was so powerful, did he not punish them for their sacrilege? Another instructor pointed out that the British were a Christian nation. Why could they not defeat the Thai and Japanese in the war?[29] The most common lecture theme portrayed Catholicism as a "fifth column," a dangerous influence that corrupted those who accepted its beliefs. In Nong Khai Province, a school principal claimed that history demonstrated how "the Catholic religion destroys every country it touches." Niyom Thongthirad told his students that France was victorious over Germany in World War I because of the assistance it received from German Catholic spies. Following the war, the Nazis eliminated the treacherous religion from their country. With Germany no longer plagued by Catholic espionage, the Wehrmacht easily defeated France in World War II. "For this reason," the principal warned, "we Thais can not worship Catholicism. Whoever accepts Catholicism is not a Thai."[30]

One reason that Thais perceived Catholicism to be a foreign religion was that many of the earliest converts in Siam were Vietnamese. The first French priests to establish the Church in the northeast had success with Vietnamese immigrants who found themselves marginalized within the Siamese community. Some families had already converted to Catholicism in Vietnam and brought their religion with them. There was also a large community of Catholic Vietnamese in the Samsen district of Bangkok. When the Thai government looked for an explanation as to why many Catholics resisted efforts to convert them to Buddhism, they saw ethnicity as the answer. In 1942, the Ministry of Interior instructed all governors to conduct a survey in order to ascertain the ethnic background of Catholic populations within their respective provinces. The governor of Chachoengsao Province reported back some startling results. Out of almost 1,600 Catholics in the entire province, 93 percent were identified as Thai, only 6 percent as Chinese, and less than 1 percent as Vietnamese.[31] Despite this evidence, some in the ministry continued to view race as the reason many Catholics refused to renounce their religion and adopt Buddhism. "[In regard to] those who return to Catholicism," wrote one exasperated official, "we can see they are not real Thais. They may have Thai citizenship under the law, but ethnically speaking they are foreign, probably Chinese or Vietnamese."[32]

Table 1. Chachoengsao Province. Ethnicity of Catholics in Chachoengsao Province listed by district.

Ethnicity	*Amphoe Muang*	*Phanom Sarakham*	*Bang Kla*	*Phoe banphot*	*Bang Nam Briaw*
Thai	855	31	372	184 Sino-Thai	27
Vietnamese	0	0	0	3	0
Chinese	29	0	14	–	6
French	1	0	0	0	0

Source: Data from the Ministry of Interior files, National Archives of Thailand. 3.1.2.10/6. Suk Anchanand to Ministry of Interior, July 19, 1942.

THE STRATEGY FOR ELIMINATING CATHOLICISM

On July 31, 1942, the governor of Nakhon Phanom Province sent a letter to the Ministry of Interior in which he wrote, "The province works very closely with the people to teach and train them on how to be patriotic citizens who have repented and continue to be good Buddhists and give alms. We never cease to follow the policy of removing Catholicism from Thailand. Those people who return to Buddhism no longer observe the [Catholic] ordinances at all. They wish to live in strict accordance with the law."[33]

The campaign to eliminate the Catholic Church from Thailand was directed by the Ministry of Interior. At the local level, it was enforced by the provincial governors and especially the district chiefs. On January 16, 1941, at the height of the Franco-Thai border conflict, Bangkok sent out a communiqué to the governors of provinces with significant Catholic communities.[34] The directive communicated the government's threefold strategy. First, local officials were instructed to close down Catholic churches and schools. Catholic services were banned. Second, the district chiefs must "invite" Catholics within their jurisdiction to return to Buddhism, the national religion. District leadership extended this invitation in ways that made it very difficult for Catholics to decline. Finally, the directive instructed provincial authorities that Church buildings located in areas of military or economic importance, principally in the northeast along the Mekong River, posed a serious danger. These buildings threatened the overall well-being and security of the nation, and governors were charged with facilitating their relocation.[35] Although all governors received this directive, implementation of the policy was left to the province's discretion. Likewise, Catholic populations across Thailand reacted in a variety of ways. Some proved more determined than others to resist conversion or relocation, and the Church-state confrontation often turned violent.

The Thai government banned Catholic services the moment martial law was declared in Thailand on November 30, 1940. Police closed down churches all throughout the east, north, and northeast, so that the "fifth column" could not use Sunday services as a cover for their espionage activities. The police informed anyone who refused to convert to Buddhism that they could display crucifixes and religious icons and pray in their own homes, but public meetings were forbidden.[36] The length of the ban varied. Governors in Udon Thani, Nong Khai, Nakhon Phanom, and Sakon Nakhon proved more rigid than others, as their provinces had large Catholic populations and were situated on the front lines of the border war. Most other provinces relaxed the ban after the conclusion of hostilities. Sakon Nakhon began permitting Catholic services in 1942 before prohibiting them once again in 1943.[37] Nakhon Phanom, which had been bombed by French planes at the outset of the conflict, was the only province to maintain its ban from 1940 until the fall of the Phibun government in 1944.[38]

One area of Thailand escaped this religious persecution altogether. The Ratchaburi mission west of Bangkok was a Salesian mission separate from those in Bangkok and the Isan. Its churches were not affected by the policies of the Ministry of Interior. In 1943, the police general in Bangkok sent out a notice to law enforcement in Ratchaburi, Kanchanaburi, and Samut Songkhram directing police not to interfere with the activities of Catholics in those areas: "Police should understand that Catholics have services at the church all the time that they may attend. Also, the duties of the priests involve going to burial services or traveling to the homes of those who are sick or injured. . . . Police officials should understand that all these activities are permitted under your supervision and protection."[39]

The Ratchaburi diocese escaped persecution because its priests and administrators were Italian, not French. Unlike France, Italy was an important ally of the Japanese and could still use its consulate in Bangkok to protect the interests of its citizens. Thus, the Phibun administration developed a policy of noninterference in the Ratchaburi Diocese's affairs even as it expelled the Church from the rest of the country. Later, the diocese would come into conflict with the state when Italian priests traveled to the northeast to minister to Catholics in that region.

In the rest of the country, appropriating Church property turned out to be a very simple process. The French priests who managed Church buildings in the northeast had been deported during the border conflict. After the priests' departure, the churches were left vacant and civic authorities declared that the status of the buildings as religious edifices had officially expired. This change in legal status allowed the government to take ownership of Catholic churches, schools, houses, and land. In Ban Wiankuk in Nong Khai Province, municipal leaders claimed that they took over property only after they could not determine who owned the buildings.[40] When Father Lacombe was forced to leave his parish in Chang Ming, he bequeathed the church keys to a sister in his congregation. When he had not returned after three months, the woman turned the keys over to a district leader.[41] Under government direction, churches were converted into office buildings, teachers dormitories, or even Buddhist monasteries. When Thailand assumed control of Champassak in 1941, police used the city church as their provincial headquarters. Authorities closed down Catholic schools and removed the religious iconography from the classroom walls before reopening the buildings as public schools. Buddhist imagery and statues replaced the torn-down crucifixes. The Catholic Church also owned a considerable amount of land, which it used as possible expansion sites or as farmland to generate revenue. In Sakon Nakhon, the district confiscated Church fields, then leased them out to citizens for planting.[42] The seizure of property provided a financial incentive for local officials to follow Bangkok's anti-Catholic policies.

Economic advantages notwithstanding, instructions from the Ministry of Interior make it clear that the primary objective of appropriating this property was to limit the influence of the Catholic Church in Thailand. Because Catholicism had been designated as a threat to the Thai nation, any churches situated near areas of economic or military importance had to be relocated. The decision over whether to relocate a church was the priority of the governor of each province, but the Ministry of Interior offered the following guidelines. In communities with substantial Catholic populations, local government must assist in finding land where the church could be resituated. Officials should ensure that Catholic buildings were grouped together and that the church's new plot was smaller than its previous plot. In towns where most Catholics had converted to Buddhism and the churches were deserted, local government should destroy the building so that it could never again be used as a meeting house.[43] By encouraging the demolition of these structures, the Phibun regime tried to prevent any returning clergy from restoring their former congregations.

The state's anti-Catholic policies encouraged vigilante violence against the Church. From 1941 to 1944, church buildings all across the country were damaged by vandalism, arson, or looting. Since the policy of the Ministry of Interior was to eliminate Catholic churches wherever possible, these attacks had the tacit approval of the government and were occasionally the result of direct orders from the province. The police did not intervene to stop mobs that attacked homes, schools, or churches, and refused to investigate these crimes afterward. Nor was anti-Catholic violence simply a knee-jerk response to the hysteria of the 1940 Indochina war. Records both from the Ministry of Interior and eyewitness accounts suggest the brunt of the destruction of property actually took place from 1942 to 1944, long after the conclusion of hostilities with French Indochina. Although both Hanoi and Bangkok cooperated with the Japanese, due to the tensions created by the transfer of territories, they were hardly allies.[44]

Several attacks against Church property provide evidence of a partnership between municipal government, police, and local mobs of Thai Blood Party members. After Bangkok ordered district officials to close down Catholic churches, the police kept a vigilant watch to make sure no one tried to reopen them and hold meetings inside. Parishioners in Tha Rae reported to Bishop Pasotti at Ratchaburi that police officers regularly prevented them from checking on the status of their church building. Meanwhile, vandals regularly slipped past the web of surveillance to destroy crucifixes, break windows, and steal valuable items belonging to the Church. Authorities in Nakhon Phanom monitored Catholic activities very closely but took no action to prevent arsonists from burning down a cathedral in Kham Toei in June 1942.[45] When parishioners in Chachoengsao Province formed a night-watch group to protect their church, the police arrested its members on false charges. These arrests effectively disbanded the night watch and allowed members of the Thai Blood Party to ransack the building the very next night. In Sakon Nakhon, Udon-Thani, Nakhon Phanom, and Loei, a total of seven churches were attacked, burned down, or vandalized from 1942 to 1944.

In some cases the government used safety concerns as an excuse for demolishing a religious edifice. In Nakhon Phanom Province, the chief of Tha Utane district requested the nuns' quarters at Ban Chiang Yeun be torn down. By 1944 most Catholics had left the area, and the empty building was considered a possible hazard because it was located near an elementary school.[46] Other demolition projects were handled in a slightly less professional manner. In neighboring Sakon Nakhon Province, a group of monks destroyed the bell tower, outhouse, and other structures located in the courtyard of the Catholic church at Phanat Nikhom. When Father Forlazini protested this development to local authorities, he learned that the district chief had preapproved the monks' actions because the buildings supposedly violated current building codes.[47] The governor of Nakhon Phanom also blamed Catholics for the destruction of their own property. He claimed that many parishioners had lost both their respect for France and their faith in Catholicism when French artillery from across the Mekong damaged the cathedral in Nong Saeng. The destruction of this sacred edifice caused many to convert to Buddhism and express their outrage towards the French by destroying some of the church buildings and offering others to the community for public use.[48] For the Thai government, this event supported the narrative of Catholicism as a form of deception. Once Thai citizens broke free from the corrosive influence of the clergy, it was only natural that they direct their anger at those who had deceived them.

Banning services and confiscating property were just two of the tactics used by the Phibun regime to pressure Catholics to convert to Buddhism. The government also adopted a "reeducation" strategy. Over a two-year period, district officials held public meetings to publicize the country's new religion policy. Attendance was mandatory for Catholics. After convening the meeting, the district chief would explain that Catholicism would no longer be tolerated in Thailand and requested that everyone present sign a petition declaring their intention to become Buddhists. Thai officials regularly used the phrase "return to Buddhism," reflecting the nationalist discourse that Catholicism was not a legitimate religion and that Catholic Thais had abandoned their true identity and heritage. By signing the pledge to become Buddhist, people underwent a process of rediscovering the path of their ancestors. The Phibun regime refused to acknowledge that Catholicism had a centuries-old heritage in Thailand. Many Thai Catholics were third-generation Church members who knew very little about Buddhism.[49] The first group invited to return was the civil servant class. In February 1941, the Ministry of Interior held a mandatory meeting attended by non-Buddhist civil servants in the Bangkok area, including Muslims and Protestants, at Wat Mahathat. Anyone who did not sign a petition stating they would adopt Buddhism could no longer work for the government.[50]

The government used this same process to convert non-Buddhist civil servants throughout Thailand. Klang Kham, a Catholic schoolteacher in Ubon Province, received a letter from the district chief informing him that he and his family must convert to Buddhism. He described his dilemma as follows: "Kamchat Phatti Suwan, the district chief, took me to his home several times during the week to persuade me. The only explanation he gave was that I must stop practicing a 'European religion.' I told him it was not a European religion. He told me that when I changed religions and had been a monk for one month, he would make me director of the school and increase my monthly salary. I told him I would have to consult with my family. He gave me one week."[51]

Klang Kham fled to Bangkok in an effort to avoid the decision, but he eventually returned to Ubon and informed the district that he would not give up his religion. Upon hearing this news, the vice prefect responded, "You must really love the Europeans. You are truly stupid."[52] Klang Kham left his teaching job and worked as a frontier runner until the status of the Catholic Church was restored, when he became a catechist.

These tactics worked on Catholic civil servants, but the government realized it needed a different form of leverage for ordinary citizens. In Prachinburi Province, a district chief organized a series of mandatory meetings at the district office, where he instructed Catholics to sign the petition to adopt Buddhism. When each person refused, he ordered them to return to the same event day after day so that they were unable to run their businesses or do anything except listen to his sermons on the evils of a European religion. Police arrested anyone who failed to attend. Faced with the prospect of financial ruin, many Catholics eventually signed the petition so they could return to their lives.[53]

The absence of strong Catholic leadership made it easier for provincial leaders to bully members of the congregation into converting. The declaration of martial law and the deportation of all French citizens deprived the Church of its most effective teachers and advocates. The state also arrested several Thai priests who were charged with conducting espionage for the French. The day after French planes bombed the Dongphraram army base in Prachinburi, police arrested Father Michel Somchin and Father Sanguen. The priests, both Thai subjects, were accused of having used flashlights to guide the French planes towards the camp and were sentenced to two years imprisonment.[54] In Nakorn Ratchasima, Father Nicholas was also arrested for being a spy. He spent three years in prison before dying of tuberculosis.[55] Nakhon Phanom witnessed the worst violence. Police murdered seven parishioners in Ban Song Khon after they refused orders to stop teaching about Catholicism or encouraging their brethren to keep the faith. The seven victims in Nakhon Phanom, along with Father Nicholas, were beatified by the Pope and became Thailand's first Catholic martyrs.[56]

When France and Thailand observed a cease-fire in February 1941, most Catholic leaders believed the government would end its harassment of the

Church. In fact, Thailand's victory only emboldened the government in its campaign against the Church. Although Bangkok rescinded the deportation order, allowing French citizens to return to Thailand, local officials refused to allow the return of French Catholic missionaries. When priests arrived at their parishes in Nakhon Phanom Province, they were arrested by the police and released only after promising to return to Bangkok.[57] Local governments continued to pressure those who failed to convert to Buddhism. In Ubon Province, a nun was imprisoned for a year for trying to convince relatives not to enter a Buddhist monastery.[58] In public schools, teachers and administrators directed abuse towards Catholic students who could no longer attend religious schools. Lawrence Khai, a student in Nong Saeng, recalled his experience when the Catholic school he attended was reopened as a state school: "At the school the teachers forced me and my friends to deny the Catholic faith and to adore the statue of Buddha. They said, 'There is no more other religion to practice except Buddhism.' The teacher set up the statue of Buddha in the hall and they forced us students to adore. We refused to obey. They hit us with sticks. They forced us to kneel in front of the statue of Buddha, pressed our heads down with their strong hands. We tried to turn our heads away from the statue of Buddha. The teachers hit us, directing our heads straight to the statue."[59]

As we have seen, the arrests and violence that occurred during the border war were only the first phase in a long-term campaign to force Catholics to abandon their religion. The Thai state reasoned that by deporting French missionaries and imprisoning Thai priests, it could pull down the pillars of ecclesiastical leadership and watch the body of the Church collapse.

THE VATICAN RESPONDS

For several months, the Catholic Church could do little to protect either its members or its property from the orchestrated efforts of the Thai government. But contrary to the claims of Thai propaganda, the Church was not solely a French institution. It could draw on the resources of a worldwide organization. In 1942, the Vatican responded to anti-French sentiment in Thailand by placing the Isan under the jurisdiction of the Salesian mission at Ratchaburi. The Italian Bishop Gaetano Pasotti was assigned the task of lobbying the Phibun regime for the return of religious freedom.[60] Over the next two years, Pasotti appealed in writing and in person to various offices within the Thai government, protesting the destruction of property and requesting an end to the ban on public meetings and a restoration of the Church's prewar status. In his correspondence with the Interior Ministry, Pasotti argued that the persecution was unjustified, because Catholic Thais were not French informants and did not represent a threat to national security. The Church taught its membership to be patriotic, law-abiding citizens. As proof, he reminded Thai authorities that the Church was not experiencing this same level of persecution in any other country within the Japanese sphere of influence. In China, Indochina, the Philippines, and even Japan itself, Catholics still enjoyed the freedom of public worship.[61] Despite Pasotti's arguments and his Italian citizenship, the Thai government refused to return Church property.

Pasotti did manage to get the government's attention, however, when he sent Italian priests into northeastern provinces to replace the French clergy that had been deported. Church authorities reasoned that since Italy was an ally of both Japan and Thailand, Italian priests could provide leadership to fractured congregations and begin the process of restoring the Church's footing in provinces where it had been the target of so much harassment. The arrival of non-French ecclesiastical leaders alarmed local authorities. The governor of Nakhon Phanom informed the Ministry of Interior that the presence of these priests in his provinces was making it difficult to keep new Buddhist converts from backsliding towards Catholicism. He warned that if these clergy were allowed to operate freely, they would soon undo all the progress local officials had made towards eliminating Catholicism from their areas of jurisdiction.[62] While municipal leaders were determined to prevent this, they recognized the need for a new strategy. The instructions provided by the Ministry of Interior applied only to French nationals. From this point forward, provincial authorities developed their own policies for neutralizing the influence of Salesian missionaries.

To discourage Italian priests from permanently relocating to the northeast, local governments denied them access to all Church property. In most cases, the state had already reappropriated these buildings for other purposes. In Nakhon Phanom, Father Albert sent a letter to the governor asking for the return of the priest's quarters so that Father Giuseppe Pinafore could live there when he arrived at Chiang Yuen. The governor responded that the house belonged to the province and was now the residence of the chief of police. The province allowed Father Pinafore to visit Chiang Yuen and Nong Saeng but would not permit him to begin religious instruction.[63] After arriving in Sakon Nakhon, Fathers Marchesi and Forlazini reported to the province as the new Catholic stewards in Chang Ming and Tha Rae. But the government prevented them from taking ownership of Church property, claiming the Italian priests were not the owners.[64] Another priest, Reverend Stocker, arrived in Donthoi to find the governor had installed Buddhist monks in the former Catholic priest's quarters. After moving into the home of a friend, he was visited by law enforcement who ordered him to leave the district. The police informed Reverend Stocker that the state had appropriated the church building and all associated properties and had forbidden the people of Donthoi to associate with Catholic priests. Therefore, what reason could there be for him to stay? Stocker, who had just come from Bangkok, expressed his amazement that the government had confiscated Church property in "Siamese Laos," while Catholic institutions in Bangkok remained completely unaffected.[65]

The arrival of Italian clergy in the northeast created sharp divisions within local communities and rekindled the animosities of the Franco-Thai conflict. Former Catholics who had renounced the faith as a result of government pressure resented the reappearance of European priests in their village, while those who remained Catholic embraced the new ministers. Thai nationalists were incensed at the sight of priests, which they assumed to be French, once again living and working in their community. Even those who realized the priests were Italian still accused them of being "an enemy to Thailand, trying to enslave the Thai people to the Italian Nation."[66] In locations where the priests resumed holding services and performing ordinances, estranged members slowly returned to religious activity. The government, in turn, feared that the Church might reestablish itself. This growing resentment led to renewed confrontation and violence. Father Marchesi received several death threats warning him to leave Tha Rae district in Sakon Nakhon Province. During the night, mobs threw stones at the house where he was staying.[67] Police and local government suggested the Italians leave the province, as they could not guarantee the priests' safety. Meanwhile, the governor of Sakon Nakhon accused the clergy of stirring up religious zealotry among Catholics after a Buddhist monk was stabbed in Phanat Nikhom district.[68] As Italian priests refused to heed government warnings to leave the northeast, the Church-state standoff escalated. Finally, the government resorted to imprisonment. Police arrested Father Pinafore in Nakhon Phanom and transported him to a jail in Champassak. Thai authorities accused him of telling his congregation that the Thai army had damaged the Catholic Church, stolen Church property, and injured a priest during its assault on Champassak the previous year.[69]

At this point, the Church's strategy of sending Italian missionaries into the northeast began to pay dividends. Pinafore's imprisonment attracted the attention of the Italian legation in Bangkok, which contacted the Ministry of Foreign Affairs that same week demanding the release of the Italian priest.[70] Bangkok officials, fearful of jeopardizing relations with an Axis member, immediately agreed to end the harassment and imprisonment of priests, but they requested that Italy confine the Salesian missionaries to the boundaries of the Ratchaburi mission. Italian diplomats refused, saying the matter could best be settled after the war's conclusion. Thailand's ambassador in Rome advised the Foreign Affairs office in Bangkok to accept this arrangement, because a few priests in the northeast were of slight importance in comparison with the thousands of Japanese troops stationed inside the kingdom. Thai diplomats had recently received pledges from the governments of Italy and Germany to endorse Thailand's independence from Japan following the war. The ambassador cautioned his home government not to risk Rome's support on such a crucial issue.[71]

Because the Thai government could no longer evict or imprison Italian priests, it increased pressure on Catholics to disassociate themselves from the Church. Police officers in the northeast recorded the names of people who met regularly with priests and kept them under surveillance.[72] Prime Minister Phibun instructed local officials that they must respect the Catholic clergy but that Thai citizens who refused to obey the government policy of converting to Buddhism must be subjected to various forms of indirect punishment. In Nong Khai, this meant that civic authorities conducted inspections of Catholic homes and found obscure reasons to levy fines. Residents could avoid paying the fine only by visiting a local temple to honor the monks or by inviting the monks for dinner at their home. Anyone who refused to follow these criteria would accumulate more fines, until they ended up in jail.[73] In Ban Nong Doen, Catholic residents received fines because their toilets were insufficiently clean. The only sure method of escaping such penalties was to convert to Buddhism.[74]

ANTI-CATHOLICISM IN CHACHOENGSAO PROVINCE

To what extent was the anti-Catholic persecution simply a by-product of the war hysteria surrounding Thailand's conflict with French Indochina? Given the close proximity of many Catholic communities to the Thai-Indochinese border, one would expect the Thai authorities to keep them under close surveillance during the martial law period. But state-sponsored anti-Catholicism was not limited to border regions, nor was it simply a side effect of military conflict. In October 1941, over a year after Phibun initiated the border dispute, the Thai newspaper *Ekkaraj* addressed the atmosphere of religious intolerance in Thailand. After acknowledging that a ban on Catholic meetings in border areas may have been necessary at the height of the conflict, the editorial pointed out that many Catholic churches in the country's interior remained closed. Why, it asked, was this necessary when hostilities had ceased and the state of the country had returned to normal?[75]

The newspaper article referred to conditions in Chachoengsao Province, just east of Bangkok. Although the area had no sizeable minority population or military installations, eyewitnesses confirmed that the harassment of Catholics in Bang Kla district mirrored what had occurred in Sakon Nakhon and Nakhon Phanom. After the border conflict began, the district chief obtained a list of all the Catholics in the district and ordered each of them to report to "reeducation meetings." Beginning in March 1941, between sixty and seventy people attended these gatherings held in the pavilion of Wat Chaeng. The district chief and assistant police chief presided and began by explaining the theme of the gathering: "We are Thai and we must act like Thais in flesh and blood, in our beliefs, and in our souls."[76] The chief set the tone early by instructing everyone, "We can no longer practice Catholicism in this area, we must renounce it and adopt a new religion. If you want to remain a Catholic, sit on the floor. If you are willing to convert to Buddhism, please sit in a chair."[77] When all but three women took their places on the floor, the chief explained the district's new policy on Catholicism. Catholics should not be so stubborn, he warned, as public opinion showed that most people were opposed to this religion. Catholicism was a French religion, and Buddhism was the religion for the Thai. When one individual countered that Catholicism was not a just a French religion, the district chief responded, "The members may not all be French, but the religion itself is definitely French."[78]

Reeducation meetings also provided an opportunity to question the civic knowledge and loyalty of Catholic Thais. The district chief questioned them, for example, concerning the meaning of the different colors in the Thai flag. When someone gave the right answers he responded, "Correct—now why don't you want to become a real Thai?" Provincial authorities conveyed the impression that Catholicism had adversely affected the country's unity. One woman from Tha Lad village who attended the meetings recalled the following exchange: "[The district leader] asked the question, 'What do we do with a mango tree that has contracted *ka fak?*' Someone answered, 'We must cut it down and get rid of it [before the disease spreads].' He replied, 'Correct. Catholicism is like *ka fak*. It must be cut out of our midst.' "[79]

The residents of Bang Kla were forced to sit and listen to this anti-Catholic tirade for several hours. Anyone who attempted to defend themselves was immediately shouted down and accused of being "fifth column." Catholics realized that speaking out would only bring more trouble, so they endured these diatribes in silence.[80] At the end of the second meeting, the district chief announced that he would no longer summon them to these gatherings. Henceforth, they should just plan on attending each day between 1 and 5 p.m. This pattern continued for weeks. Because this reorientation took up the entire afternoon, Catholics had to abandon their stores and jobs, and many had to travel long distances from their villages to the district center. The costs, both in terms of money and time, gradually wore down Catholic resolve. At the end of each meeting a handful of people would sign their names to the petition. Their signature indicated that they now understood their duties as Thai citizens, and they became exempt from further meetings.[81] But as the majority of Catholics continued to keep the faith, the district chief began to warn them that the environment in Bang Kla was becoming increasingly dangerous. As one resident in attendance recalled, "The district chief told us how hard he was working to keep the Catholics safe. He was watching the church very carefully, not to spy on us, to keep us safe. He said to us, 'Catholics go to church without weapons, so if someone came to make trouble, what could you do? The Thai Blood Party has hundreds of members to cause problems. Do you know how many times I've stopped them from causing harm? I heard rumors they were going to do something and I was worried about my people. So I encourage all of you Christians not to dissent because they think you are all fifth column.' "[82]

Whether these instructions constituted a genuine warning or a subtle threat is unclear, but it awakened Catholics in Bang Kla to the reality that they could not rely on the authorities to protect their lives or property. They formed a night-watch group to protect their church building. Each night several volunteers spent their night watching over its grounds.[83] As Catholics could not legally possess weapons, they could offer little resistance if a mob decided to attack, but their presence deterred Thai Blood members from attacking their house of worship.

The arrival of two Italian priests from the Ratchaburi Diocese sparked widespread violence and caused Catholics to abandon the area for several years. Father Constonzo Gavalla was reassigned from Kanchanaburi to Chachoengsao Province in the hopes that he would provide leadership and guidance to the membership there. Father Gavalla traveled from Bangkok by boat to the village of Tha Kwian, where he disembarked. Many locals were not pleased to learn of his arrival. An eyewitness traveling in the same boat recalled overhearing two men threatening about how they would "break that priest's neck" later on that night.[84] That evening Father Gavalla reported to the civic authorities as required by law before retiring to spend the night in the priest's home next to the local church. Within hours, the entire community knew about the arrival of another Catholic priest. On the night of March 14, 1941, a mob attacked the priest's quarters in Tha Kwian and looted the church. Father Gavalla later recalled his experience:

> At 11:30 p.m. while we were asleep, over twenty people came to the house. They used an axe to destroy the door and enter the home. They used axes, large knives, and clubs, and began destroying things within the house. When I was fully awake, I decided to try to flee, since I knew I could not fight with so many people. When I reached the market (about thirty meters from the house) the assailants caught me and ripped off my clothing. They took all the money in my bag (ten baht) and also my watch, boat and train tickets, my travel documents, and other personal papers.
>
> Then the mob dragged me face down and threatened me so I wouldn't turn over. If I disobeyed they would kill me. Those who remained punched, kicked and hit me. There were two men. The first hit me in the head with a club. Finally they dragged me over and tied me to a tree near the church. All this caused me to lose consciousness momentarily. When I came to I saw a boy walk by and asked him to free me. He refused, saying that if he helped me he would be in trouble. I struggled until eventually I was able to free myself.[85]

Father Gavalla then returned to the priest's quarters and noticed that the house had been ransacked and many items stolen. After two hours, both the district chief and the police chief paid him a visit. When he attempted to recount the home invasion, the district chief interrupted him, saying that they had no interest in last night's events. Instead they wanted to ascertain whether the Italian priest was in Tha Kwian to conduct espionage. After searching the premises and posing several questions, the police chief concluded Father Gavalla was not a spy. The district chief drew up a statement affirming the priest's innocence and declared that the district was not responsible for the damages to the house. He then ordered the priest to sign it. That afternoon Father Gavalla returned to Bangkok, stopping only to file a police report at Baed Raew station before checking into the Hospital General St. Louis to recover from his injuries.[86]

The home invasion in Tha Kwian provided local officials with the pretext they needed to deal with Catholicism in other areas of Bang Kla district. The day after Father Gavalla's assault, police arrested seven Catholics in the village of Tha Lad on charges that they had robbed and assaulted an Italian priest in Tha Kwian.[87] Most of the detainees were also members of the watch patrol. These men were sent to a detention facility in Phanom Sarakham subdistrict. After three days a police official visited the prisoners to inform them that the district would drop the charges if they agreed to give up Catholicism. They would be released immediately and their guns would be returned. Each of the men signed a statement and returned to Tha Lad. During their absence, the night watch had disbanded, making the church an easy target for the Thai Blood vigilantes. A local Catholic woman recorded the violence that occurred the first night after the arrests: "While those men were imprisoned at Phanom district, one night many people came to ransack the church. I don't know how many there were because I took my children and fled in a boat along the river. It sounded like many people because I could hear the sounds of destruction and people shouting, '*Chaiyo!*' The next day I reported to the district chief to renounce Catholicism. He informed me that there were over four hundred people who attacked the church. After that I no longer had to attend the meetings."[88]

The state understood that the church was more than a gathering place; it was the soul of the Catholic community. The building's desecration marked the beginning of a hiatus for the congregation in Tha Lad, one that would last until the end of the war. When Thong Ma, one of the members of the night watch who had been arrested, returned from jail he learned that the village leaders had formed a committee to itemize and sell all the belongings taken from the church. Some Church property was also sold, including the priest's belongings. The building was abandoned and eventually demolished when the village decided to build a road through the property. In 1944 when the Thai government began making restitution to the Catholic Church for property seized or destroyed, it conducted a survey of the district. It found that the Catholic Church leased out its only remaining buildings, and that there were no longer any Catholics worshipping in Bang Kla.[89]

The case of Chachoengsao Province suggests that the government security concerns were merely a pretext for their agenda of religious uniformity. Chachoengsao was not a northeastern border province, it had no military installations, and most of the Catholics self-identified as ethnic Thais, not

Vietnamese. For a campaign of such intense persecution to occur in this province suggests two things: first, that the anti-Catholic movement was an important part of Phibun's domestic agenda of nation building, and second, that provincial and district leaders employed their own discretion in implementing the directions of the Ministry of Interior.

THE END OF PERSECUTION

Support for religious persecution began to wane once it became clear that Japan would lose the war and the Allies would return to Southeast Asia. After Phibun resigned as prime minister in 1944, the country's new leaders abandoned his rhetoric of National Humiliation and attempted to cultivate support among the Allies.[90] The anti-Catholic movement was one of the first policies to be scrapped. The Thai government realized that the Vatican could be a useful ally if the country was to avoid British occupation following the war. The government of Khuang Aphaiwongse publicly affirmed its commitment to the principles of religious freedom enshrined in the Thai constitution. For years, Bishop Pasotti had written to all levels of government concerning the abuse of Church members and property with almost no response. Suddenly, it was the Ministry of Interior that initiated correspondence with the bishop, informing him that the state was working to expedite the return of Church property.[91] In November 1944, the governor of Nakhon Phanom sent out a memorandum notifying district leaders of the province's updated policy regarding the Catholic Church. Government organizations occupying Church buildings must either vacate or request permission from Catholic leadership to remain. In Loei Province, Pasotti instructed civic leaders to vacate the church, which had been used as a public school, and to transfer ownership to leading Catholic citizens who acted as transitional caretakers.[92] Anyone who had taken any Church possessions or valuables was instructed to return the items to their district office. The district must compile records of Church property destroyed over the past three years. Finally, Catholic worship would be permitted under the supervision of the local police.[93]

Bangkok's abrupt policy reversal meant government agents responsible for harassing the Church now found themselves in an awkward position. After the fall of Phibun, these agents watched in bewilderment as state support for their efforts quickly evaporated. The case of Nai Roen Trisathan illustrates how the government recruited individuals to carry out their nationalist religion policy and then abandoned them once the policy became untenable. Nai Roen had been recruited in January 1941 by authorities in Phitsanulok Province, who requested that he take charge of the Catholic question in the Nikorn Laks area. After accepting the offer, he began enforcing the state's three-pronged strategy of banning meetings, converting Catholics to Buddhism, and secularizing Catholic schools. Nai Roen received police protection while he carried out these responsibilities, which he viewed as his duty to the nation. While Thai troops fought to regain the *lost territories* and defeat Western imperialism, he would purge the enemies within. For his efforts, he received a lucrative position as the manager of the community slaughterhouse and became an administrator at the former Catholic, now public, school.[94]

As the war turned against Japan, however, Nai Roen noticed that local government slowly retreated from its own anti-Catholic policy. He wrote to the governor of Phitsanulok explaining that a Catholic group, which had formerly administered the church and school, had begun pressuring him to return their property so they could once again hold meetings. He complained that the new district chief refused to give him the political backing he had previously enjoyed and the police no longer protected him. Without the backing of these institutions, Nai Roen felt that his life was in danger from resurgent Catholic elements that would hold him responsible for their persecution in Phitsanulok. He resigned his position soon afterward.

Bishop Pasotti seemed amenable to the idea of using Vatican influence to support leniency for postwar Thailand once the government had proved its willingness to support religious tolerance. Instead of railing against Thailand for injustices suffered during the war, he expressed his gratitude towards the new government for restoring the Church's property and official status as an acceptable religion: "This action reflects the government's new policy of establishing religious freedom for everyone, which the constitution protects, and which the Regent Pridi supported on Dec 8th, 1944. We believe it will also have influence on Thailand's foreign relations as well. . . . Our devotion to Thailand is unchanging and we promise to make every effort to help increase the nation's honour and prestige and growth in the future."[95]

The evidence from the final months of the war suggests that Catholics returned to the Church once it was permissible to do so. More research must be done in order to ascertain the extent to which the Church was compensated for confiscated or damaged property as part of the postwar reconciliation. It seems clear, however, that the Catholic Church quickly rebuilt its organization in Thailand after enduring an intense four-year period of government persecution. To be sure, Catholics were not the only denomination to suffer scrutiny during the Franco-Thai conflict. The Phibun government created an atmosphere of religious nationalism designed to pressure all religious minorities to conform to the majority faith. As religion became an indicator of one's civic allegiance, Muslims also found their religion subject to state interference.[96] In fact, Muslims were an ideal target for this type of irredentist movement, as they also inhabited the border of regions deemed lost to Western imperialism. Unlike Catholics, however, Muslims were not accused of being fifth column or labeled a danger to the nation's well-being. There were two important reasons for this difference. The southern territories in question had been transferred to Britain, not France, and Phibun had no interest in stirring up animosity towards the British. Also, Islam did not fit within the discoursive framework of National Humiliation, since no Islamic imperialist power had intervened in Thailand. Thus, although discrimination against Muslims did occur, its intensity did not match that of the state campaign against Catholics. In the Interior Ministry's official correspondence regarding religious policy, only the Catholic Church is repeatedly mentioned by name as a threat to national security.[97] Within the National Humiliation narrative, the Church was more than a foreign religion; it was a symbol of imperialism.

CONCLUSION

For over three years, Phibun's military state described anti-Catholicism as an important step on the pathway to complete independence. His supporters viewed the Catholic Church as part of the imperialist apparatus that disregarded the country's laws and obstructed self-government. Priests such as Reverend Stocker were considered subversives because they discouraged Catholics from participating in civic ceremonies that included Buddhist rituals. As we have seen, the level of Church persecution varied in different parts of the country due to a variety of factors, including geography and regional initiative. The most intense harassment occurred in the northeast, while congregations in Bangkok and the north were relatively unaffected. The exception of Chachoengsao Province, however, indicates that more research is necessary if we are to understand how each region responded to the anti-Catholic policy emanating from the Ministry of Interior.

The outbreak of war in Asia allowed the Thai state to promote its anti-Western agenda without jeopardizing its independence. In 1941, Thai newspapers celebrated the dawn of a new era in which past injustices would be avenged. Europeans living in Bangkok grew increasingly alarmed at the antiwhite sentiments expressed in the city's newspapers.[98] Phibun's nation-building philosophy received strong popular support because he used National Humiliation discourse to emphasize the need to restore national honor and elevate Thailand's international status. This process of restoration required the recovery of territory ceded to European imperialists and the removal of any institution that had participated in Thailand's semicolonial subjugation. As one of the most recognizable symbols of European influence in Thailand, the Catholic Church naturally became a primary target of this political scheme.

4

Thailand and Pan-Asianism

Few topics in Thai history garner more attention from scholars than the alliance with Japan during World War II. Historians often cite the alliance as the definitive example of *bamboo diplomacy,* arguing that Phibun entered into a patron-client relationship with Japan to prevent Thailand from becoming a battlefield. It is true that Phibun wanted to preserve the country's independence. But he also saw the Japanese Empire as a vehicle for expanding Thai influence in Southeast Asia. It was a pragmatic decision based on the changing balance of power in Asia, one that required a new discourse to explain the basis of a Thai-Japanese partnership. In the absence of cultural or historical links between the two nations, Phibun touted the strong ideological parallels between National Humiliation discourse and Pan-Asian rhetoric. Wartime propaganda claimed that both countries had been victimized by Western imperialism. The Thai state demonstrated considerable dexterity in adapting National Humiliation imagery to suit the new climate of international politics, presenting Thailand as semicolonized to certain audiences or perpetually independent to others. Seen from this perspective, the war in East Asia was simply an expansion of Thailand's struggle against colonialism. Meanwhile, the Phibun regime used the dislocation and disorder of war to continue its pursuit of a Greater Thailand.

THE DECISION

As 1941 drew to a close, it became increasingly apparent that Japan was positioning itself to strike against additional targets in Southeast Asia. Any showdown between Japan and Britain would certainly bode ill for Thailand, wedged as it was between the British Empire and Japanese forces occupying French Indochina. The Thai government remained neutral regarding the conflicts in Europe and in China, but Phibun understood the country could not wait out the war. A Japanese assault on Burma or Malaya would require passage through Thailand. During the buildup to the 1941 border conflict with French Indochina, Phibun signed a secret agreement granting Japanese troops safe passage to attack Britain on condition that Tokyo supported his territorial claims. Japan had delivered the Tokyo Peace Accord, and Phibun knew he would be expected to reciprocate. In effect, the prime minister had negotiated himself into a corner. He could not admit Japanese troops without reneging on his promise to maintain Thai neutrality. For several months he watched and waited, hoping for a turn of events that would release him from his obligation.

On December 8, 1941, Phibun ran out of time. Japanese forces invaded Thailand along its eastern border with Cambodia and at several points along the western side of the southern peninsula. After a few hours of resistance, the Thai government agreed to an armistice. The treaty that followed permitted Japanese troops to pass through the country, but more importantly it preserved the Thai army, the source of Phibun's political power. Over the next few weeks, Phibun's confidence in Japan's ability to defeat the Allies increased and he began to express more enthusiasm for the Axis cause. In January 1942, Thailand declared war on Britain and the United States.

Phibun's declaration of war dictated the government's strategy—its fate was now linked to Japan—but it also raised a critical secondary issue. How would the government explain its sudden shift in loyalties? How would it manufacture public animosity towards Britain and support for Japan?[1] Despite all the scholarly attention paid to Thailand's "flexible" foreign policy, the country had been pro-British dating back to the mid-nineteenth century. Britain was the first European nation to negotiate a trade agreement with Thailand. It maintained a central role in its economy, and still wielded enormous cultural influence over the country's political elite. By comparison, Thai-Japanese relations had a much shorter history. Japan was a much smaller market for Thai exports, especially rice, and most people felt no cultural affinity for their fellow Asian nation. During the secret talks that followed the signing of the Thai-Japanese treaty, Phibun acknowledged that popular support could be a serious problem. Aside from the military, most bureaucratic officials maintained favorable attitudes towards Britain and the United States, and a number of civilian functionaries even expressed anti-Japanese sentiments.[2]

In an effort to sell the new alliance, the government attempted to link Japan's Pan-Asian rhetoric with the narrative of National Humiliation that had already gained widespread acceptance in Thailand. Phibun explained that his regime declared war on Britain because the British had repeatedly taken advantage of Thailand in the past. The war, he argued, would increase Thailand's level of independence by reducing British influence over its culture, economy, and former vassal states. Conversely, Wichit's writings portrayed Japan as an empathetic ally that, like Thailand, had suffered the indignations of Western interference. Through its alliance with Japan, he reasoned, Thailand was now engaged in a campaign to liberate all Asia. After the Western imperialist order had been swept away, Thailand's noncolonized status would give the country a powerful position in the "New Order" that would rule Asia. Phibun and Wichit wanted to emulate Japanese political and military success. They saw the conflict in Asia as an opportunity to liberate territories under Western control, which would then become part of a "Greater Thai Empire." Throughout the war, these leaders claimed that Thailand had already begun driving the French out of the Golden Peninsula. The next step was to help Japan eliminate Western imperialism in Asia.

Once formulated, this discourse was disseminated through a variety of media outlets. Newspaper articles chronicled the long tradition of cordial relations between the two Asian nations and explained Japan's strategy in Southeast Asia. Dailies also printed summaries of public speeches by Phibun, Wichit, Prince Wan, and other prominent leaders outlining the necessity of going to war. The government printed new irredentist maps that documented the amount of territory lost to Britain. In a demonstration of solidarity with colonized peoples, the Phibun regime allowed independence organizations, especially the Free India movement, to broadcast their anticolonial messages from its radio transmitters.

In 1942, Bangkok's only radio station was owned and operated by the Department of Publicity, which produced a popular show featuring two entertaining personalities known as Nai Man and Nai Khong. The program was created to publicize the regime's new pro-Japanese policy and intensify animosity towards the Allies.[3] Each night people tuned in to hear Nai Man and Nai Khong celebrate Japanese victories, discuss how Western nations had wronged Thailand in the past, and inform listeners of new cultural policies. The pair became an important outlet for directing accusations against the enemy while refuting charges made by their radio counterparts in New Delhi, Rangoon, and Singapore.

The Thai state censored all mass media outlets during the war in an effort to control public opinion. Following the treaty with Japan, the government organized a press conference with the Japanese ambassador, who instructed reporters that certain topics regarding Japanese-Thai relations were off limits.[4] Thailand did have an underground resistance movement run by Pridi, known as the Free Thai (Seri Thai) movement, which opposed the alliance with Japan and favored the Allies. Occasionally this group distributed leaflets attacking government policy. Due to Phibun's overwhelming popularity early in the war, however, the Seri Thai had only minimal influence on public discussion.[5] The existence or absence of competing nationalist visions lies outside the boundaries of this study, whose objective is not to identify any particular discourse as legitimate or illegitimate. Rather, this chapter seeks to demonstrate how the official (state-sponsored) dialogue concerning Thailand's place in Greater East Asia evolved out of preexisting narratives on National Humiliation.

PROMOTING THE ALLIANCE WITH JAPAN

The news of Thailand's surrender to Japanese imperial troops shocked the nation. Many citizens were stunned at the ease with which they had been defeated and occupied. Many Thais shed tears at the sight of Japanese soldiers marching through Bangkok. They believed their country had lost its independence.[6] The Department of Publicity faced the urgent task of somehow convincing citizens that Thailand's relationship with Japan was a partnership, not an occupation. On December 10, 1941, Phibun outlined the government's new policy in a radio broadcast to the nation. The prime minister stated that Thailand could no longer avoid the war that engulfed the rest of the world. The Thai government agreed to cooperate with Tokyo's demands to preserve the nation from being annihilated. Japan had no desire to fight Thailand, Phibun insisted, but merely required passage through its territory to fight its real enemy, Britain.[7] The government had negotiated an agreement that allowed Japanese soldiers to enter the country in return for Japan's pledge to respect Thailand's independence and sovereignty. Phibun concluded with a plea for unity. If all citizens placed their faith in their prime minister, he would guide the country through this period of uncertainty.

Thai leaders worked hard to produce public sympathy for the Axis' war objectives and dispel the notion that Japan was a threat to Thailand. Bangkok newspapers printed articles sympathetic to Japan during Thailand's period of neutrality, including explanations of Japanese expansion. In May 1941, just after the signing of the Tokyo treaty, *Nikorn* carried a two-part story detailing the demographic pressures confronting Japan. The article began with late-nineteenth-century Japan, which was considered a "have-not" country in comparison to Britain and France, because its territory was insufficient to support its growing population of agrarian laborers. While 50 percent of the population was farmers, only 15 percent of the land was arable due to the mountainous nature of the Japanese archipelago. The Japanese government explored migration to China and Manchuria, but these areas were already overpopulated and living standards there were low. So it turned its attention to the "southern lands," where there was plenty of open land and the climate was well suited to the Japanese constitution.[8]

These newspaper stories asserted that Western powers had robbed and humiliated Japan just as they had done in Thailand. Another article in *Nikorn* explained that Western imperialists tried to prevent Japanese industrialization by limiting their access to raw materials and foreign markets. Despite this interference, Japan succeeded in producing manufactured items whose fine quality and affordable price allowed them to begin competing with European goods for market share throughout Asia.[9] The Western powers responded to this challenge by levying tariffs on Japanese goods or establishing quotas on imports entering their colonies in India, Indochina, the East Indies, and the Philippines. These protectionist policies awakened Japan to its own economic vulnerability. Its leaders realized that continued industrialization required the acquisition of its own colonies, just as Western Europe had done. This realization caused Japan to take possession of Formosa in 1895, Korea in 1905, and later Manchuria (Manchukuo) in 1933. The article concluded that Japan's new policy had opened the way to increased economic development and enhanced national security.

A similar article in *Santi rasadorn* titled "The Origins of the Pacific War" argued that the United States and Britain had conspired to strangle the Japanese nation.[10] The Allies feared a resurgent Japan would challenge the existing imperialist order and worked to deny Japanese businesses access to the Chinese markets. When these measures became insufferable, Japan had no recourse except to launch a war to liberate China from Western imperialist control and open its markets to other Asian powers. An editorial in *Sri krung* contended that Britain and America had tried to limit Japan's armed forces using the 1922 Washington naval treaty and were now sending weapons to Chiang Kai-shek. The British and Americans wanted the Nationalist Chinese to sacrifice themselves defending the Western imperial hierarchy. When this strategy failed, the article suggested, the Allies began an oil embargo and enacted other economic sanctions in an attempt to starve Japan, which was now locked in a struggle for its own survival.[11]

The Bangkok media denounced the West as imperialists while touting Japanese efforts to "liberate" China. Certainly Thai leaders were aware of Japan's record in Manchukuo and even suspicious of their intentions for Thailand. But the Japanese also represented an Asian nation that had been humbled by the West but that had quickly recovered and grown into a modern industrial state and formidable military power. Japan's success fascinated the junta that ruled Bangkok. For decades, Thai reformers had watched with envy as Japan rapidly modernized its institutions, arguing that Thailand could follow the Japanese example of blending modernity with tradition.[12] As far as Japanese imperialism was concerned, Phibun understood that the New Order in Asia could serve Thai interests. The arrival of Britain and France in Southeast Asia had initiated the decline of the Thai empire, but Japanese hegemony in the region might create suitable conditions for its revival. By 1942, Japan had assisted Thai expansion into areas of French Indochina and was considering Phibun's petition for control of the Shan states in British Burma. Thai propaganda claimed that the purpose of the Thai-Japanese alliance was the "destruction of the old order under the heel of Britain and the United States," but clearly Bangkok had plans to restore its own imperial glory.[13]

THE CASE AGAINST BRITAIN

"Britain has wronged us again and again. We will not forgive them."

Radio Bangkok, January 8, 1942

The notion of a Japanese-Thai alliance confronting British tyranny functioned well at a rhetorical level; but leaders from both countries acknowledged that Thai citizens remained fascinated with British society and culture. Japanese military attaché Asada Shinsuke observed how Bangkok's elite continued to follow British sports, history, and the tradition of the royal family, even after Thailand's declaration of war. More Thai officials spoke English than any other foreign language, and many adopted English customs including tennis, tea, and country clubs. During his time in Thailand, Asada didn't recall ever meeting a Thai who spoke Japanese or displayed much enthusiasm for Japanese culture. Given the country's craving for European sophistication, he estimated it might take a century of propaganda to completely remove Western influence from Thailand.[14] All of this complicated the formation of an effective anti-British propaganda campaign. Generating antipathy towards France was simple by comparison. French culture had not permeated

Thailand in the same way, and the Franco-Siamese crisis became the foundation of a historical narrative on National Humiliation. Vilifying Britain would require a much more nuanced approach.

To formulate its anti-British discourse, propagandists returned to the Franco-Siamese crisis, this time to evoke the theme of betrayal. In speeches, newspaper articles, and radio broadcasts, the Thai state accused Britain of abandoning Thailand by refusing to assist the monarchy during the 1893 crisis. It was true that Thailand enjoyed close relations with Britain in the past, but what had it profited them? British pledges of friendship were mere ploys to maximize their trading profits; they abandoned their friends at the first sign of trouble. If Britain had been careful to avoid directly humiliating Thailand, it was only so that they could lull its leaders into complacency while exploiting the country's resources and annexing its territory.

Through its use of the betrayal narrative, the state revised Britain's role in the events of 1893 in order to absorb that country into its larger discourse of National Humiliation. The new historiography on the Franco-Siamese crisis rejected the conventional wisdom that British diplomacy acted as a restraint on French expansion into Siam, suggesting instead that Britain (and even the United States) had abandoned Siam to its fate. Phibun's declaration of war specifically referenced British and American neutrality during the crisis as one of his reasons for declaring war on the Allies.[15] Newspaper commentaries accused the British of being two-faced. An article titled "Pain Serves as a Reminder" attacked Britain's reputation as an ally of Thailand: "Britain claims we should be more grateful to them for helping us preserve our independence during RS 112. Who are they trying to fool? They never did anything to help us, they only helped themselves."[16]

In an effort to rewrite the history of the crisis, state narratives blamed Britain for using Siam's predicament for its own advantage. The Franco-Siamese crisis helped establish a lasting balance of power between British and French empires in Southeast Asia without compromising Britain's monopoly on Siamese trade.

By framing the events of 1893 in this manner, the government used historical precedents to justify its entry into the Axis camp. Thai leaders adopted the position that it would be a mistake to rely on Britain in the upcoming conflict. In a newspaper interview, Phibun suggested that Churchill wanted to utilize the Thai army as a shield against the Japanese march on Singapore. Thai soldiers would be asked to fight and die to preserve British hegemony in Malaya and India.[17] Ultimately, the army would have been destroyed and the nation occupied while British generals retreated towards their next line of defense. This notion that Britain first manipulated and then discarded its allies became an important theme of Thai propaganda during the early months of 1942 when the Allies were retreating across Europe and Asia.

Radio broadcasts pointed out that Britain did little to save Norway, Poland, France, or Belgium from their collective fates but was now using infantrymen from those countries to safeguard its own interests.[18] In their nightly radio program, Nai Man and Nai Khong frequently criticized Britain's use of colonial soldiers to defend its empire while the British themselves remained safe on their island. Canadians had been captured during the battle of Hong Kong, Egyptians fought in Europe, and Australians guarded Singapore even with Japanese forces poised to invade Sydney.[19] In response to Churchill's famous declaration that his country would never surrender, the radio duo mocked Britain's willingness "to fight to the very last Indian."[20]

Figure 2. **British Deception.** A political cartoon showing a British soldier holding up Thailand as a shield against an attacking Japanese soldier. The caption reads, "English Deception: England's secret plan would lead to Thailand's destruction. The way to save Thailand is to join the Japanese assault on England." (National Archives of Thailand)

Figure 3. **Britain Is Our Enemy.** Thai and Japanese soldiers push Britain out of the Malaysian peninsula. The caption reads, "England is Our Enemy: Let's unite our spirit and our strength and destroy the invader together. May Thailand continue to grow and prosper in order to help achieve the New Order in Asia." (National Archives of Thailand)

Meanwhile, Radio Bangkok declared its empathy for the "enslaved peoples" of the Anglo-American empires, claiming that Britain had similarly forced the Kingdom of Siam to fight on its behalf during World War I. British advisors, they argued, used the unequal treaty system as leverage to convince Rama VI to declare war on the Central Powers. Then after benefiting from Siamese support during the war, London did nothing to address the subject of extraterritorial privileges. Vajiravudh had been awarded the Star of India in recognition of his service to the United Kingdom. His acceptance of a decoration normally awarded to colonial subjects would be interpreted later as demeaning to his status as the king of an independent country. For Nai Man and Nai Khong this act symbolized Thailand's inferior semicolonial relationship with Britain.[21] Phibun explained his refusal to join the Allies by declaring that he would not allow Thailand to be treated like another colony. The media in Bangkok repeatedly invoked the phrase, "We will not die for Britain's sake," as though it were a declaration of independence.[22]

As part of this process of historical revision, the state provided several examples of how Britain had undermined Thai independence in the past. Nai Man and Nai Khong filled entire broadcasts with claims that Britain had sought to colonize Siam since its arrival in Ayutthaya 300 years ago. During one program, the duo explained how Siamese kings had generously welcomed English traders to the kingdom, even offering royal protection against Dutch attempts to force them out. Later when Dutch naval vessels began seizing Ayutthaya's ships, the English refused to assist in the monarchy's defense. During the reign of King Narai, the East India Company threatened to blockade Mergui, Ayutthaya's most important Indian Ocean port, unless the king agreed to pay compensation for actions taken against the English governors. In response, Narai declared war on the English and forced them out of Mergui and Tenasserim.[23]

At its inception, National Humiliation discourse and the concept of *lost territory* referred only to lands taken by the French; but this changed after the Thai declaration of war on the United States and Britain. Irredentists argued that Britain was equally guilty of seizing Thai lands to add to their empire.[24] They accused the East India Company of conspiring to take Penang in 1786, while Rama I was distracted by the war with Burma.[25] According to Thai radio broadcasts, Britain had once turned the governor of Kedah Province against Bangkok, offering the sultan protection while he raised troops to assist Burma against the Thai king. In their lust for natural resources, the British continuously renegotiated the border between Thailand and Burma, thereby cheating the Thai out of vast amounts of northern terrain. As for the south, Phibun's regime now claimed that British officials pressured Chulalongkorn to sign away the four Malay states in order to rescind the most humiliating aspects of the unequal treaty system.[26]

The state's revised history of British-Thai relations illustrates the extent to which National Humiliation discourse employed geography to convey a sense of victimhood. Phibun's irredentist maps depicted client kingdoms such as Kedah as fully integrated units within the Thai nation-state. In reality, Kedah had been a semiautonomous state that paid tribute to the Siamese monarchy and that later accepted the suzerainty of the British Empire. Thongchai has described these cartographical constructions as "the encoding of desire." Their purpose was to act as a two-dimensional representation of what was otherwise an intangible notion of loss and betrayal. Without the idea of the geobody, it would have been very difficult for Phibun to chronicle a history of violence committed against the Thai nation. Even radio personalities Nai Man and Nai Kong analyzed historical maps of the Thai kingdom in an effort to explain Thailand's legacy of territorial loss:

> KHONG: When I look at this old map I feel stunned.
>
> MAN: Why wouldn't you feel stunned? In the north, [Britain] trampled on our head. They used chains to bind our feet. Both arms have been tightly bound. That's something anyone can understand.
>
> KHONG: You said that in the north they trampled our head. I'm curious about the Greater Thai states, our own flesh and blood, when did they get swallowed up?
>
> MAN: Britain took it after they defeated Burma. They casually gobbled it up without any real justification. Their real purpose was to monitor our activities in the north. They frantically seized northern territory before the French could get it. This almost led to a war with France.
>
> KHONG: This injustice is our inheritance. For several decades our borders have shrunk all over the country.[27]

Despite the efforts of state media, the attacks against Britain failed to arouse the same anger and resentment as the anti-French campaign of the previous year. There are several possible explanations for this result. First, the government began publicizing the amount of territory lost to France much earlier than territory lost to Britain. At the height of Franco-Thai hostilities in 1940, when the Thai government was busily printing and distributing thousands of irredentist maps, Phibun sent explicit instructions to the Ministry of Interior to print maps displaying territorial concessions to France, but not other losses.[28] The prime minister saw no benefit in needlessly antagonizing London while he was already locked in a struggle with the Vichy government. One popular explanation is that Thais felt the loss of territories to French Indochina more acutely because the inhabitants of those regions were considered ethnically Thai, while the people in lands ceded to Britain were either Burmese or Malay.[29] Bangkok's newspapers often referred to the Shan peoples as "Greater Thais" in an attempt to convince readers that these people had strong cultural connections with Thailand.

The failure of National Humiliation discourse to generate anti-British hatred can best be understood if we take into account Britain's method of acquiring its territories from the Thai monarchy. According to Suphaphorn Bumrungwong, the loss to France became more meaningful to Thailand because the defeat had been so humiliating for the monarchy, whereas territorial concessions to Britain involved diplomatic negotiation.[30] Over time, the shame of the 1893 loss was transferred to the Thai armed forces, which did not fight another foreign war until 1941. The opportunity to restore the military's reputation as defenders of the nation first motivated the People's Party to attempt a recovery of *lost territories.*

State media also analyzed the history of trade relations to find additional evidence of British exploitation. Newspaper articles recounted instances where Britain had strong-armed the monarchy into allowing it access to Siam's abundant natural resources and labor force or control over its exports. Siam also became a market for British manufactured goods and began to adopt its civilizing influence. As Europeans gradually took hold of Thailand's major industries, they displaced Thai entrepreneurs, which crippled the country's long-term development. Nai Man and Nai Khong cited northern Thailand's teak industry as an example, claiming that Britain obtained huge teak concessions from the monarchy through deception and military leverage. When Thai logging businesses proved unable to compete with the large European firms, their owners went bankrupt and its employees went to work for the British. Over several decades, Britain dominated the teak industry, extracting lumber worth millions of baht from Thai forests.[31] Nai Man concluded that Churchill's request for an alliance with Thailand was motivated by his fear of losing access to such valuable natural resources.

Thai leaders also revisited the narrative, first established by legal scholars during the 1920s, that the Bowring Treaty inaugurated an era of semicolonialism for Thailand. "The white races kept us shackled for more than seventy years," one commentator stated, "because of Britain's example. Every treaty signed by Rama IV followed the same format as the British treaty, so that our own authority gradually eroded."[32] Such diatribes accused John Bowring of deceiving Siam by professing friendship while crafting a contract that would gradually deprive the country of its sovereignty. The treaty imposed three important restrictions on the monarchy: limiting tariffs, restricting Siamese industry, and enforcing extraterritoriality.[33]

In addition to the effect on self-governance, commentators in Thailand and Japan suggested these types of unequal treaties had a paralyzing effect on economic development in Asia. Phibun's ideologues reasoned that Thailand's development lagged behind Japan and other civilized countries because Thailand had been a virtual colonial possession of Britain for almost a century. In 1893, approximately 93 percent of Siam's exports passed through the hands of British traders.[34] In 1941, a Japanese report estimated that London still handled as much as 83 percent of Thai exports: "Under the circumstances, it is not too much to say that the national economy of Thailand is virtually under British control. Thailand has attempted several times to reform its currency system, but has been forced to accept the British plan in every instance. Since Britain's influence has penetrated deeply into every nook of Thai commerce and industry, it will not be easy for Thailand to eradicate this evil."[35]

The Thai state used these statistics as evidence that a semicolonial relationship had existed between Thailand and Great Britain for the past century. If Thais remained loyal to the West, they reasoned, it was only because they remained ignorant of how Britain had exploited their country. This semicolonial analysis was a reversal of traditional narrative developed by Prince Damrong: that Thailand remained independent as it evolved from premodern kingdom to modern nation-state. Within the new framework, the Chakri monarchs appeared as beleaguered vassals struggling to prevent the erosion of sovereignty and loss of territory; rather than confident diplomats who protected Siamese interests by playing the great powers against each other. The narrative of victimization transformed the war into a choice between self-determination or continued subjugation. "We must kill the British tiger," Bangkok radio warned, "before it recovers and kills us."[36]

JAPAN: OUR TRUEST FRIEND

Turning opinion against the British was not the only public relations challenge facing the government; it also had to build confidence in Thailand's new ally. Certain media outlets took their lead from the state and published articles describing the rich historical legacy of Thai-Japanese relations. *Nikorn*'s writers insisted that the peoples of the Golden Peninsula had maintained an association with Japan based on Buddhism for almost a thousand years.[37] During the era of Mongol dominance, the people of Nan Chao celebrated Japan's victory over the armies of Kublai Khan, who had also attacked the Thai. The kings of Ayutthaya welcomed in Japanese Christians exiled by the Tokugawa shogun, and they also had a group of Samurai serving in their armed forces. During the reign of the Meiji emperor, the two countries signed an important trade agreement.[38] For the past century, the growing British influence in Thailand had steered it away from Japan. This changed, however, as the new military rulers began to reconnect the country with its Asian neighbors. In 1933, Thailand's delegate to the League of Nations abstained from voting on a motion to censor Japan for its aggression in China. Although this vote reflected Bangkok's strategy of neutrality, it was interpreted by the Japanese as an opportunity for the two nations to draw closer throughout the decade.[39] Thai nationalists argued that the long-standing Japan-Thailand friendship made it natural for Thais to empathize with Japan in their struggle with the West.

Phibun's government attempted to reshape perceptions of Japan by juxtaposing images of a greedy, manipulative, disloyal, oppressive, racist West with a generous, benevolent, just, egalitarian East. The state reevaluated history and contrasted the contributions of Britain against those of Japan in an effort to define Thailand's truest friend. The recent war with Indochina served as an illustration. Japan had assisted Thailand in recovering its lost provinces, while the Allies obstructed Thai efforts and insisted on maintaining the status quo.[40] The 1941 Tokyo Peace Accord helped Bangkok's efforts to portray Japan as a friend of Thailand and an advocate of Asian solidarity.[41] In an interview published in a Tokyo newspaper, Wichit Wathakan, then a minister without a portfolio, articulated how the issue of the *lost territories* affected Thai relations with Japan: "I have every sympathy for the people of Nippon in their efforts at establishing the East Asia co-prosperity sphere. I heartily agree with Prince Konoye's sincere statement at the time of the formation of his Cabinet in which he said that Nippon would devote herself to wiping out inequalities and replacing them with a just order of things. Since Thailand has been one of the greatest victims of the old unjust order and since she is now endeavoring by dint of her own strength to right some of the old wrongs, there is no reason why Thailand should not cooperate with Nippon."[42]

Wichit embraced the concept of a Greater East Asia largely because he believed Thailand would play an important role in its realization. "I believe," he said, "that in demanding the return of the lost territory from French Indochina, Thailand has taken the first step in the establishment of a New Order in East Asia."[43]

The Thai state repeatedly invoked the traumatic memory of territorial concessions to convince the country that the Japanese were more trustworthy than westerners. In the same interview, Wichit noted that Thais were being bombarded by Allied propaganda warning them that the Japanese were imperialistic, but that

> we have complete faith in Nippon and teach our people to trust her. We have three reasons for this:
>
> The first is that Nippon has never threatened us in the past. The second is that Nippon has not taken one inch of territory from Thailand. The third

reason lies in the fact that politically speaking, Nippon has no need for Thai territory but hopes rather for Thailand's increasing strength.[44]

Following the Japanese attack on Thailand in 1941, the media evoked the image of a benevolent Japan to remind the nation that imperial soldiers were comrades, not conquerors. Bangkok radio promised listeners that Thailand's new allies could be trusted to keep their pledge of noninterference because "Japan has never been anything but supportive and helpful to us, they have never hurt us in the past."[45] By transferring Malay territory to Thai jurisdiction in 1943 Japan hoped to bolster its image as protective patron. Initially, Phibun hesitated to accept such a gift; but Wichit viewed the transfer as an opportunity to remind the Thai public of Britain and France's past sins, which would heighten "war consciousness and promote friendship and dependence on Japan."[46]

In his 1942 New Year's address to the Japanese troops, Phibun invoked a blessing upon the soldiers, calling them the brethren of Thai people and soldiers, so they would be victorious and set free the peoples of Asia. He reminded his audience that a strong and independent Thailand was essential to helping Japan complete the creation of a "co-prosperity sphere" in Asia.[47] Despite these assurances, many observers remained skeptical. When Japan's ambassador to Thailand met with Bangkok reporters in April 1942, he faced a slew of questions over whether his country's soldiers really understood that they were "guests" in Thailand and not an occupying force.[48]

INVENTING ASIANNESS

Thailand's place within the Greater East Asia Co-Prosperity Sphere is a topic that has yet to be addressed in sufficient detail by historians. Although a great deal of scholarship has been produced on the appeal of Pan-Asian rhetoric to colonized peoples working towards self-government, Thailand exists as an anomaly in Southeast Asia because it was already an independent state with an internationally recognized government. As the head of a sovereign state, Phibun had more leverage in his relationship with the Japanese than either Sukarno of the Dutch East Indies or Aung San of Burma. He recognized the Greater East Asian Co-Prosperity Sphere as a euphemism for empire; but like other nationalist leaders, he also understood that the changing order in Asia provided an opportunity for Thailand—and for himself. The destruction of the Western imperialist hierarchy would release Thailand from its semicolonial status and allow it to take a greater leadership role in regional affairs. Japan's rhetoric of "Asia for the Asians" could easily be packaged with preexisting Thai propaganda on humiliation and loss. The Phibun government embraced the Pan-Asian narrative, not due to an affinity for Japanese culture, but because it presented the best prospect for satisfying the regime's ambitions.

In 1940, Japan announced its intentions to create a Greater East Asia Co-Prosperity Sphere, transforming Asia so that it "was no longer to be a colony or semi-colony of the Anglo Saxons, but was to be delivered from alien aggression and restored to the Asiatics."[49] The removal of Western influence would allow Asia to remember its common past and create a spiritual awakening that would cause it to unite culturally and politically. In his commentary on the idea of a Co-Prosperity Sphere, Japanese philosopher Okawa Shumei wrote that Asia had a common political destiny and shared worldview that would eventually allow it to overcome superficial differences. He believed that all Asian cultures could be traced back to a great "Eastern Culture" that existed in China during the Tang dynasty. The intrusion of Western imperialism in the nineteenth century had fractured the cohesion of this cultural community. Europeans gained power over Asians in part by demeaning their culture and rewriting their history. According to this theory, political independence in Asia would lead to a "resurrection of the ancient glory of the spiritual life of Asian peoples."[50] Having avoided European colonization and the trauma of cultural discontinuity, Japan still possessed the spiritual heritage of ancient Asia and could reimplant it in recently liberated peoples of Asia. This ideology strongly resembled and may even have been the origin of Thailand's own discourse of rupture among the peoples of the Golden Peninsula. Since Thailand had only been semicolonized, the Phibun regime saw itself as sharing Japan's burden of cultural leadership.

The formation of a Greater East Asia was an intoxicating idea, but it lacked a precise definition or boundaries. Who were the Asians? What were the common characteristics that would decide membership in the Co-Prosperity Sphere? Once this category was thrust on them, non-Western elites from many countries proved adept at appropriating and redefining it in an effort to promote national values under the guise of Pan-Asian unity.[51] Thailand's military elites were no exception. Intellectuals such as Wichit understood how the process of defining Asia could be used in order to privilege Thai culture within an emerging regional hierarchy. Several qualifications emerged from the discourse, some more inclusive than others. Asia was supposedly inhabited by a variety of "yellow-skinned peoples," as opposed to the white European colonizers. Such a distinction ruled out India, whose inhabitants the Thai have traditionally disdained in part because of their much darker skin tone.[52] Buddhism, which Thais saw as the foundation of their own national identity and also a link to Japan, was another universally Asian attribute. In this case, the Philippines and the East Indies, predominantly Christian and Muslim respectively, could certainly not be considered Asian. Yet if we look closer at the dialogue, we see another concept emerge, one that speaks to the common experience of the Eastern peoples but maintains cultural distinction from the West. For Thai intellectuals, the word "Asians" referred to peoples who could benefit from the Thai example of overcoming Western imperialism.

In his public speeches, Phibun often remarked that the unique bond between the Japanese and Thai peoples was built on the common experience of defeat and humiliation. Japan empathized with Thailand, he said, because they both had sacrificed honor and territory in the face of Western aggression: "Our histories have followed a similar course. Japan has been bullied in the same manner as Thailand. In 1864, warships from the four nations of England, Holland, France, and America simultaneously attacked the city of Shimonoseki in Japan and forced the Japanese to pay the amount of 3 million gold coins to all four countries. Thirty years later in 1893, French warships invaded the Chao Phrya River and forced Thailand to pay 3 million baht. You can see that our countries have met with the same type of hardship."[53]

Thai leaders imagined their country following the path of recovery blazed by Japan decades earlier. In their minds, Admiral Perry coercing the Tokugawa Shogunate out of isolationism was analogous to Sir John Bowring forcing Mongkut into a trade agreement with Britain. Like Siam's monarchy, the Meiji emperor had worked to modernize his country and eliminate the unequal treaties. Thai nationalists believed Japan understood its own obsession with the *lost territories* because they had been forced to cede Sakhalin Island to the Russians in 1875.[54] Japan's phoenixlike recovery and ascension to the status of world power made it the ideal nation to lead the huddled masses of Asia into a bright new future. The Thai monarchy had never shown much interest in identifying themselves as Asian, but the military elite now adopted this moniker with pride. The Phibun government portrayed Japan as having restored the honor of all yellow peoples by successfully building a modern industrial society.

NAI MAN: Our entire nation should understand that the main reason the white races do not despise us the way they do the black races is that Japan, a yellow race, has become a world power.

NAI KHONG: If Japan were defeated, the yellow races of Asia would be treated no better than the black races are treated now.

NAI MAN: Those of us with yellow skin who travel abroad feel proud to be treated with respect because we have yellow skin like the Japanese. Asians from many countries who travel to Europe and America are respected just like the Japanese.

NAI KHONG: The Japanese example helps Asians everywhere.[55]

To enlist support for its cause, the Thai state argued that the fortunes of all Asians depended on a Japanese victory in the Greater East Asian war. A Japanese defeat would mean an end to all the progress made towards racial equality. This war would decide the fate of all Asia.[56]

Bangkok celebrated its partnership with Japan as an important milestone in the history of Asia—the first military alliance between two Buddhist nation-states. Phibun planned an elaborate treaty ceremony and chose a location that symbolized an Eastern spiritual connection. Instead of hosting the function at a royal palace or government building, representatives of the two countries signed the document at the Temple of the Emerald Buddha, one of the nation's holiest sites. Bangkok radio told listeners it was fitting for this sacred temple, which represented the pinnacle of "Asian architecture," to host the signing of the Thai-Japanese accord, itself a triumph of Asian solidarity and diplomacy.[57] Although the Japanese recognized Shintoism as their state religion, the Thai media depicted Japan as a predominantly Buddhist country like itself. Japanese reverence for the emperor paralleled the Thai people's respect for their monarchy. These shared values helped promote the notion of a uniquely Asian culture that could exist in opposition to the Western European tradition. This war was a struggle over values, and Asia's spiritual strength would prevail over Western materialism. Continued association with Japan, which embodied spiritual ideals, would surely strengthen Thai culture just as prolonged exposure to Western values had weakened it.[58]

National Humiliation discourse envisioned the Co-Prosperity Sphere as a new hierarchical system that would rank Asian peoples according to their level of sophistication and cultural achievement. Their own nation would occupy a status slightly lower than Japan, but it would be well above the colonized peoples of the Dutch East Indies, British Burma, French Indochina, and the Philippines. Government propaganda described Thailand as a bridge between Tokyo and the freedom movements popping up across Asia. Bangkok's leaders claimed an ability to empathize with other Southeast Asian nationalists because their country had also been maltreated by European imperialism. It was the traumatic loss of territory and bitter indignation suffered during the events of 1893 that awakened a sense of nation-self: "The majority of old men living in Thailand know well the humiliating concessions of these regions to France under pressure of military might. This bitter memory afire with indignation has finally grown into a great torchlight for the Thai aspiring after the restoration of their regions lost to French Indochina."[59]

Thus, Thai nationalists claimed they had already faced down the adversary still confronting most of Asia, which made their country an ideal role model for other nations. Despite these similarities, they felt Thailand should be considered more advanced than its neighbors due to a highly developed sense of national consciousness.[60] This consciousness had allowed the nation to rapidly progress towards complete independence. Thailand was not as sophisticated as Japan, which had managed to throw off European hegemony earlier on and began its journey towards modernity much sooner. Nai Man and Nai Khong discussed the relationship between full sovereignty and national development.

> Nai Man: When the branches of government of any country are controlled by the people of that country working together, that nation can begin a process of unlimited growth.
>
> Nai Khong: Especially in the case of Japan, which managed to reform itself. It had complete independence before Thailand and so was able to progress much faster than us in many areas.[61]

Thai nationalists argued that the country's unique status made it an important advocate of the Co-Prosperity Sphere in Southeast Asia. Radio Bangkok devoted a great deal of programming to explaining the Japanese agenda, soliciting support from other nationalities, and refuting the accusations of Allied broadcasts. The message was simple: the war represented the dawning of a new age of cooperation. Japanese forces fought to free Asia, not to enlarge its own empire. The nations of Asia, which had long slumbered under the rule of foreigners, were now beginning to awake. Under Japanese and Thai guidance, these peoples would throw off the yoke of Western tyranny and establish sovereign nation-states. Whereas the so-called democratic nations of the world had promised self-government for decades, Japan was now making that dream a reality. Asian labor and natural resources would begin to facilitate the economic and cultural development of the Co-Prosperity Sphere, instead of simply enriching the cities of Europe. "Fellow Asians: wherever and whenever you encounter a Japanese or Thai soldier, please put down your weapons," Radio Bangkok entreated. "They are not your enemies."[62]

Japanese leaders hoped that other nations would follow the Thai government's example of cooperation and support for Pan-Asianism. Japan used Thailand to call on the Kuomintang to abandon the war in China.[63] On December 22, 1941, Phibun broadcast a shortwave radio message to Chiang Kai-shek, urging him to abandon the destructive war that was pitting Asians against each other. The Thai prime minister assured his Chinese counterpart that the Japanese would keep their promise to liberate Asia and that they were indeed a virtuous and trustworthy people. He further promised Chiang that he was not being coerced by the Japanese to send this message, which represented his true feelings on the matter.[64]

The media also beckoned China to follow Thailand's example and cast its lot with Greater East Asia rather than continue a fight that prolonged Western hegemony in Asia. Thai newspapers compared China's history of loss with its own, detailing how Europeans grew rich off the backs of Chinese laborers and humiliated a once proud people by gradually eroding its autonomy. "China was just like us," declared Bangkok Radio. "It escaped colonization only because the great powers couldn't agree on how to divide it."[65] If Britain now offered to help the Chunking government, it was only to divert the Japanese away from India. Overseas Chinese communities in liberated areas already supported Japan's vision of a free continent; now it was left to Chiang Kai-shek to grasp the vision and end this pointless conflict. The Thai government also hoped to use Pan-Asianism as a tool to secure the compliance of the large Chinese community in Bangkok. In addition to their control over several key industries, the Sino-Thai population was an important source of revenue for the Kuomintang. During their occupation of Thailand, the Japanese military did not interfere with Bangkok's policy towards the Chinese, who offered the government their reluctant support.[66]

Under the auspices of Pan-Asianism, Phibun supported a variety of Southeast Asian independence movements in an effort to expand Thailand's sphere of influence and destabilize the British and French empires. This was a reversal of traditional Thai foreign policy. Under the Chakri monarchs, Siam had cooperated with European governments in suppressing revolutionary activities. Josiah Crosby, the British consul in Bangkok during the 1930s, speculated that the monarchy profited from the stability of the status quo and had no wish to see either Britain or France leave their respective colonies.[67] The sentiments of the ruling elite slowly changed after the military came to power in 1932. In the 1930s the Japanese presence in Thailand increased, cooperation with European states became less important, and the prospects of Thai expansion became more enticing. During the 1940s, several nationalist organizations used Bangkok as a base of operations for their anti-imperialist activities. Throughout that decade, Thailand offered direct and indirect assistance to insurrectionist movements in India, Burma, Laos, Cambodia, and even Vietnam.[68]

Thai military leaders used their own narrative of victimization to build relations with neighboring revolutionaries and act like loyal participants in the Co-Prosperity Sphere. One example was Thailand's encouragement of the Indian independence movement. Beginning in 1941, the Thai state began supporting the Free India campaign in order to use it as a weapon against the British. Prominent members of Bangkok's Indian community established the Indian National Council (INC), an organization committed to the Indian National Congress Party and the realization of self-government. In December, the Japanese organized a large meeting at Silpakorn Theatre to convince Indian residents that both Thailand and Japan supported their cause. In June 1942, factions of the independence movement met at the Bangkok Conference, also attended by Wichit, who was then deputy foreign minister, to adopt a resolution on the purpose and leadership of the INC. Many Indians living in Thailand volunteered for the nascent Indian National Army (INA) and began their training at a camp southeast of the capital near Chon Buri. Thailand served as a major supply center to the INA during their disastrous Imphal campaign and even provided assistance to facilitate the evacuation of Indian troops from Burma.[69]

In addition to simply providing space for training and meetings, the Thai government also provided the INC with airtime to broadcast "The Voice of Free India" over Bangkok radio. Both Thai and Japanese officials supervised the scripts for these broadcasts. The program was an important part of the strategy to win the hearts and minds of Indians throughout Southeast Asia and to refute British propaganda coming from Delhi. The Thai-Indian partnership brought legitimacy to both parties. Phibun's patronage of the movement reinforced Thailand's image as an emerging leader in Asia while insulating the INC from accusations that it was an Indian Manchukuo. When Radio Delhi dismissed the INC as a Japanese quisling, the Free India broadcaster reminded listeners that their support came from Thailand, not Japan.[70]

Thai involvement also helped to appease certain factions within the Indian independence movement that did not trust Japan and intended to reject Japanese leadership once the British had quit India.[71] Indian nationalists rationalized their cooperation with Thailand as a natural consequence of the Hindu-Buddhist tradition shared by the two countries, thereby deflecting concerns about Japanese manipulation.

The Free India radio network consistently defended Thailand's government against accusations from Britain's Radio Delhi concerning the decision to join Japan. These attacks only increased the prestige of Thailand, it argued, by demonstrating that Britain must now respect a country they once considered to be inferior. Rather than blaming Thailand, the British should examine themselves to find an explanation for why they were losing the war.[72] It was foolish for Delhi radio to constantly criticize Thailand, the broadcasters continued, when it was obvious they knew nothing of actual conditions inside the country. Only Indian residents of Bangkok were qualified to explain the differences between Thailand and British India. The radio broadcasters pointed out that Indians in Thailand were free to criticize British authority, while those who spoke out in Calcutta or Bombay were imprisoned by the thousands.[73] Thai newspapers promoted the INC by publicizing its meetings, which occasionally were attended by government officials. For these Indian nationalists, Thailand was the real democracy, a place where the concepts of free speech and rights of assembly still existed. "England and America are not democracies, they are hypocrisies," claimed a Free India announcer. "They use the word 'democracy' to deceive the rest of the world."[74] He added that India should reject offers of friendship from the United States, which was interested only in recruiting proxies to fight the Japanese on their behalf. Thailand, India's true friend, offered its assistance out of a spirit of gratitude for Indian culture and religion, without asking anything in return.[75]

This shared cultural heritage made Thailand the ideal nation for India to follow on the path towards independence and modernity. INC broadcasts reiterated the historical narrative of a virtuous kingdom defiled by rapacious foreigners, which struggled for decades to redeem itself. "The Thais are Buddhist, they worship the Buddha as a great teacher, and the teachings of the Buddha have an important place in the hearts of the Thai people. This is why the Thais are among the most generous people in the world. It is regrettable that foreign nations have exploited this generosity for the past fifty years to satisfy their own greed."[76]

Indian nationalists identified with Thailand's discourse on removing British influence from their country and admired Phibun's ability to rouse the nation from the slumber of semicolonialism. On July 14, 1942, the Free India broadcast included a special birthday salute to Phibun, calling him a leader who was sent from heaven to save the country in its moment of peril. For months the prime minister had held the "tiger by the tail" before safely guiding Thailand into an alliance with the Japanese.[77] Thailand had once been a weak and divided country, but under the unifying influence of Phibun Songkhram the nation had come together and earned the respect both of their fellow Asians and the Western powers. Free Indian patriots congratulated Thailand on its achievements during the National Day celebration of 1942:

> Today Thailand has an important role in creating solidarity among the peoples of Asia, because it has grown strong under the leadership of Phibun Songkhram. Celebrating this National Day makes us think of India's national day, January 26. On January 26, 1930, India proclaimed its independence in spirit. Since that day we Indians have been independent in spirit. National spirit is important. Was it not because of their strong spirit that Thailand successfully changed their own government [in 1932]? Was it not also this strong spirit that gave Thailand Phibun Songkhram?
>
> We congratulate Thailand on this special day and we hope they will pass safely through this conflict. Let us also hope we Indians one day have independence and strength of spirit like Thailand.[78]

The Thai government was equally effusive in its praise of the Free India movement's efforts to win self-government for India. Radio Bangkok called the organization "an important contribution to the creation of the New Order in Asia" and encouraged all colonized peoples to form similar parties.[79] In his speech delivered at Silpakorn Theatre on December 23, 1941, Wichit told Bangkok's Indian community that all peoples have the right to govern their own land. He reminded them that the Thai understood the importance of driving white people out of Asia, because they too had many bitter memories of the *farang*.[80] Thai leaders such as Wichit believed Indian nationalism would not only help eliminate Western influence from the continent, it could also help position Thailand as the ideal power to help fill the resulting political and cultural vacuum. By acknowledging that Thailand was ahead of India in terms of its political maturity, the Free India broadcasts helped establish Thailand as standing above the crowd of Asian nations clamoring for independence.

While the Thai government professed that its sympathy for anticolonialism stemmed from its own history of National Humiliation, its real strategy involved weakening Western empires in order to expand Thailand's influence. Phibun's speeches and writings clearly indicate that he intended to replace Western authority with Thai cultural hegemony wherever possible. His government made plans to project Thai influence throughout mainland Southeast Asia as the British presence gradually receded. Again borrowing from Japanese discourse, Phibun saw Thai culture as the least affected by Western involvement because the country had not been directly colonized, and therefore it was the most authentically Asian. At the Bangkok Conference in June 1942, Thai leaders evoked their noncolonized status to enhance the country's prestige in comparison to other Asian nations. The function of the conference was to celebrate the idea of India as part of Greater East Asia, featuring flags from each participating country and pictures of prominent Indian nationalist leaders, including Gandhi. Phibun's message, however, was another characteristic example of Thai chauvinism: "During the period when India had to contend with foreign aggression and fell under the domination of a race alien in language and in culture, resulting in Indian Culture being deprived of support and maintenance which in time brought on a gradual decay, Thailand undertook the duty of safeguarding Indian culture. If you visit our National Museum, you will find that we have preserved ancient relics and objects of the Art of India in a better state and to a greater amount than those to be seen in the Indian Museum in Calcutta."[81]

For Thailand's military regime, Pan-Asianism was little more than a vehicle for expanding its interests into the vacuum left by the disintegration of Western empires. Phibun cooperated with Japan's construction of the Thailand–Burma railway, which caused the deaths of thousands of Malay and Burmese corvée laborers, because it was an important means for projecting Thai hegemony west of the Salween River. In his note approving the construction project, he wrote, "It's all right for Japan to build it. We will follow behind the Japanese army and spread our culture. That's cooperating as an ally."[82]

Bangkok saw the proposal of a Thai-Japanese cultural agreement as a similar opportunity to enhance its regional standing. Wichit wanted to include other nations in the agreement and hopefully establish Thailand as the cultural center of Southeast Asia. Phibun felt that even Japan could benefit from Thai expertise in agricultural technologies suited to the Golden

Peninsula. He wanted to invest heavily in these fields, thereby pressing Thailand's advantage so that it could "become the school for all Asians."[83]

Anticipating an eventual departure of the British from Burma, the Thai government expected the region would fall within its sphere of influence. Bangkok had quietly supported Burmese anticolonial activities even before the outbreak of the Greater East Asian war. In 1939, Crosby reported to his superiors in London concerning rumors of a joint Thai-Japanese attack on British Burma. The British ambassador was convinced Wichit was involved in a conspiracy to ship arms by way of his sister-in-law, a student at Rangoon University, to rebels in Burma.[84] The Thai government was complicit in Japan's secret training of Aung San's Thirty Comrades and the creation of the Burman Independence Army (BIA). In December 1941, the BIA crossed from Thailand into Burma to begin the liberation of their homeland.[85] The Bangkok media praised the heroism of these revolutionaries, as they had done with India, and encouraged all Burmese to unite with Thailand in a fight to remove the British yoke from the necks of all Asian peoples.[86] Thai Radio broadcasts criticized the arrest of U Saw as another example of British hypocrisy, promising democracy but enforcing martial law. The Thai government hoped to convince their neighbors that they had rejected joining the Allies because Britain expected them to fight against "our Burmese brothers."[87] The desire to see Burma free convinced Thai leaders to allow Japan's passage through its territory, which in turn led to Thailand's entry into the war.[88] No amount of British plotting could prevent the Thai and Burmese from reestablishing their precolonial era friendship. In an astounding revision of history, the Thai media claimed the two countries maintained a close relationship for hundreds of years prior to Britain's arrival in the peninsula.[89] National Humiliation narratives focused only on the European enemy and avoided mentioning the centuries of conflict between the Thai and Burman kingdoms, punctuated by Burma's sack of Ayutthaya in 1767.

While Bangkok's media showered praise on Burmese efforts to achieve independence and self-government, the government was busy planning to annex portions of its territory. Prior to the war, Thailand professed a strict devotion to neutrality. Even after Phibun began to mobilize the army, he assured the country that it was strictly in preparation for a defensive war and that the government had no intention of fighting outside its current borders.[90] Japan's invasion of Thailand and the subsequent war with Britain and America nullified existing territorial boundaries and increased the regime's appetite for expansion. "We have already added four provinces," crowed Bangkok radio, "and soon we will add even more."[91] Early in 1942, Phibun requested Japanese approval of a Thai military campaign in Burma, involving the Shan states in the North and Tenasserim Province in the east.[92] The desire to "recover" these territories was a determining factor in the rush to declare war on the Allies. Despite Japan's reluctance, Thailand's Phayap army invaded the Shan states in March, occupied the city of Keng Tung, and eventually proceeded northward until it reached the border of Yunnan Province in China.[93]

The invasion of Burma provides evidence of how Bangkok hoped to use Pan-Asianism to serve its national interests. Phibun endorsed Asian solidarity and liberation from British imperialism because he felt it would allow Thailand to reconquer territory it had "lost" two centuries ago. The Greater East Asia Co-Prosperity Sphere provided the ideal conditions for the creation of a Greater Thailand, something that had been inconceivable while the Western powers dominated Asia. Prior to its military campaign, the Thai government issued decrees declaring that the Shan, Karens, and Mons of eastern Burma were all members of the Thai race that had been cut off from their own people and forced to live under the political rule of an alien race. Provincial officials in northern Thailand were instructed to treat these peoples as Thai nationals and to offer them assistance when possible, whether they lived within or without the boundaries of Thailand. As Eiji Murashima points out, these measures were consistent with actions previously taken to serve the Lao and Khmer during the 1941 Indochina war. In both cases, military expansion was disguised as part of a noble effort to emancipate all members of the race from Western imperialism.[94] In the Thai media, the capture of Keng Tung was an incredible military triumph that confirmed the military's role as savior of the nation. Previous monarchs, including Rama III, had attempted to conquer the Shan states. Where they had failed, Thailand's modern soldier had succeeded.[95] Newspapers celebrated the idea that the Shan states had been "restored" to the nation and thousands of Thais could be reunited with the homeland. One newspaper carried an article describing the people of Keng Tung, noting that in dress, culture, and religion, they were "just like us."[96] Accounts of the 1942 National Day celebrations noted that hundreds of "Greater Thais" in the newly acquired territories dressed themselves in traditional attire and participated in parades, expressing their gratitude that they were now free from the constraints of British imperialism.[97]

FEARING THE *FARANG*

In the final chapters of the historical novel *Four Reigns,* members of Phloi's family sit down to discuss how Thailand's surrender to Japan will affect the future. The divergence of opinion over the government's new direction is best reflected in the conversation between the older, more traditional Uncle Phoem and his idealistic nephew Sewi. Phoem believes the Thais have lost their country and become the newest vassal of the Japanese Empire. He reacts with skepticism to Sewi's assurances that the alliance with Japan saved the country from complete destruction, reminding his nephew that the war is not over. The new treaty simply thrusts Thailand into a larger conflict, where it will have to contend with the powerful enemies of the Axis. His uncle's stern warning seems to amuse the youthful Sewi, who responds: "Your questions don't surprise me, Khun Uncle. You stand in fear of the farangs because you were born and bred and spent your most impressionable years in the age of farang supremacy. That age has come to an end, Khun Uncle. Japan is ridding Asia of the farang powers, driving them out of the Philippines and Malaya at this very moment, and is going to drive them out of Burma, Java, Borneo, India . . . even Australia might have to bow to Japan one of these days. When the smoke clears, Khun Uncle, Japan will be leading Asia, with us as their partner, because we've had the foresight to join with them from the start."[98]

Sewi's comments reiterate the narrative circulated by the Phibun government and represent the attitude of a younger, seemingly more confident generation. He dismisses Uncle Phoem's apprehension as the product of an earlier semicolonial era, when Thailand was weak and easily intimidated into giving up its territory to the invincible Western powers. For Sewi, that world no longer existed. The century-long Asian fear of *farangs* was being smashed under the tank treads of the Japanese Imperial Army along with American and British fortifications. Men like Sewi expected to assist Japan in its crusade to remake Asia, believing that they would also remake Thailand in the process.

CONCLUSION

This chapter has examined the Thai-Japanese alliance during World War II by focusing on the discursive parallels between Japan's Pan-Asianist rhetoric and Thailand's own ideology of National Humiliation. The Phibun government invented a new historical narrative that praised Japanese friendship and condemned British duplicity. Thailand's support for Japan may have been motivated by self-preservation in the beginning, but it quickly evolved into something far more ambitious. In the early months of 1942, the military regime contemplated the construction of a new Thailand built on the ruins of the British and French empires. As Reynolds has already argued, the actions of the Thai government were not merely "defensive efforts to protect national interests in troubled times."[99] Phibun's wartime policies of external expansion and internal purification reflected his desire to increase his own power by building a Thai empire. He claimed that he was merely avenging past humiliations and restoring Thai honor. The war was an opportunity to redefine Thailand as the equal of the West and to establish its cultural hegemony throughout mainland Southeast Asia.

The Thai state was engaged in a process of nation building, but it preferred to describe that process in terms of "restoration" or "emancipation." Government propaganda suggested that the nation had always existed but had been lulled into a state of lethargy. This great conflict between East and West then became an opening for Thailand to reassert itself, to break free from the Western colonial order, and to increase its sovereignty. Declaring war on the Allies paid immediate economic benefits for the government, which was able to cancel unsatisfactory contracts and take control of industries formerly dominated by foreign companies. The Thai state, which had gone to great lengths to educate people of the evils of extraterritoriality, now congratulated itself on the apparent demise of the old system of unequal trade relationships:

> NAI MAN: Logging concessions, mining concessions, and other concessions given to our enemies expired upon our declaration of war. Who will take charge of these industries? We Thais will be in charge. From now on Thais will have complete control over commerce, logging, mining, and industry. If foreigners are involved at all, it will be because we welcome them in, not because they exercise special rights as in the past.
>
> NAI KHONG: We have complete control over our own country, and we control our own natural resources in the earth and in the water. We should feel proud that we are achieving greater mastery over our own house.[100]

This growing sense of political and economic autonomy also provided a measure of political legitimacy for the ruling elite that took power after 1932.

The original manifesto from the People's Party asserted that a change in government was necessary for the country to overcome European obstruction and narrow the achievement gap between itself and the West. A decade after toppling the absolute monarchy, Phibun claimed that his government was becoming both modern and completely independent. In the months following his alliance with Japan, he silenced detractors by arguing that anyone who favored either the monarchy or alliance with Britain wanted to return Thailand to the state of subservience.[101] The Thai state's wartime policy was a direct product of National Humiliation discourse, which depicted the past half century as a continuous effort to climb out from under the burden of inequality and shame associated with 1893. Pro-Japanese propaganda was designed to demonstrate an innate symmetry between Thailand's efforts to drive out the French in 1940 and Japan's determination to drive all westerners out of Asia in 1942. Both campaigns seemed connected to the idea of avenging a sense of loss and reestablishing Thai prestige within the international community.

Ultimately, the promise of a New Order in Asia wherein Thailand would play a leading role failed to materialize. By the end of 1942, a string of Allied victories planted seeds of doubt in the minds of Thai leaders concerning the final outcome of the Greater East Asia War. As Japan's stock fell, the territories appropriated by Thailand during the war became a liability. Phibun, who had survived this far by forming close ties with Japan, gradually distanced himself from the ideas of Pan-Asianism and the Co-Prosperity Sphere. Japan became unable to honor its commitment to help develop Thailand's light industry and pressured Bangkok to extend it larger and larger amounts of credit. In 1944, caught between growing resistance from the Free Thai movement and increasing tensions with the Japanese, Phibun resigned as prime minister. Historians credit Phibun with helping to preserve Thailand from the devastation inflicted on other countries during the war, but they seldom examine the consequences of his alliance with the Japanese. Much that he achieved during the war would be undone in the postwar settlement, including his greatest triumph: the acquisition of the *lost territories.*

5

1946: Postwar Reconciliation and the Loss Reimagined

Thailand's World War II experience required nationalist historians to demonstrate impressive intellectual dexterity in their insistence that the country had *never been colonized*. Many scholars argued that Thailand was unaffected by the Greater East Asian war, it being the only country in Southeast Asia to maintain its independence throughout the entire ordeal. Thamsook Numnonda argued that the Thai viewed the Japanese not as an occupying force but as a "guest army." In spite of Phibun's cooperation with Japan, which included a declaration of war on Britain and the United States, by September 1945 Thailand had somehow ended up on the side of the Allies and was hoping to avoid the embarrassment of defeat and occupation that awaited the Axis. For Thamsook, this apparent contradiction was easily explained: Thai diplomacy saved the nation.[1] This narrative borrows the analytical framework of the Franco-Siamese crisis and superimposes it on the events of World War II. By emphasizing survival as the country's solitary goal, Thamsook downplays the loss of the four provinces and prestige while maintaining the illusion that the nation maintained its independence. Her interpretation facilitates continuity by mending what would otherwise be an embarrassing tear in the fabric of the past.

Other historians have taken issue with this survivalist discourse, claiming it does not adequately account for the 1940s as a break from the past. E. Bruce Reynolds has argued that the Thai government's efforts to militarize the nation and transform Thai culture constitute a separate "Fascist Era" in Thai history brought on by the admiration of the Thai elite for the accomplishments of Mussolini and Hitler.[2] During this period Thailand's goal was aggressive expansion, not self-preservation. On more than one occasion between 1940 and 1944, Phibun jeopardized the nation's sovereignty in his quest to enlarge its boundaries. Rather than simply survive the war, Bangkok attempted to build a Greater Thailand, whose borders and national identity would encompass all the Tai peoples of Southeast Asia. From this perspective, the fall of Phibun, the repudiation of his regime's ethnic theories, and the failure to resurrect an imagined Thai empire from an invented past all point towards 1945 as a moment of defeat. Although Reynolds' approach certainly improves on the survival thesis, it has the effect of portraying the wartime era as an anomaly in Thai history, a period disconnected from the eras that precede or follow it.

This chapter examines continuity and rupture within the Thai historical narrative by viewing Thailand's postwar experience through the lens of National Humiliation. As previous chapters have already argued, Thai supporters of the Indochina conflict and ensuing Greater East Asian war viewed those events as opportunities for redemption that signified the end of Thailand's subservience to the West. The Allied victory, however, destroyed the dream of a Greater Thailand and marked the return of Western imperialism to mainland Southeast Asia. Thailand had not been "saved." Its imperial ambitions had been thwarted, its government forced to resign, and its people left to deal with the demands of occupation, financial reparations, and territorial readjustment. "The war has left us a crippled nation," one press editorial admitted. "That is the price we must pay for our mistake."[3] Like the crisis of 1893, the end of World War II represented a potential rupture in the historical continuum. Therefore, the event required the adoption of a new narrative, one that rehabilitated the past by ignoring failed attempts at expansionism and instead emphasizing the country's commitment to international peace, as embodied by the United Nations. National Humiliation discourse, so prominent during the Phibun administration, became a liability as Thailand struggled to find acceptance in a new international order. Yet the ideology of "The Loss" continued to exert influence. Even as the postwar Thai government condemned Phibun's anti-Western policies and worked with the United States to restore Thailand's international standing, it continued on with Phibun's anticolonial agenda and refused to give back the *lost territories.*

WORKING THEIR PASSAGE HOME

Postwar Thailand faced numerous political and economic difficulties. The economy was in shambles, crime was rampant, and war profiteering created rice shortages throughout the country. The new government, led by members of the Seri Thai faction that had opposed Phibun during the war, blamed these problems on the wartime regime. This was also Pridi's strategy for avoiding a long-term Allied occupation and the anticipated imposition of financial reparations. As a symbolic gesture of the country's new direction, the government even changed the English name of the country back to Siam.[4] While the Allies drew up plans for postwar Southeast Asia, the United States and Britain were at odds over whether to treat Thailand as friend or foe. U.S. policy favored a lenient approach towards Thailand, which it viewed as an occupied country during the war. Washington considered Seni Pramoj and Pridi Banamyong to be the legitimate leaders of wartime Thailand and agreed that Phibun should be held responsible for the declaration of war on the Allies.[5] Britain, on the other hand, favored a much harsher approach. Phibun's cooperation with Japan had real consequences for Burma and Malaya. British officials dismissed the Seri Thai movement as political window dressing and argued that Thailand had betrayed them by helping facilitate the Japanese invasion of Singapore. Therefore, Siam would have to conform to Allied policy in order to "work its passage home." The United States interpreted these arguments as a British attempt to reestablish their sphere of influence over Siam, which it was determined to prevent. In the end, the U.S. government succeeded in convincing Britain to withdraw many of its demands. American intervention in this matter allowed the new Siamese government to write off the expansionist and anti-Western policies of the Phibun era as an abnormality and establish its credentials as a peaceful, pro-Western nation.

In 1942, the American Legation in Bangkok prepared a "General Report on the Conditions in Thailand." The report attempted to ascertain the nature of the country's relationship with Japan and its true attitude towards the Allies. Written by Second Secretary John Holbrook Chapman, it concluded that the Thai-Japanese alliance was a fiction and that the "informed public opinion" in Thailand was one of hostility, fear, and hatred towards the Japanese.[6] In contrast, Thai attitudes towards the West (particularly Americans) were quite favorable. Chapman therefore concluded that the Thai people should not be held responsible for the collaborationist practices of their authoritarian government: "There is a small group of government leaders at the very top who undoubtedly are pro-Japanese either for ambitious reasons or for personal profit. This group controls all the means of dissemination of information to the public such as the radio and the press, and it is responsible for the propaganda, under Japanese tutelage, to convince the world that Thailand is a willing and enthusiastic participant in Japan's Co-Prosperity Sphere in Greater East Asia."[7]

Figure 4. **Trust the Leader.** A cartoon blaming Phibun for the country's difficulties after World War II. The caption underneath reads, "Trust in the Leader, and the country will be lost." (National Archives of Thailand)

Chapman believed the Allies should not consider wartime Thailand as an independent country. He maintained that Thai policy agendas originated with Japanese military planners, who relied on the Thai army and civic administration for publication and enforcement. The report concluded that the Japanese were in complete political control of Thailand, even speculating that each of the government ministries contained a Japanese advisor responsible for ensuring the preservation and advancement of Japanese interests in Thailand. Following Phibun's resignation in 1944, the Office of Strategic Services (OSS) also commissioned a separate study that declared the field marshal solely responsible for Thailand's declaration of war on the Allies.[8]

This interpretation suited the policy aims of both Bangkok and Washington. From the U.S. perspective, absolving the Thai of collaborationist charges would reduce British leverage with Thailand's new rulers and instead create an independent postwar government that could gradually be drawn into an American sphere of influence. Eager to avoid a long-term British occupation of Thailand, Pridi and the Seri Thai were only too happy to place blame for the war on Phibun. Thus, the Thai embraced the narrative that their country had been occupied during the war in order to ensure national sovereignty once it was over.

As part of its attempt to rehabilitate Thailand's image, the United States assisted in rewriting the country's wartime history. The U.S. Army and diplomatic corps fed stories to the American press claiming that the two countries had never truly been at odds. In 1945, Secretary of State James Byrnes announced that Siam had maintained a secret alliance with Washington for the past three years.[9] Since the United States had no imperialist presence in mainland Southeast Asia, it was not difficult to invent a Thai-American friendship that projected far into the past. "Our relations with Siam have always been friendly," gushed the *New York Times*. "American advisors helped lead the nation out of its medieval barbarism."[10] U.S. publications were careful to portray the Thai as a happy and carefree Oriental race, very different from the aggressive and militant Japanese: "Of all the Orientals, the Siamese are certainly the jolliest. They like to think of themselves as 'sanuk'—jolly, carefree, gay. In fact, the Siamese are so 'sanuk' that in 1932 they rebelled against the traditional absolute monarchy on the revolutionary leaders' promise that the new regime would be more fun than the old."[11]

Such stereotypes helped convince Americans that a people as fun-loving as the Siamese would never have gone to war with the United States on their own initiative. The declaration was made with the Japanese in complete control of government, after the Thai "became a catspaw and their homeland part of the strategic ambush from which Japan planned to steal an empire."[12] This reasoning allowed Americans to make the case that Thailand should be considered an occupied nation during the war, not an enemy combatant. While the Phibun government was simply a cog in the Japanese war machine, the majority of Thais supported the Pridi-led Seri Thai movement that resisted the Axis and provided intelligence for the Allies. Although the Seri Thai never engaged in military combat, its very existence was evidence that Thailand was an ally of the United States. A former OSS agent assigned to Thailand claimed that by war's end, the Seri Thai had been prepared to put 150,000 men into the field to fight against the Japanese. By pretending to help the Japanese while secretly working against them, the Thai accomplished the "biggest double-cross in history."[13]

As the pro-Allies image of Siam gained acceptance, even Phibun would claim he had supported the Allies during the war. In an attempt to avoid a war crimes tribunal, the field marshal sent a letter to several Bangkok newspapers stating that his government also conspired to deceive the Japanese. Knowing the Thai army couldn't defeat Japan and recognizing that the Japanese couldn't win the war, Phibun claimed his one remaining choice was to lull the invaders into a false sense of security. The "Follow the Leader" campaign and the decision to declare war were mere ploys to accomplish this task. Having done so, he proceeded to work against the Japanese by restricting their access to foodstuffs, textiles, land, and raw materials. He reminded people that he had refused to attend the Greater East Asia Conference in Tokyo and that he had not allowed Japanese to be taught in public schools. At the end of his letter, the former prime minister assured the country that he had "never nurtured any dislike for the Allies as, unlike the Japanese, they have never wantonly invaded our country."[14] Although few people took Phibun's letter seriously, his arguments illustrated the larger process of historical revision taking place in postwar Siam.

While the Americans proved eager to reconcile with Siam, the British did not. Phibun's decision to allow the Japanese passage through Siam proved devastating to British interests in Southeast Asia and helped complicate the postwar relationship. Initial treaty proposals in 1945 made it clear that the British intended to treat Siam as an enemy combatant requiring occupation. Britain demanded that Bangkok not only accept Allied (British colonial) occupying forces for an indefinite period but also underwrite their cost.[15] Furthermore, the British government held that the Siamese government must compensate Allied nations for all property damage during the war and declared that the Allied Military Authority would supervise key industries such as tin, tea, rubber, and rice in order to help alleviate world shortages.[16] Fortunately for Siam, the U.S. State Department intervened and convinced Whitehall to modify its demands. The revised agreement, which Siam signed September 8, 1945, did not give Britain control over strategic industries but still required the presence of an occupying force. As part of a later economic agreement, Siam was required to provide a quota of rice shipments to the UN to help alleviate world hunger.[17] In Siam, reaction to the settlement was mixed. Thais were dismayed by the arrival of 20,000 Indian troops, which helped further alienate the country from Britain. An editorial in *Sri krung* reflected the mood in the capital: "Since the Japanese entered Siam we have witnessed bitter suffering in our lives. We have tried and prayed to rid our land of this unlawful gang, but our prayers were not heard and we were bound hand and foot. We were greatly relieved at the end of the war for the termination of Japanese might, only to be replaced by the black and white troops who came in to disarm the Japanese."[18]

The presence of another occupying force (or was it a "guest army"?) contradicted the idea that Siam had been on the winning side of the conflict and provided yet another challenge to the historical dogma of perpetual independence. On the other hand, most informed citizens understood that only American intervention had saved the country from a worse fate. The Bangkok media praised U.S. influence for allowing Siam to "lift up its head among the nations," and expressed gratitude for the sympathy of the American people.[19]

THE ISSUE OF THE *LOST TERRITORIES*

Siam's treaties with the United States and Britain removed important roadblocks along its path to redemption, but others appeared in their place. The De Gaulle government, based in London, had refused to recognize the 1941 Tokyo Peace Accord signed by the Vichy regime. At war's end, French representatives in Kandy informed Thai delegates that a state of hostilities still existed between France and Siam and would continue to exist until the four provinces were returned to French Indochina. Although it had anticipated that France would make territorial demands, the Thai government was surprised to learn that the French considered the two countries to be at war. Even at the outbreak of hostilities in 1941 there had never been a declaration of war between France and Thailand. Marshal Petain and Prime Minister Phibun had legally authorized the transfer of territory while both governments were aligned with the Axis; now both the Free French and Seri Thai sided with the Allies. On what basis, the Thai government asked itself, could a state of hostilities possibly exist?[20] The French responded that the Tokyo Peace Accord was invalid because French representatives had signed under pressure of Japanese intervention. By virtue of its seat on the UN Security Council, France now had the authority to veto Siam's application for membership in the United Nations if the Thai did not agree to give up the territories in question.

Given the Siamese government's eagerness to repudiate Phibun's actions and its enthusiastic compliance with Allied demands, its stern rejection of the new French ultimatum warrants discussion. It is significant because it demonstrates the government's success in using National Humiliation imagery to make irredentism a truly national issue. Pridi renounced Siam's interest in both the Malay and Shan states only days after Japan's surrender, but he made no mention of the four provinces taken from French Indochina.[21] Several factors might explain this discrepancy. First, Phibun and Wichit's irredentist campaign, based as it was on National Humiliation and ethnic origins, convinced many Thais that Siam had a legitimate claim to the four provinces.[22] By comparison, the history of the Malay and Shan states was less controversial, and the people living there were considered only marginally Thai. Second, Siam obtained the provinces through the blood and sacrifice of its soldiers, and the conflict had ended when both parties signed a legal and binding treaty. If France felt coerced by Japan, it was certainly no more coercion than they had applied to the Siamese monarchy in 1893. Finally, the Thai viewed France as a defeated power that was now simply hanging onto the coattails of the British and Americans.[23] Having collaborated with the Axis, the French seemed ill-suited to the moral high ground they were now trying to occupy. Most importantly, at the height of tensions in 1941, the Thai military elite had explained the acquisition of the *lost territories* as an essential step towards the ultimate goal of national redemption. To concede the four provinces now would be an acknowledgment that Siam remained inferior to its western counterparts. It would reopen the wound of 1893.

In October 1946, Khuang Aphaiwongse visited Paris as part of a special Siamese delegation charged with defending the country's position on the border issue. When negotiations opened, French officials accused Siam of opportunism, saying that they took advantage of France's 1940 occupation in order to steal away the border provinces. In response, Khuang invoked the National Humiliation narrative constructed during the Phibun regime. He explained that the four provinces were just a sliver of colonial territory to the French; but to his countrymen, those territories were a powerful symbol of suffering. The tragic memory of Siam's defeat in 1893 had been handed down from generation to generation, Khuang argued, so that it still lived in the souls of the Thai people.[24] After Japan occupied French Indochina, public opinion demanded that the people living in the *lost territories* be reunited with the

Thai nation. The 1940–1941 border war had been an attempt to provide the country with a sense of closure on this issue. Back in Bangkok, newspaper editorials echoed this narrative: "If France is broad-minded enough to sacrifice a slice of territory back to Siam, after careful consideration, such a friendly gesture will forever eradicate the antagonism held between the two nations. A slight sympathy shown by France will help put an end to the bitterness entertained by both sides. There is no other good chance for France and Siam to come to a compromise than this."[25]

It is clear then, that while postwar Siam was willing to repudiate almost all aspects of the Phibun agenda, it viewed the acquisition of the *lost territories* with a great deal of pride, part of a process that would allow past wounds to heal. For the nation to again be defeated by France would reverse this therapeutic process. When added to the surfeit of problems already facing the postwar Thai government (food hoarding and shortages, reparations, increased crime, Allied troops), the prospect of losing this territory—of losing face in this way—was alarming. Thai politicians understood that allowing this new humiliation would have serious political consequences.

In light of this realization, the Pridi faction that now ruled Siam proposed several alternatives to avoid compliance with French demands. Bangkok proposed submitting the matter to an Anglo-American arbitration committee. When that proved impossible, the Thai government offered to relinquish control over the territories to a four-nation commission, which would then conduct a plebiscite in the border provinces. In November 1945, the Seni Pramoj government suggested the two parties refer the matter to the United Nations.[26] Each of these requests reflected Siam's desire to avoid direct two-party talks with the French. Since both Britain and the United States supported a return to the pre-1940 status quo, Siam's leaders understood it was unlikely that they would be able to keep all four provinces. It was essential, however, for the government to avoid the appearance of capitulating to France. In early 1946, the U.S. State Department conducted an assessment of the political situation in Siam, which concluded that an unfavorable settlement regarding the border situation could destroy the democratic system of government. One American official described public opinion as more united over the *lost territories* than on any other domestic or foreign issue.[27]

The Thai military, which took credit for obtaining these provinces for Thailand, adamantly opposed ceding them to France. Prince Wan, a central figure in the 1941 Franco-Thai negotiations, speculated that any attempt at retrocession might trigger the collapse of the elected government and the military's return to power.[28] This scenario became even more likely after the unexplained death of King Ananda Mahidol in June 1946 and the rumored involvement of Prime Minister Pridi Banamyong. Although he supported France's claim to the territory, Dean Acheson recognized that allowing the Thai government to save face in the matter was crucial if the country hoped to avoid a return to dictatorship.

On the other side of the negotiating table, France was determined to use the negotiations to rebuild its own prestige. From the beginning, France's goal was to retrieve the territories in a way that humiliated Siam. George Picot, the French representative at Kandy, stipulated that the Thai must officially renounce the 1941 Tokyo Peace Accord as a precondition of talks between the two countries. In addition to the return of the four provinces, a French proposal from October 1945 also demanded the return of the Emerald Buddha, a religious icon taken from Vientiane and installed at Wat Prakeow almost two hundred years earlier. The Bangkok government interpreted the condition as an insult, responding that no self-respecting leader of Siam would consider giving up the country's most sacred image.[29] In the ensuing weeks, when word of the French request was leaked to the public, it helped generate a new wave of anti-French sentiment in Bangkok.[30] France withdrew the demand only after both Britain and the United States reacted negatively.

By July 1946, the United States attempted to broker a deal that would replace the top echelon of Thai administration in the four provinces with an American contingent that would govern the region until its fate could be decided by the International Court of Justice (ICJ). France again refused, insisting on the immediate removal of all Thai personnel, including police, from the provinces before the matter could be submitted to the UN. As Larry Niksch has argued, France's demands exasperated American intermediaries because they "represented a formula for humiliating the Siamese, the very outcome the State Department wished to avoid."[31]

SIAM AND INDOCHINESE INDEPENDENCE

France's condescending demeanor produced unanticipated results. In addition to prolonging territorial negotiations with Thailand, it also undermined the much larger task of reasserting French hegemony over former colonial possessions in Indochina. Japan's rampage through mainland Southeast Asia interrupted French colonial security operations, allowing the reorganization and growth of indigenous nationalist forces. The sudden collapse of the

Japanese Empire then became an opportunity for the Viet Minh, Free Lao, and Khmer Issarak forces to assert themselves as the legitimate ruling authorities in their respective regions. By 1946, each of these groups engaged in a protracted guerilla campaign to stall the reestablishment of French imperialism in mainland Southeast Asia. Meanwhile, the government of Siam proved an enthusiastic, if clandestine, ally. During World War II, the Phibun regime claimed its expansionism was really an attempt to drive the Western imperialist influence from Asia. Even after the war, Siam's left-leaning governments also had a vested interest in preventing the return of the colonial order. France's designs on the four provinces and the disdainful manner with which they treated the Thai smacked of the prewar colonial mindset that the Thai had found so demeaning, and it helped ensure Siam's continued support for the revolutionary movements spreading across French Indochina.

Christopher Goscha has argued that the secret relationship between the Thai government and Viet Minh was based on the two parties' mutual antipathy towards French imperialism. As early as 1937, before Phibun's ascension to the premiership, Thailand amended its immigration policy to encourage Vietnamese, Lao, and Khmer to settle in its northeast provinces. Bangkok viewed immigration as an important strategy to boost border populations, which in turn would help it secure these regions against the threat of French encroachment. By 1941, the Thai government reported that 13,000 Vietnamese had immigrated into Siam. These populations offered important recruiting potential for the Viet Minh and served as ideal hideouts for refugees who crossed the Mekong to escape French security forces. It also allowed Vietnamese guerillas to regain control over bases previously established in northeast Siam.[32] At the end of 1941, the Thai government announced the creation of two groups: the Independent Indochina Party and the Khmer Issarak Party. These organizations worked to restore independence to Vietnam and Cambodia, respectively. As part of his quest for a Greater Thailand, Phibun envisioned a "restoration" of the Golden Peninsula as he imagined it existing before the arrival of European imperialism, with the Thai ruling over the Lao and Khmer and the Vietnamese completely independent.[33]

Pridi did not endorse the National Humiliation agenda created by Phibun and Wichit, but he did share their antipathy towards French imperialism. In the years following World War II, Pridi and his supporters offered various forms of covert aid to several anti-French factions. The disarmament of Japanese troops in 1945, combined with numerous Allied arms drops during the war, left the Siamese in control of a sizeable arms cache. As leader of the Seri Thai, Pridi had access to these weapons and helped direct them into the hands of the Viet Minh. Vietnamese Communists had important contacts within the Seri Thai government, the Royal Navy, and the Thai police and made frequent trips to Siam to purchase munitions. In eastern Siam, the Aphaiwongse family also operated a business that supplied the Viet Minh with weapons. Chawalit Aphaiwongse, once the assemblyman for Battambang Province, secretly provided the Viet Minh with rifles, machine guns, and antiaircraft guns.[34]

Siam assisted the revolutionary struggle in Indochina for two reasons. First, both the Seri Thai government and the public sympathized with the indigenous movements fighting in Indochina out of a sense of ethnic solidarity. The governor of Nong Khai Province harbored Lao Issara leader Prince Souphanouvong and protected him from capture by the French.[35] In Roi-Et Province, secret groups distributed leaflets asking the populace to donate money to the monks at Wat Burapha on behalf of the Free Lao movement.[36] Pridi's wife would reflect on the cooperation between Thai and Indochinese people years later by commenting, "We helped. . . . We were after all, Asians together."[37] On the other hand, it would be misleading to characterize Siam's actions as altruistic. The Thai supported these resistance groups because it was in their self-interest to do so. According to Goscha, Bangkok's decision in May 1946 to allow the Vietnamese to train their troops inside Siam was a response to France's aggressive stance on border negotiations.[38] That same month, France vetoed Siam's initial application to join the United Nations. Siam's only hope for retaining its annexed territories and safeguarding its prestige was to help prevent the reestablishment of French rule in Indochina.

At the same time, Siam continued to rehabilitate its international image by maintaining a façade of impartiality concerning the hostilities. When the British Legation contacted the Foreign Ministry to request that Siam stop providing assistance to the independence movements in Laos and Annam, Thai officials responded that they had no knowledge of any such activities.[39] The French chargé d'affaires had already officially protested the pro–Viet Minh coverage in Bangkok's newspapers. Such prejudicial coverage, he argued, would needlessly jeopardize the ongoing negotiations between the two countries. Foreign Ministry official Visutr Anthayukti responded that the Thai government was a democracy that respected the freedom of the press and could not control its activities. He added that Thailand had consistently taken a neutral position on France's activities in Indochina, but if the French were unhappy with Bangkok's press coverage on the conflict, they should provide the newspapers with their own version of events.[40] In fact, the Thai media had adopted a pro–Viet Minh tone dating back to the Franco-Thai tensions in 1940. Under Phibun's direction, newspapers informed the public that the militants fighting for freedom in Indochina should be referred to as "revolutionaries," which implied a greater sense of legitimacy than "rebel groups," the term used previously in media coverage.[41] This depiction of the Indochina conflict continued even after World War II ended.

The Thai government's refusal to vacate the four border provinces and encouragement of revolutionary groups threatened to draw the country into a second border war with French Indochina. On May 5, 1946, a group of nearly two hundred persons crossed the Mekong from Siam into French Indochina to attack the Lao town of Hin Bu, killing several persons and capturing firearms before fleeing back across the river. The French retaliated by bombarding the town of Nakorn Phanom and firing at Siamese riverboats suspected of ferrying Vietnamese rebels. Two weeks later a similar outbreak of violence occurred in Nong Khai Province. A group of Free Lao attempted a raid on Vientiane and engaged French forces before fleeing into Siam and taking refuge in the border village of Tha Baw. In their pursuit of the Lao fighters, French soldiers temporarily occupied the village and exchanged gunfire with Thai police, causing several casualties.[42] Desperate to avoid escalating the military conflict with France, Pridi followed American recommendations to withdraw all Thai troops from any area under attack. These two incidents cultivated rumors, which would last throughout the summer, that France was on the verge of invading Siam to retake the border provinces.[43] Bangkok newspapers translated the content of Radio Saigon, which was busy celebrating the French capture of Luang Prabang from the Free Lao. The broadcasts assured listeners that once France had defeated the remaining rebels, it would also restore the Lao territories stolen by Phibun Songkhram.[44] In early June, the Thai newspaper *Thamthada* reported a massive mobilization of French troops taking place just outside Thailand's borders: "A coastal city in Battambang will be attacked by warships that are close to Thailand on three sides. Planes and infantry are encroaching on our borders and preparing to cut roads through the jungle. Inside sources claim the French are preparing warships and airplanes for a massive invasion of Thailand. These circumstances indicate France is preparing an invasion larger than the one launched in RS 112."[45]

Public anxiety over these border clashes only increased in the ensuing months. In early August a combined Viet Minh–Khmer Issarak force attacked and temporarily held the French-administered town of Siem Reap, near the border of Phibun Songkhram Province. After French forces retook the city, the French accused Siam of aiding the incursion and even claimed that Thai regulars had participated in the attack.[46] The Thai government denied involvement. Many of its officials believed that France was secretly provoking these clashes as a way to justify an invasion of the disputed territories.[47] The Siem Reap incident proved to be a turning point in the negotiations process. On August 26, France notified the United States that it would withdraw its offer of arbitration by the International Court of Justice on the question of the border dispute, citing alleged Thai complicity in the attack on Siem Reap as the reason.[48] French authorities then proceeded to move an additional thousand troops to the Thai border as Radio Saigon began proclaiming France's intention to take the four provinces by force. Unable to control the movements of refugees and guerilla forces and faced with the prospect of invasion, Siam closed its border with French Indochina in late August.[49]

DEBATE IN THE NATIONAL ASSEMBLY

By the end of September 1946, the prospect of returning territory to France seemed inevitable. France, Britain, and the United States were quickly running out of patience with Siam, which could no longer stall the negotiations. The Bangkok press speculated that changing conditions in Siam would place pressure on the Thai government, under Prime Minister Thawan Thamrongnawasawat, to resolve the dispute before the end of October. After the Siem Reap raid in August, French forces along the border adopted an aggressive posture. The rainy season had ended and as the river flooding began to subside, it would become easier for France to ferry its colonial troops across the Mekong into Thai territory. Moreover, the Indian occupying forces were scheduled to evacuate Bangkok on October 31. This would mean that France could invade Siam without the extra complication of having British colonial forces caught in the ensuing conflict.[50]

Recognizing the urgency of the matter, Prime Minister Thamrong convened a special session of the National Assembly beginning on October 14, 1946. He explained that the government had recently received an updated proposal from France and requested the assembly's advice on how Siam should respond. Following this introduction, Foreign Minister Direk Jayanama stood before the membership body to read the text of the treaty document, which can be summarized as follows:

Article 1: The government of Siam would accept the agreement of May 9, 1941, as void and transfer control of the disputed territories to French authorities.

Article 2: The aforementioned action would end hostilities between the two nations. If Siam agreed to withdraw its complaint to the Security Council, France would no longer bar Siam's entry into the United Nations.

Article 3: The two parties would establish a Conciliatory Commission composed of two representatives from each country and three representatives from neutral countries.

Article 4: The commission would reevaluate the border delineation based on all applicable ethnic, geographic, and economic arguments.

Article 5: Negotiations would eventually be opened to determine the amount of compensation to be paid to France by Siam.[51]

In his speech, Direk stressed that the government remained committed to the lost provinces and was not advocating their return to France. It raised this issue for debate because acceptance of the proposal would involve altering the nation's boundaries, which according to Article 76 of the 1946 Constitution required the approval of the National Assembly. Throughout the first day of discussion, Prime Minister Thamrong refused to divulge his stance on the French proposal, preferring instead to allow the legislators to ask questions and present their own opinions.[52] The assembly's reaction to the government's presentation revealed the extent to which the issue of the *lost territories* had become a political hand grenade. Several officials denounced the meeting as the government's obvious attempt to dump the matter in the lap of the parliament. Chiang Mai representative Suwit Phantaset claimed Thamrong had the process backwards. The government had the power to negotiate with foreign countries and should only approach the assembly once it had a signed treaty to submit for a vote.[53] Most assembly members understood the reality of Siam's situation, and they feared the government was only soliciting their opinion in order to avoid responsibility for making a necessary but extremely unpopular decision.

The text of the French proposal only added to their worries. Several representatives criticized the draft as another attempt by France to restore its own shattered prestige by humiliating Siam. The assembly's main objection focused on Article 1, which required Siam to declare the 1941 agreement null and void. Although it had ended up on the losing side of the Greater East

Asian war, the Siamese remained proud of their military's performance in restoring territories they perceived to have been taken away unjustly decades earlier. To renounce the Tokyo Peace Accord as invalid would have the effect of apologizing for Siam's conduct during the war. Elected officials felt it would dishonor the memories of those soldiers who sacrificed their lives to reunite the four provinces with their homeland (NAP 241). They expressed regret that recently liberated populations in the border regions would fall back under the yoke of French imperialism and feared the reaction of their own electorates once it became known that these territories were lost yet again. The heated debate in the assembly demonstrates how these territories, by now an icon of Siamese humiliation, had existed for the past five years as a symbol that the nation had regained its honor. The victory over France had been one of the greatest triumphs in the country's history, temporarily erasing the legacy of defeat inherited from the monarchy. Now a new generation of Thai politicians feared they would have to experience their own moment of partition. This potential outcome was so painful that many representatives urged the government to reject the accord, even if it meant war.

Assembly members who spoke out against acceptance of the peace plan did so for a variety of reasons. Foremost on the list was a refusal to submit to French bullying yet again. One of the most vocal opponents of the proposal was Chawalit Aphaiwongse, brother of opposition leader Khuang Aphaiwongse and a newly elected representative of Battambang, one of the provinces in question. In his speech before the assembly, he argued that it was essential for Siam to avoid capitulating to French imperialism. He reminded his fellow representatives of the bitter history of humiliation that characterized Franco-Siamese relations over the past half century and of the many times France had strong-armed Siam into an unequal treaty. "If this proposal had been put forward by a neutral party I would not disagree so strongly," Chawalit admitted, "but this proposal is from France, a nation that considers itself an enemy of ours, and who has always intended to take this land from us and make its people their slaves" (NAP 266). He warned that France's ultimatum was specifically designed to debase Siam, and that its acceptance would only delay the inevitable conflict for future generations. Former prime minister Seni Pramoj agreed that France was being unnecessarily harsh with Siam in an attempt to restore its diminished status as a power in the East. France was a defeated power like Siam, he reasoned, but the confrontation over the four provinces offered them an opportunity to act like a superpower (NAP 283).

The spirit of defiance expressed by the assemblymen echoed the attitudes of Young Siam, the political faction that led the country into the Franco-Siamese crisis a century earlier. Like their ancestors, Siam's representatives remained convinced that France was trying to cheat them out of territory obtained legitimately. They believed France and Siam had followed similar policies of self-interest during World War II. Both Phibun and Petain surrendered to the Axis and chose to form occupation governments rather than face annihilation. Each country gave birth to resistance movements that worked alongside the Allies—the Free French led by de Gaulle and the Free Thai under Pridi Banamyong. After the war, these freedom movements took power and repudiated the policies of their wartime predecessors. Despite these parallels, Siam had been denied membership in the UN, while France had been given a coveted seat at the Security Council.

Early on in the border negotiations, French officials claimed they would not honor the 1941 treaty because it had been signed by the Vichy government. Certain members of the assembly pointed out the flaws in France's logic. As Chod Khumphan (Nakorn Ratchasima) observed, "If Vichy was the recognized government, then the treaty was legal. How can we be expected to rescind it?" (NAP 232) Such a course held Bangkok accountable for its actions while granting France immunity. Moreover, France's accusation that Siam had obtained the territories illegally was considered irrelevant, because the French employed gunboat diplomacy to obtain them fifty years earlier.

As the assembly discussed previous episodes of victimization, their fear that history would repeat itself began to increase. All legislators agreed it was essential to join the United Nations, but some questioned whether France would honor their own proposal even if Siam agreed to their demands. French behavior in the past demonstrated a consistent disregard for treaty conventions and international law. One representative questioned whether France would alter the new agreement once it had been signed, pointing out that only a few months ago Paris had reneged on a deal to allow World Court mediation. If Siam gave up the territories in good faith, it had no bargaining chips left. What response could it muster in the event that France continued to veto its UN application? Khun Radab Khadi (Sukothai) reminded the assembly of the fallout from the French occupation of Chantaburi and Trat provinces from 1893 to 1907. Although France eventually ceded the provinces back to Siam in return for Lao and Cambodian concessions, it had refused to return Kong Island (NAP 222). Other members raised possible scenarios of French duplicity. Perhaps France would retaliate against the populations of the four provinces once they had been returned, or it might convince the Soviets to veto Siam's application on its behalf. Sombun Panthid (Nan) warned that France would use these negotiations as a pretext from grabbing even more territory. If the Thamrong government agreed to give up Lan Chang, the French might try to seize neighboring Nan Province as well (NAP 273).

The most powerful argument for rejecting the proposed settlement involved the question of how the public would react to the loss of the four provinces. The four disputed provinces had been a central issue of the national election only a few months earlier. Khuang Aphaiwongse remarked that people out on the campaign trail had constantly asked him whether he would be involved in the negotiations over the border dispute and his opinion on a possible outcome (NAP 238). Several representatives expressed the opinion that the people of Siam were not ready to give up the provinces and would blame the assembly for surrendering to France and dealing the country another crushing defeat. Although all elected officials feared this outcome, some would be affected more than others. In 1941 when French Indochina ceded the strip of territory opposite Luang Prabang to Thailand, most of the land became the new province of Lan Chang, but a small portion was divided into five districts that became part of nearby Loei Province. Not surprisingly, Loei's newly elected representative, Songkran Udomsit, was a staunch opponent of any plan to return those districts to French Indochina: "When I was elected I received support from those five districts," he told the assembly. "How can I be responsible for giving them back?" (NAP 296) Saw Sethabut (Thon Buri) criticized the government for ignoring the will of the people when formulating its policy on the border dispute. "As we discuss this matter we must consider the feelings of the Thai people. I've changed my opinion on this matter after meeting with several people last night, including fellow representatives. The prime minister has stated that the public will probably be very upset over this matter. I think this is worse than upsetting; it is like ripping the nation's heart out!" (NAP 307)

The heated debate surrounding retrocession proved that National Humiliation imagery continued to shape popular opinion. Wichit's racial theory, which designated the people in these provinces as ethnically Thai, framed the matter as a choice over whether to send these ethnic Thais back into French bondage. Whatever the outcome of the Greater East Asian conflict, most Thais still believed their war against French Indochina had been a just cause. In an emotional speech before the assembly, Kamon Chonsuek recalled his experience as a soldier in the Indochina campaign. He remembered hearing children singing a new song titled "Monthon Burapha Once

Belonged to Us." At the conclusion of hostilities, young and old had celebrated the Tokyo Peace Accord, because it had restored Thai honor and freed the lost provinces. Kamon himself was wounded in a clash with French troops, but he considered his injuries insignificant compared to the reward of returning the "eastern territories" back to their homeland (NAP 224).

Now that Siam had lost the war, the same discourse on loss made the prospect of returning the provinces populated by people who only months ago had voted in their first election feel like condemning an innocent man to the gallows. "We just obtained their release from prison," Chawalit Aphaiwongse (Battambang) opined, "and now we're hurrying to send them back" (NAP 268). Most representatives knew that Thai citizens empathized with the plight of people they considered to be fellow Thais and were concerned about the fate of these peoples under a French administration. Saw Sethabut (Thon Buri) suggested that the government demand France provide Siam with a date for Lao and Cambodian independence as a condition of transferring the territories. This would at least provide some evidence of Bangkok's concern for the plight of the border provinces. As Saw explained it, "The prime minister claims this [France's future plans for the territories] is none of our affair. I see it as very much our affair, because the people of these four provinces are our flesh and blood. If these peoples are persecuted, it is the same as if we are persecuted" (NAP 309).

The government also demonstrated its concern for the border peoples by offering assistance to those who wished to emigrate from the four provinces in the event they were returned to French Indochina. The prospect of thousands of refugees once again streaming out of French-occupied lands towards Siam invoked the privation of the past. Ararathaphorn Phisan (Trat) recollected the hardship undertaken by families who left his home province in 1904, after Chulalongkorn ceded it to France. "The events of 1904," he declared, "will forever be inscribed on the hearts of every resident of Trat Province" (NAP 298).

Such pronouncements suggest how the *lost territories* continued to function as a representation of the *chosen trauma*. Collectively speaking, the nation imagined itself reliving the tragic events of the original Franco-Siamese crisis. These historical associations help explain why several representatives ultimately voted to risk armed conflict rather than accept France's humiliating ultimatum.

As debate continued, Siam's difficult dilemma became more and more apparent. France's uncompromising position of power presented the assembly with two very unattractive options: either surrender or fight. To choose the former would be to throw away the objective of the 1941 Indochina campaign, rendering the sacrifices of citizens and soldiers completely meaningless and dooming fellow Thais to French hegemony. To choose the latter would require enormous sacrifice at a time when the nation was ill-equipped to do so. The logic of National Humiliation theory had forced the country into a moral dilemma—properly honoring the blood of the fallen would require more blood.

The Thai government searched for ways to retain its dignity long after it had given up on retaining the four provinces. As stated earlier, the Thai government wished to avoid the appearance of capitulation to France, and the most promising strategy for accomplishing this was by involving a third party—preferably the United Nations. In 1946, the UN was still in its formative stages. The rhetoric of peaceful coexistence had not yet been crushed by the realities of the Cold War. Despite their conviction that France was abusing its status on the Security Council to fulfill its imperialist ambitions, Thai leaders still had enormous respect for the UN. They saw the world body as a small nation's best hope for international justice and the ideal organization to help mediate their current dispute. Chod Khumphan (Bangkok) argued that if the UN was going to designate itself as the "father of the world," then the Thai government should simply refer the matter to their judgment (NAP 208).

Siam was under no illusion that the UN would allow it to keep possession of the four provinces, but deferring to the international body might be of value. The UN's decision in the matter, even if it decided in France's favor, would carry enormous credibility with the Thai people.[54] As Phetchabun representative Chuea Sanamueang observed, a UN directive ordering Siam to relinquish the provinces would cause far less public bitterness than simply acquiescing to France's demands (NAP 232). Also, UN deliberation over the matter would shine the light of international scrutiny onto France's past and present dealings with Siam. Thai leaders such as Saw Sethabut were confident that if they could discuss the border dispute in a high-profile forum, the world community might sympathize with their plight (NAP 308). Perhaps the media and people of the Western democracies would lobby their governments to adopt a less rigid policy towards Siam. Seni Pramoj had already employed this strategy to Siam's advantage by disclosing confidential information on Britain's twenty-one demands to an American newspaper reporter. Although the UN was certainly the country's best hope of eluding embarrassment, France's privileged position within the organization caused some representatives to doubt whether the world body would entertain their plea. "If the United Nations is as devoted to peace as the foreign minister claims," asked Thamnun Thianngen (Chon Buri), "why has it said nothing while France has repeatedly invaded our borders?" (NAP 300)

As part of Siam's UN strategy, several representatives still clung to the hope that the territorial issue could be decided by the World Court. In August, France had withdrawn its participation from court proceedings after alleging Siam's involvement in an attack by Khmer rebels on a French garrison near Siem Reap. The Siamese government consistently denied the allegations and offered to help form a fact-finding commission that would prove its innocence. Now that Siam had been vindicated, Luang Ararathaphorn Phisan proposed that the government resubmit its case to the International Court of Justice (NAP 218). At this suggestion, Foreign Minister Direk reminded the assembly that only UN member nations could submit petitions to the ICJ. The previous submission had been possible only because the French agreed to sponsor the process, but it was not likely they would do so again (NAP 200).

If the UN would not decide the fate of the four provinces, the next best solution would be a referendum within these territories themselves. Chuea Sananmueang (Phetchabun) was one of many representatives who supported an election allowing the contested areas to vote whether they would prefer to stay part of Siam or return to French Indochina.[55] The proposal seemed consistent with the postwar political atmosphere. After all, the Allies were already busy lecturing the rest of the world about the principles of self-determination as contained in the Atlantic Charter. Siam's border dispute with Indochina offered an excellent opportunity to put those ideals into practice. Other assemblymen advocated pulling out Siam's administration and conferring independence on the four provinces. The government would give up the provinces but not bear the shame of surrendering to France. As an added incentive, if the French chose to take possession of the territories they would have to account for their invasion of a sovereign nation. Direk again stood to explain why neither a referendum nor independence was a viable alternative. A foundational principle of the Atlantic Charter involved a return to the prewar status quo (NAP 311). It was not enough to simply give up the territories; they must be returned to French Indochina if Siam expected the Allies to support their UN membership application.

After spending the first day of the National Assembly debate fielding questions and listening to opinions, Prime Minister Thamrong began day two by offering a cautious analysis of Siam's situation. He reminded the assembly that all postwar prime ministers, including Seni, understood the country had little chance of keeping the four provinces. Up to this point, there had been hope that Siam might win some compromise whereby it could retain a portion of the territories or at least minimize the repercussions from ceding territory. Those hopes had been dashed by France's recent ultimatum (NAP 253). Thamrong exhorted the assembly to adopt a realistic approach to the country's dilemma: "The four provinces can be compared to a terminal patient," Thamrong explained. "The question is no longer whether that patient will live or die. There is only a question of how long until he dies and under what circumstances" (NAP 250). The prime minister went on to list three important reasons Siam had little choice but to accept the French proposal. First, a strong relationship with the United States was the cornerstone of Siam's postwar foreign policy, and retention of the territories could only complicate that relationship. American officials made it clear that retrocession was one of the steps Bangkok must take to atone for its alliance with Japan during the war. Undersecretary of State Dean Acheson also advised Siamese officials to withdraw their complaint from the Security Council and negotiate directly with France (NAP 235). Second, admission to the United Nations was essential if Siam hoped to rehabilitate its image and reenter the community of respected nations. Rejecting France's ultimatum would sever relations between the two countries and delay entrance to the UN indefinitely.

Finally, Thamrong impressed upon the assembly the real possibility that France would invade the four provinces if Siam failed to relinquish them voluntarily. He felt that some representatives failed to appreciate the disastrous repercussions of another war.[56] The military was in no condition to defend the country against a French assault, and if Siam was defeated the terms of surrender would be much less favorable (NAP 302). Neither the United States nor Britain would intervene, and armed conflict would place more strain on an economy already plagued by inflation and burdened by mandatory rice shipments to the UN. Even worse, French forces might occupy more territory than the provinces in question, in which case Siam would have to offer further concessions to get it back (NAP 276). Border tensions had already led to a French incursion from Vientiane across the border in Nong Khai Province. Phan Inthuwong (Nakorn Phanom) testified that the French had periodically shelled border towns in his home province. Citizens of Nakorn Phanom had patiently endured these attacks in the interest of supporting the government and maintaining peace, he continued, but they also realized that their province would suffer greatly from a war with France (NAP 244–245).

After presenting Siam's predicament in sufficiently gloomy terms, Thamrong attempted to soften the blow by referencing Articles 3 and 4 of the proposed peace accord. These two clauses detailed the formation of a Conciliatory Commission, which would recommend alterations in the eastern boundary between Siam and French Indochina according to principles of ethnicity, geography, and international law. The committee would consist of a delegate each from France, Siam, and three other impartial countries. If the government cooperated by transferring administration of the territories to France, Thamrong suggested, the United States would use its influence to look after Siam's interests. There was a reasonable chance the committee would endorse Siam's claims to a portion of the four provinces, but for now they must give all of it back (NAP 212). In his concluding remarks, the prime minister reminded the assembly that by accepting France's offer, Siam would begin winning back the respect of the international community and enhance its reputation as a peacemaker (NAP 278). Following the prime minister's speech, most members were ready to accept the inevitable. The assembly eventually voted 91 to 27 to grant the government authority to rescind the treaty of 1941 and return the disputed territories to France.[57] Seni's comments towards the end of the debate reflected the sense of fatalism that gripped the assembly: "If we return the provinces, let it be Siam's sacrifice for the achievement of world peace. We will give up these lands, which contain our flesh, our blood, our brethren, or France will never let the issue rest. France already has colonies all over the world; it should stay in Europe instead of interfering in Asia. We have already lost much including our honor, and now we must swallow this bitterness, because France will never give up this fight."[58]

On October 18, Thamrong addressed the nation to announce his government's decision to give back the four provinces. The prime minister's reasons for complying with France's demands were clear. Siam must follow the advice of the United States and Great Britain. Second, this course of action would demonstrate the country's commitment to world peace. Finally, Siam must follow the principles of the newly established United Nations in order to secure membership. Thamrong's remarks stressed his own disappointment that Siam was once again giving up the *lost territories,* referring to the decision as "yet another sad chapter in Thai history."[59]

Figure 5. **Price of Admission.** A political cartoon showing Prime Minister Thamrong handing a paper to a French official, in order to pass through the doors of the UN and obtain membership. The paper reads, "Special price for ticket to enter the UN = four provinces." The man with the mustache remarks, "If you want to see the UN show, you have to pay the ticket price." (National Archives of Thailand)

PUBLIC REACTION

In anticipation of a possible violent reaction to the announcement that it would yield territory to France, the Thai government printed thousands of leaflets detailing its course of action to the public. Still, the prime minister's statement shocked and angered a nation already suffering through a postwar malaise involving inflation, crime, rice shortages, and rampant corruption. The day after Thamrong's speech, *Nakorn sarn* expressed its sentiments on the issue: "Today our newspaper joins fellow newspapers in mourning for Siam over the loss of the four provinces to France."[60] The editorial in *Thai rashdr* lamented, "We are stricken with grief over the news that our million Siamese brethren are going to leave us. . . . We have shed our tears of worry and regard for our brothers on this heartbreaking departure."[61] Bangkok papers received hundreds of letters demanding that Siam go to war with France rather than endure the shame of admitting defeat once again.[62] In December 1946, 5,000 people turned out at Bangkok's Sarapram Gardens to protest the official return of Battambang and Phibun Songkhram provinces to French Indochina.[63] In spite of its grief, the Thai media proved surprisingly moderate in its criticism of the government. Rather than immediately blaming present or past leaders for the embarrassment, editorials adopted a tone of resignation, accepting the fact that the entire nation bore responsibility for this tragic turn of events. As the editor of *Naew na* wrote, "The dream that a one-time government has endowed upon the Thai is now disappearing. We are facing a terrible fact. No matter how bitter this fact is, we must face it squarely. It is selfish to fuss around, placing blame on this person or that person for being the cause of this. It is a fact that this idea bloomed during the Phibun government, but not without the general consent and support of the people themselves. We have shown our wholehearted support and delight with mass demonstrations, and so forth. Now that the matter has come to a tragic end, let us not lay blame on each other."[64]

Instead of blaming government, most newspapers blamed France. The political cartoon "Price of Admission" depicts how once again Siam had to endure the humiliation of accepting France's terms and giving up territory. In the illustration, Prime Minister Thamrong appears much smaller (and lower) than his French counterpart in order to signify the international status of each figure. Through the entire process of negotiations, the French refused to make any major concessions and eventually relied on the threat of force to achieve their objectives. In effect, France in 1946 possessed the exact attitude as in 1893, acting as a great imperial power dictating terms to an uncivilized people. Thai newspapers commented on how France's actions in Indochina were completely out of step with the more conciliatory policies pursued by Britain in India and the Americans in the Philippines. "We wonder," wrote a *Tawan* columnist, "why a country like France, which is the greatest worshipper of freedom, brotherhood, and equality as well as the unsurpassed originator of democratic principles, never practices her own concepts."[65] Others took comfort in their belief that France had won a hollow victory. In the months leading up to retrocession, thousands of residents of the four provinces poured over the borders into Siam proper, allowing the Bangkok media to point out once again that these people had no desire to live under European colonial rule.[66] France could use their superior military to possess the land, *Bangkok rai wan* observed, but the people's hearts will always belong to Siam.[67]

In addition to anger, Thais also felt disillusioned regarding the precarious position of their country in an uncertain world. In August 1946, two months before the issue was decided, *Siam nikorn* commented that the fate of the *lost territories* acted as a barometer on whether the rights of small nations would be respected in the coming age.[68] When neither the Allies nor the UN moved to counteract French bullying, many in Siam interpreted this as a sign that the new political climate would be no different than the old. The Thai felt their claim to the four provinces was supported by history, ethnicity, and geography, but in the end none of these factors proved relevant. "History shows that might rules the world," wrote *Sri krung*. "The treaty of 1941 was declared void due to France's superior military power."[69] In 1946, just as in 1893, Siam self-identified as the virtuous Buddhist kingdom, deceived by a foreign aggressor.

The media responded to the territorial trauma by reverting back to Royal-Nationalist narratives of the past. Commentators focused on the historical parallels with the Franco-Siamese crisis in order to describe the retrocession as a small victory for Siam: "Siam's resolute decision to return the four provinces to France should by all means be regarded as most timely and sensible. Siam was forced to do so once before in the reign of Chulalongkorn. The astute king ceded the territory to France in order to divert the political clouds hanging over Siam, as a way of sacrificing the finger to save the hand. And his clever policy saved Siam throughout. The present government policy may be likened to that policy."[70]

The nation mollified its grief by glorifying the Fifth Reign. On October 23, only days after Thamrong's radio address, Siam commemorated the death of Chulalongkorn. In their assessment of the king's legacy, pundits drew lessons they felt could be applied to the country's current predicament. In its editorial titled "A Beloved Monarch," the newspaper *Democracy* credited Chulalongkorn as the driving force behind the country's modernization at the end of the nineteenth century: "King Chulalongkorn woke Siam from her complacent basking in the sun, and put her feet firmly on the road to progress and advancement. He shrewdly realized that if Siam was to maintain her independence and prosperity she must march with the times. She had to be strong and at the same time tactical if she wanted to avoid the fate that was overtaking her neighbors."[71]

This quote is a microcosm of Royal-Nationalist history. The leadership of the monarchy, its ability to blend tradition with modernity, allowed Siam to avoid colonization and remain independent. Under the guidance of the king, the country rapidly advanced in knowledge and status and would soon deal with the West on an equal footing. The events of 1946, however, had derailed Siam from its intended path. Instead of helping Siam continue forward, the domestic and foreign policies followed by Phibun caused a decline in the nation's fortunes. In the words of the *Democracy* editor, "Unfortunately, for the past five years we have been cut off from the rest of the world due to the war. We are lagging behind in all fields of human endeavor as a result of being out of touch with the latest developments. . . . We would do well today to ponder the achievements of our great and beloved king. We should go further and understand what his plans were for this country. Finally, we should always place before us his reign as an example—an example to be followed."[72]

By portraying the country as having been asleep for the past five years (since the border war with Indochina), the author argued that the Phibun era existed as a historical interlude, disconnected from eras that preceded and followed it. *Siam nikorn* offered similar analysis by arguing that the country's experiment with fascism had severely damaged Siam's prestige. The entire world became suspicious of Siam following the Japanese-mediated treaty of 1941, as evidenced by the U.S. refusal to deliver warplanes to Bangkok.[73] In this way, Siam's defeat in World War II represented a reversal of the historical paradigm that gained acceptance at the war's beginning. The victory over French Indochina had once symbolized Thailand's achievement of parity with the West; now it represented a nightmarish episode that had dishonored the nation and brought its economy to ruin. The decision to return the provinces to France was portrayed as a necessary step forward towards undoing the damage wrought during the fateful years of 1941–1942. It would help the nation return to normalcy and replace the narrative of defeat with a more comforting notion that Siam had "survived" the war. By returning the provinces, Siam pledged its support to adhere to the principles of the United Nations. The resulting gain in prestige would perhaps compensate for any sense of regret felt at the loss of the border provinces. As a journalist from *Democracy* expressed it, "What we must convince ourselves is that we 'have not lost face' over this affair. There is no such thing as 'saving' or 'losing' face today. We are all members of a family of nations. Internationalism and not watertight nationalism is our ideal today. If members of a family quarrel with each other and one has to give way, is it a 'loss of face?' "[74]

France's hard-line stance during postwar border talks helped Siam shed its wartime image of an aggressor nation and instead present itself as a victim of imperialist attacks. The recasting of Siam as a "peaceful nation" was essential if it hoped to secure membership in the United Nations. The country was already performing its penance by providing rice shipments to the UN to alleviate the famine in postwar Asia. The French attack on Nong Khai in May and the August incident at Siem Reap disrupted rice production and allowed the Thai media to reframe the territorial debate in moral terms. Editorials portrayed Siam as a humanitarian nation whose foremost concern was worldwide famine relief but whose noble efforts were being obstructed by the unprovoked assaults of a selfish imperialist power.[75] The media applauded the government's nonviolent response to French attacks, a policy that it characterized as "throwing bread to the man who throws stones."[76] Siam's new strategy of peaceful coexistence meant it could not directly confront France, so it requested international intervention to help ensure its continued delivery of rice shipments. Siam's admission to the United Nations in December 1946 was an important step towards glossing over its past military aggression. "Siam can never hope to take a dominant role in the affairs of the world," wrote the *Bangkok Post,* "but she can become . . . a model for other nations of the Far East."[77]

Even after the transfer of territory and Siam's entry to the UN, many politicians still viewed the border dispute as unresolved. The nation still had aspirations that some portion of the four provinces might be returned, and those aspirations rested with the organization called the Conciliatory Commission. As 1946 drew to a close, the Thai media called on the international community to right the wrongs France had inflicted on Siam. An editorial in *Suwannaphum* seemed relieved that "it is now up to the Conciliatory Commission to decide who will take and who will give,"[78] while *Nakorn sarn* called on the international body to "show its generosity and justice."[79] In a newspaper interview, a Thai delegate to the United Nations expressed confidence that Siam would probably get back one or two provinces and perhaps even all four.[80] Many within the Thai government shared that optimism. Siam's official request involved the return of all territory lost to France since 1893, including Battambang, Champassak, Lan Chang, and the entire left bank of the Mekong. Secretly, Thai officials believed the commission would award Champassak and Lan Chang back to Siam as part of a suitable compromise.[81]

Once again, Siam's irredentist petition was denied by the international community. On June 27, 1947, the commission announced its decision rejecting all outstanding Thai claims to additional territory. A separate commission, set up to consider the issue of reparations, determined that Siam owed

France U.S. $518,000 in compensation for damages accrued during the 1941 border war.[82] In August, the National Assembly convened to deliberate on an appropriate response to the findings. Concerned over public opinion, Thamrong ordered the printing of five hundred copies of the commission's report for public distribution.[83] This time, however, the country would not be as understanding of the government's failure to salvage some portion of the nation's territory and dignity. Opposition members charged the government with overstating its case. Seni criticized the decision to ask for all land east of the Mekong, which he believed made the Allies suspicious of a possible expansionist agenda. Khuang argued that it was foolish to ask for anything east of the Mekong, when Siam should have been satisfied with a request for Champassak and Lan Chang.[84] In September, Thammasat University organized a public forum to allow citizens to state their opinions that the border provinces were an integral part of Siam. The meeting drew a large gathering, including members of the assembly on both sides of the issue. Representative Chuea Sanamueang of Petchabun Province acknowledged that the public had the right to be dissatisfied with the commission's ruling, but he defended the government, explaining that it would be impossible to go against the United Nations and the Allies. Others adopted a more aggressive tone. Assemblyman Pramuan Kunmatya urged young people to adopt a stronger spirit of nationalism so that Siam would be better able to defend itself from imperialism in the future.[85]

Public hostility to the commission report paralyzed the Thamrong government, which could not decide whether or not to accept the report's recommendations. A few months later, the prime minister was relieved from having to make such a difficult decision. On November 8, 1947, a military coup removed Thamrong from office. The commission report sat on a shelf until a second coup returned Phibun Songkhram to the office of the prime minister. The field marshal renounced any Thai claims to the four border provinces and agreed to pay the proscribed reparations to France.[86] The durable premier wanted to stabilize his new government and close the book on his irredentist past.

VICTORY MONUMENT: COMMEMORATING THE LOSS

Located at the center of one of Bangkok's busiest traffic circles, Victory Monument stands as a reminder of Thailand's ambivalent relationship with its own past. Today, the memorial is one of the city's most recognizable landmarks and a common rendezvous point for locals and tourists alike. Few Thais, however, know the origins of this monument or its contested history. The intended meaning of this famous shrine has largely disappeared from public memory because it evokes an era that Thais would prefer to forget. Instead of celebrating the triumph of 1941 as the Thai state originally intended, Victory Monument silently acknowledges the loss of 1946. The memorial has evolved into a cultural marker associated with National Humiliation imagery, preserving the memory of defeat for future generations.

The Thai government began construction of Victory Monument in the summer of 1941, laying the first cornerstone at a special National Day ceremony.[87] At the time, the nation was still celebrating its great triumph over France and the addition of four new provinces to the national space. Phibun Songkhram's popularity was at its zenith. The Thai nation was unified and optimistic about its prospects for the future. The prime minister envisioned a marvelous edifice that would capture the spirit of the age. At the center of the monument sits a fifty-foot-high column designed by artist M. L. Phakun, an obelisk-shaped structure composed of five bayonet blades placed together. Renowned artist Silpa Bhirasri and his assistants cast five bronze statues representing the army, navy, air force, police force, and civilians to stand at the base of the memorial. Each image stands twelve feet high and assumes a heroic pose. When combined with the obelisk, the structure conveys a sense of unity: five branches of society become one to protect the nation.[88]

On June 24, 1942, one year after the project began, Phibun dedicated the monument and spoke of its symbolic qualities. He expressed his hope that the nation would take pride in the monument and always remember that it was a memorial. Victory Monument became the final resting spot of those brave soldiers who had given their lives in the service of their country. The names of the fifty-nine individuals killed during the war with French Indochina were inscribed at the base of the monument. Underneath this plaque sat ornate hooks on which visitors could hang wreaths or flowered leis in respect for the deceased. In his speech, Phibun told the crowd that the bodies of these soldiers had expired, but their bravery and endurance would live forever as an inspiration to the country: "This important monument . . . will help motivate and train future generations of Thais to develop bravery and endurance so they will not fear death when serving their nation. And it will increase their patriotic spirit. Whenever our countrymen pass by this monument they will reflect on these qualities and renew their desire to protect our freedom and independence, which must be defended to the last drop of blood. Victory Monument represents the capacity of our people to unite our hearts and minds in order to preserve Thainess within Thailand forever."[89]

For Phibun, Victory Monument was much more than a tribute to the dead; it would be a powerful icon of national redemption, announcing to the world how Thailand had erased a debilitating legacy of shame and defeat. Starting in 1893, the *lost territories* existed as a symbol of the royal elite's disgrace, and it eventually became a reminder of Thailand's inferior relationship with the West. The recovery of four provinces, though only a small portion of the land ceded to European imperialists, offered the nation an opportunity to bring closure to the painful event. "Victory Monument," Phibun told the crowd, "will function to remind every Thai citizen that Thailand has salvaged its sacred honor with the help of the five branches of the armed forces: the army, navy, air force, police, and civilians who all sacrificed for the Thai nation."[90] It also allowed the Thai military to amend its own unimpressive record. The 1941 conflict was the country's first foreign engagement since its army had been so thoroughly outmatched during the Franco-Siamese crisis of 1893.[91] The conquest of Monthon Burapha removed the disgrace borne by the military for almost half a century. Despite being a memorial, both the name and the design of Victory Monument were intended to convey a message of military triumphalism. It announced that Thailand was emerging, under the guidance of the military, from semicolonial status into the ranks of developed nations.

As Apinan Poshyananda has argued, the construction of Victory Monument should also be seen within the context of the government's renovation program that had produced Democracy Monument, the Bridge Honoring the National Day, and the reconstruction of Rachadamnoen Road. Phibun planned to remake Bangkok in the image of a modern city.[92] During the early years of the Greater East Asian war, the memorial also became an important symbol of Asian solidarity and the anticipated defeat and removal of Western hegemony from the continent. In July 1943, when Indian revolutionary leader Subhas Chandra Bose arrived in Bangkok to meet with Axis leaders, his first scheduled event was a wreath-laying ceremony at Victory Monument.[93]

Thailand's defeat in the war and the ensuing debate over the future of the *lost territories* transformed Victory Monument into a site of contested meaning. The political cartoon featured on page 154 depicts Thai and French officials making presentations in an effort to convince Britain, the United States, and China of their rightful claim to the disputed provinces. The French officer attempts to portray Thailand as a nation of warmongers. He wants to focus attention on the picture of Thai tanks and planes on the right, while distracting attention from the "taxes" and chained-up colonial subjects behind his back. Meanwhile, Pridi and Khuang use a picture of a dove to convince the Allies that Thailand is a historically peaceful nation. Their argument, however, is undermined by the picture of a Victory Monument surrounded by human skulls. The cartoon suggests that the monument is a symbol of military expansion and ethnic chauvinism, which is the real legacy of Phibun's hypernationalistic policies.

The 1946 retrocession of the four provinces was the final blow in a series of setbacks that once again left Thailand defeated and disgraced. As we have already seen, those politicians who favored resisting French demands argued that giving back the provinces would dishonor the soldiers who died to obtain them. In 1941, the Thai navy had been decimated at Koh Chang, the Thai government paid reparations to France, but the acquisition of the east-

Figure 6. **Our Next Problem.** A Thai political cartoon depicting the postwar debate over the *lost territories*. Pridi and Khuang try to portray Siam as peaceful, while a French general tells observers from China, Britain, and the United States that Siam is a violent country. The caption reads, "Our Next Problem." (National Archives of Thailand)

ern territories allowed the country's leaders to make a plausible claim of victory. The four provinces had been the symbol of redemption, the reward of so much sacrifice. Now those lands were part of French Indochina again and the entire country was left to question the purpose of the border conflict. The meaning of Victory Monument was transformed during the ensuing period of disillusionment. After the Conciliatory Commission's announcement in August 1947 that Thailand would not receive any portion of its territorial demands from France, former Battambang representative Phra Phiset suggested that Victory Monument should be painted black to signify a state of national mourning.[94]

The landmark's redefinition continued throughout the next decade. Although Phibun returned to power in 1948, his agenda as prime minister was radically different. He soon proved himself eager to atone for his former pro-Axis policies and reinvented himself as a rabid anticommunist. Victory Monument would no longer be associated solely with the Franco-Thai border war. Instead, it would become a monument to Thailand's dead from all foreign wars. The names of Thai soldiers killed in the Greater East Asian war were inscribed on the monument's base, and later, casualties from the Korean and Vietnam wars would also be added. Later regimes deepened the ambiguity of the monument. After seizing power in 1957, Sarit sought to resurrect the monarchy's role in politics while discrediting Phibun's legacy. In the 1960s the government made plans to demolish Victory Monument and replace it with a Tomb of the Unknown Soldier. Despite its relatively ambivalent attitude towards the structure, the public opposed its destruction on the grounds that it was the final resting place of the soldier's cremated remains. Prayoon Chanyawongse published a political cartoon depicting the spirit of a deceased soldier pleading with the prime minister to spare the memorial.[95]

After failing in its attempt to replace Victory Monument, the Thai state has been largely successful in depriving the monument of its meaning. Its sole function now is that of a war cemetery. The public can visit Victory Monument only on Veterans Day, when the army holds an official ceremony, and people can purchase flowered leis to place beneath the plaque honoring fallen soldiers from several conflicts. For the rest of the year the monument is completely inaccessible. It is enclosed by a large, black iron fence and surrounded by one of Bangkok's busiest and most dangerous intersections, requiring potential visitors to cross multiple lanes of traffic. Victory Monument is now surrounded by large buildings, enormous billboards, and the tracks of the new sky train, all of which distract from the structure and obscure its visage. Like most public spaces in Thailand, it also hosts an enormous portrait of the king. The process of altering Victory Monument and allowing it to be crowded out of its own public space represents a parallel process of encouraging the events it commemorates to fade from public memory. The government wishes to honor the heroic sacrifice of its soldiers while detaching that sacrifice from a specific historical event. The structure commissioned by Phibun does not just memorialize the dead; it also evokes the demise of Thailand's dreams of triumph over Western imperialism and the loss of its beloved territories. This fact more than any other explains why it has been rendered increasingly irrelevant over the past several decades. Victory Monument now stands as a constant reminder of the nation's defeat.

CONCLUSION

This chapter has argued that the outcome of World War II represents a very painful defeat for Thailand, rather than a triumph of diplomacy. In 1946, Thai irredentists felt themselves reliving the humiliating experience of 1893, complete with Allied occupation, reparations, and the loss of territory. In order to reconcile the loss of territory with the long tradition of uninterrupted independence, the Thai state reverted back to Royal-Nationalist narratives that embraced the ideals of peaceful internationalism. This transformation allowed the country to reenter the community of nations, but it did not reduce the bitterness towards the West that had gripped the country five years earlier. The discourse of loss and humiliation continued to smolder within the hearts of Thai nationalists, fueled by the prospect of taking back the *lost territories.* Since 1946, the territories have been redefined as the four provinces. Thailand escaped the devastation of the war, and its status as the centerpiece of the American postwar strategy for Southeast Asia smoothed its transition into the postwar world. In the end, however, Siam could not avoid returning the four provinces and so adopted a magnanimous attitude in complying, as though the country was letting go of the past and moving forward towards a brighter future. After assessing the agreement with France and the transfer of the provinces, an editorial in *Democracy* stated, "We have now buried an issue, which however justified we considered ourselves in supporting could only remain a source of friction."[96]

The editor's choice of words was revealing. Indeed, Siam had "buried" the issue of *lost territory* rather than confront it. In this book, I argue that National Humiliation discourse resulted from the state's unwillingness to accept the consequences of its defeat in 1893. Instead, Thai leaders chose to nurture this historical grievance and reinforce the narrative of Siam as a victim of Western Imperialism. The transfer of the four provinces in 1946 was a critical moment in the continued development of this discourse. Although the new Siamese government surrendered the *lost territories,* it failed to repudiate the ideology that helped the Phibun regime to acquire them. As the *Democracy* editorial suggests, the country's irredentists still believed that the provinces represented Thai soil, which had been stolen yet again by French imperialists. This mentality allowed National Humiliation discourse to resurface in the next decade, when it played an important role in the Preah Vihear dispute with Cambodia.

6 Preah Vihear

A Thai Symbol of National Humiliation

On June 24, 2008, Thailand's Foreign Minister Noppadon Pattama signed a joint communiqué endorsing Cambodia's efforts to have Preah Vihear, an eleventh-century temple complex on the Thai-Cambodian border, declared a World Heritage site. This seemingly innocuous document triggered a firestorm of criticism and protest in Bangkok. For the past half century, both Cambodia and Thailand had staked claims to the land surrounding Preah Vihear. Critics argued that listing the temple as a World Heritage site would mean international recognition of Cambodian sovereignty over the ruins. Bangkok newspaper editorials accused the ruling People Power Party [Phak Phalang Prachachon] of selling out the country in exchange for gas and casino concessions in Cambodia's Koh Kong Province.

As media outlets stoked the fires of public outrage, the political opposition saw an opportunity. Citing the Preah Vihear affair as evidence of governmental mismanagement, the Democrat Party [Phak Prachathipat] called for a no-confidence vote against Prime Minister Samak Sundaravej and his entire cabinet. Meanwhile, the People's Alliance for Democracy (PAD) filed a lawsuit with Thailand's Constitutional Court claiming that the joint communiqué threatened the country's sovereignty and was therefore unconstitutional. Out in the streets, yellow-shirted PAD supporters demonstrated in front of the Ministry of Foreign Affairs before moving to the Government House. For his role as signatory of the joint communiqué, Noppadon Pattama faced an impeachment hearing in parliament and elected to resign.[1] The Thai cabinet eventually reversed its position and declared its opposition to Cambodia's application, but it was unable to affect the final outcome. On July 9, 2008, the World Heritage Council added Preah Vihear to its list of World Heritage sites, recognizing it as a Cambodian landmark. Since that time, there have been several outbreaks of violence between Thai and Cambodian soldiers stationed along the border.

The recent controversy over Preah Vihear is only the latest outbreak of tensions that began during the Cold War era. After World War II, the Thai army illegally occupied the ancient ruins, which belonged to Cambodia according to a 1907 treaty between the governments of French Indochina and Siam. Prince Sihanouk responded to this perceived aggression by suspending diplomatic relations between the two countries, launching a xenophobic press campaign and encouraging citizens in Phnom Penh to demonstrate outside the Thai embassy. The intensity of this reaction caused some observers in Thailand to wonder whether it was prudent to jeopardize trade and risk possible military conflict over a few square kilometers of territory. At a 1958 news conference in Bangkok, reporters asked Minister of Interior Praphas Charusathien why the government was taking an unnecessary gamble. "If we give up the temple, the dispute is over," a journalist observed. "Are commerce and trade not more important? Preah Vihear is just a pile of stones."[2]

The reporter's question conveyed a sense of confusion over the Thai government's willingness to further destabilize the region, just to take possession of a formerly insignificant landmark. In the early 1950s, few people in Thailand were aware of Preah Vihear's existence; by 1960 it had attained national prominence. Perhaps the answer lies in Praphas' response to the reporter: "I will never allow one stone of Thai territory to be surrendered." Although the Thai government had signed treaties recognizing Preah Vihear as located outside its borders, the military still considered the temple site to be an integral part of Thailand. This chapter explains this contradiction by demonstrating how the ancient ruins have evolved from an obscure archaeological site into the focal point of a state discourse on National Humiliation. From the perspective of the Thai state, Preah Vihear's importance has less to do with its architectural or religious significance than its connection to the *lost territories* and the legacy of Western imperialism in Thailand.

THE HISTORY OF PREAH VIHEAR

If Preah Vihear was truly part of Thailand, as Praphas told reporters in 1958, when did Bangkok first claim sovereignty over the area? Furthermore, when did the Thai state first identify Preah Vihear as an important heritage site worthy of preservation? Prior to the twentieth century, the Bangkok elite demonstrated an interest in historical preservation and the cultural value of temple ruins, but their attention was fixed exclusively on Angkor Wat. By contrast, there is no evidence to suggest they were interested in Preah Vihear.[3] Given the temple's remote location in the Dangrek Mountains, the monarchy in Bangkok was probably not even aware of its existence until it was first "discovered" by the Siamese high commissioner in 1899.[4]

The origins of the Preah Vihear controversy begin with Siam's efforts to revise certain provisions from its 1893 treaty with France. The most pressing objective involved obtaining France's withdrawal from Chantaburi and later Trat provinces in order to regain sovereignty over the Siamese people in those areas. By 1907, Siam had concluded agreements ceding the administrative district of Monthon Burapha (Sisophon, Siem Reap, and Battambang districts) to French Indochina in exchange for the two "Siamese provinces." The resumption of sovereignty over Siamese peoples and the end of French protection for Asiatic protégés restored a measure of honor and prestige to the Thai monarchy. It was an important step towards restricting foreign intervention and Siam's eventual inclusion within the ranks of civilized nations. For Chulalongkorn and his advisors, these goals were certainly worth the price of a few Cambodian lands. The French were equally satisfied to have fulfilled their role as protectors by resolving the problem of Cambodia's "Alsace-Lorraine."[5] The Siamese were reluctant to give up their claim to Angkor Wat, but neither party concerned themselves with Preah Vihear.[6]

The new treaties were important steps towards mapping the frontier between Siam and French Indochina, and a joint Franco-Siamese border commission was formed. The Siamese government, however, took little interest in the border commission's activities, which would lead to such contentious border negotiations a half century later. From Siam's perspective, the border's location had been settled in the text of the 1907 treaty, which stated that the boundary line would follow the watershed of the Dangrek Mountains.[7] The cartographical process became an exclusively French operation. Under the leadership of Lieutenant Colonel Bernard, French officials surveyed the frontier and drew up the necessary charts. In 1908, the Siamese government received a series of maps reflecting the new delineation of the border with French Indochina.[8] Although both royal and provincial officials had access to these maps, neither party was well versed in how to interpret Western cartography. The European model of mapping still represented a "new technology of space."[9] Moreover, Siamese leaders did not see the need for such spatial representations, because to them the boundary was clearly reflected in the natural geography. As Seni Pramoj, Thailand's attorney during the 1961–1962 trial before the International Court of Justice (hereafter the ICJ), would later argue, "No map was needed to find where the frontier was. . . . In fact, if a map had been shown to them, I doubt very much whether the inhabitants would have been able to read it or whether it would have shown the frontier to them with any greater clarity."[10]

Because the Siamese delegation failed to investigate the accuracy of the French maps, they remained unaware that the sketches drawn by Lt. Col. Bernard deviated slightly from the frontier description in the text of the official treaty. The border commission's maps depicted a border that ran east-west along the Dangrek divide until it reached the Preah Vihear temple site, where it turned north into Siam, arched around the temple complex, and returned to the watershed. This almost imperceptible revision placed the ruins completely within the boundaries of French Indochina, despite being located on the Siamese side of the watershed. French Indochina did not notify the Siamese Legation of their minor supplement to the treaty, and so it went overlooked. Even if the Siamese had noticed the change, it is questionable whether they would have protested, as very few people were aware of the temple's existence.[11] If Chulalongkorn was willing to give the French control of Angkor, why would he have protested the loss of a relatively unimportant site such as Preah Vihear?

It would remain so for two decades more until a visit by historian and brother of Chulalongkorn, Prince Damrong Rajanubhab, brought the ruins and their confused geography to the attention of the Siamese elite. In 1930, Damrong led an archaeological expedition to catalogue Khmer temples and monuments throughout the northeast. Upon arriving at Preah Vihear, the prince was surprised to see a flagpole flying the tricolor of France and a French archaeologist living in a nearby hut.[12] According to Damrong's understanding of the boundary, the temple site was north of the Dangrek watershed and therefore located in Siamese territory. Yet as he toured the monument accompanied by a French resident, the prince made no mention of the issue of sovereignty. He stated only that he had come to see the temple and was not acting in any official capacity.[13]

Thirty years later, the ICJ interpreted Damrong's failure to protest the archaeologist's presence at Preah Vihear as a sign that Siam recognized French sovereignty over the site. The Thai attorneys, however, offered several alternative interpretations of his actions. First, it was not uncommon during the era of high imperialism to see Europeans hoisting their national flag within the kingdom of Siam. There are reports of Thai villages, which had converted to Catholicism and accepted the ecclesiastical authority of French priests, displaying the French flag as evidence of devotion to their new religion.[14] Certainly such a move did not imply French sovereignty over the township. Second, the prince had enough foreign relations experience to know that protesting the matter would achieve little, other than to needlessly antagonize the French. Damrong's daughter, who had accompanied him to Preah Vihear, later explained her father's silence by referring back to the trauma of Siam's past: "It was generally known at the time that we only give the French an excuse to seize more territory by protesting. Things had been like that since they came in to the river Chao Phrya with their gunboats and their seizure of Chantaburi."[15]

Fearing another international incident, Damrong exercised caution and consulted with the British Legation at Bangkok, which advised him not to raise the matter with France. In his report on the matter, a British official commented, "I do not feel that the presence therein over a period of days of a French archaeologist installed in a hut, even though this be aggravated by his flying his national flag near at hand, need necessarily constitute a claim by France to possession of this territory. For the moment we can be content to wait and see."[16]

Moreover, none of the French residents present at Preah Vihear during Damrong's visit informed him that France had laid claim to the site as part of its Indochina possession. Both parties avoided discussing political matters, preferring instead to keep the encounter relatively cordial. Hence there was nothing concrete for the prince to protest against. Although Damrong remained convinced the temple was part of Siam, he lacked the cartographical evidence to prove it. The Siamese still relied on maps provided by France. It was not until 1934 that Siam conducted its own survey of the border region and discovered the discrepancy between the map boundary and the Dangrek Mountain watershed.[17] At this point, the Thai government's cause for concern was not the loss of Preah Vihear but that the French had deviated from the terms of demarcation laid out in the 1907 treaty and created a boundary that, from their point of view, violated international protocol.

The Thai leader who transformed Preah Vihear from an anonymous archaeological site into a national memorial was Phibun Songkhram. In 1939, after careful study of the Annex I map, Luang Wichit urged the prime minister to include Preah Vihear in its irredentist campaign and eventual border negotiations with Indochina (see figures 1–3).[18] That same year, Preah Vihear was featured on maps of Thailand's historical sites published by the Department of Education.[19] Still, the temple was of minor importance, one of several similar historical sites in the northeast, all of which were secondary in importance to Angkor Wat. In 1941, after months of publicly demanding that France return the *lost territories,* Thailand invaded French Indochina. The Tokyo Peace Accord, which ended the border conflict, resulted in Thailand retaking possession of most of Monthon Burapha (including Preah Vihear). In the negotiations, the Thai government lobbied hard to have Angkor Wat included in the settlement but could not extract this concession from the treaty's Japanese mediators. In an effort to hide its embarrassment, the Phibun government created a press campaign to publicize the beauty and historical importance of the temple it did obtain in the peace settlement—Preah Vihear. In March 1941, Thai newspapers carried the government's announcement concerning the prize won by the nation's military: "It is announced that in Amphoe Stung, which is part of the territory recently restored to Thailand, there is an important ancient temple that is very well known and very sacred to all Thailand. This sacred place is Preah Vihear. It is very well known for its beauty and is just as important as Angkor Wat."[20]

This was the beginning of the Thai myth of Preah Vihear, from which point onward the temple was to become synonymous with the *lost territories* and an integral part of National Humiliation historiography. In media coverage, Preah Vihear signified a process of restoration. Its return to Thailand confirmed that Phibun could repair the nation and regain all the territory and prestige lost during the period of absolute monarchy that concluded in 1932. Newspaper stories introducing the temple site to the public avoided any mention of Siamese conquest in the nineteenth century and instead focused on accusations that France had stolen the sacred shrine from its rightful heirs. Articles waxed poetic concerning the majesty of the ancient ruins, describing its layout, stone reliefs, and scenic backdrop in minute detail.[21] Within this narrative, Preah Vihear represented Thailand itself. During the era of high imperialism, the temple had fallen under Western control, which left it in a state of decay and disrepair. Now that the Phibun government had taken possession of Preah Vihear, it would ensure its preservation. Phibun allocated 2,000 baht of his own money to begin the restoration process.[22] Maurizio Peleggi has argued that the prime minister took a personal interest in the conservation in order to "appropriate prerogatives that were customarily associated with the monarch."[23] This not only helped him project a paternalistic public image but also to transform the ruins into a focal point of his discourse on the *lost territories.* In its rhetoric on Preah Vihear, the Phibun government juxtaposed imagery of French decay with that of Thai renewal, suggesting that Thailand had overcome the shame of its past. It is this association with past trauma, particularly the theory that France had "stolen" the temple, that would later make Preah Vihear a focal point of National Humiliation discourse.

Japan's surrender in 1945 meant that Thailand would return to the prewar status quo and relinquish all territory obtained from the conflict with

French Indochina four years earlier. As a member of the UN Security Council, France stipulated that Thailand must return its four new provinces of Lan Chang, Champassak, Battambang, and Phibun Songkhram (Siem Reap) to French Indochina before it could be admitted to the United Nations. Thailand, which had so recently celebrated its victory over France as vindication for the crisis of 1893, watched the undoing of its great victory over Western imperialism in disbelief. A new generation of Thais experienced the "partition" they had only read about in textbooks or editorials. In the National Assembly, opposition leaders accused the government of betraying the nation by allowing it to be bullied by the French. Citizens wrote letters to newspapers clamoring for war with France rather than relive the bitterness of territorial loss. After much debate, the Thai government voted to accept its fate and sign the treaty. The memory of loss would endure. A decade later, the nation's resentment would find expression in the symbol of Preah Vihear.

The Washington Accord of 1946 reestablished the border set forth in the 1907 treaty, giving France control over Preah Vihear once again. In 1953 the Thai government, once again led by military strongman Phibun, renewed its interest in the nation's ancient heritage, starting with an enormous renovation project at Sukhothai.[24] Cambodia achieved independence that same year, and the Thai government viewed France's departure as a natural opportunity to reopen the question of Preah Vihear. When Sihanouk shocked the Western world by announcing his neutralist stance and subsequent refusal to join the Southeast Asia Treaty Organization, Thailand quietly established a police post just north of Preah Vihear and hoisted its flag over the temple site.[25] Although this move represented a modest territorial expansion, it would also give Thailand the moral high ground in the upcoming dispute with Cambodia. With its soldiers currently stationed at the temple site, Thai lawyers and commentators claimed the Annex I map was a recent fraud and that Preah Vihear had always been part of Thailand.

THAI WOLF, CAMBODIAN LAMB

The Cambodian government interpreted Thailand's presence at Preah Vihear to be an infringement of its national sovereignty. The two countries bickered over the matter for several years before the Thai government extended an invitation to formal talks regarding a more precise delineation of the border. The negotiations took place over a period of months during 1957–1958 and covered a range of topics including commerce and cross-border traffic.[26] As the conference progressed, Preah Vihear gradually came to dominate the agenda. Each side exploited the issue to express resentment over historical injustices and promote a domestic political agenda. Press coverage of the negotiations heightened public interest in the mountain temple. Prince Sihanouk used the border dispute to argue that Cambodia was threatened by Thailand (as well as Vietnam) and convince his government of the wisdom of a neutralist foreign policy. Ignoring its more recent experience under French rule, the Cambodian government instructed its people that the real danger to the nation had always been Thai imperialism. For Phnom Penh, Thailand's attempted annexation of the heritage site was a contemporary reminder that the Thai were attempting to conquer its lands and subjugate its people as they had done for centuries.

From 1958 to 1960, Cambodia took the initiative in transforming the battle over Preah Vihear into a war for domestic and international public opinion. Dissatisfied with the status quo and frustrated with the negotiation process, Sihanouk launched the first salvo in what would become a protracted conflict. In March 1958, thousands of students, policemen, and civil servants marched past the Thai embassy in Phnom Penh to protest against a perceived lack of respect from Thailand. The demonstrators carried signs celebrating Cambodian nationalism and attacking Thailand, such as "Thais Invade Their Neighbors," "Thais Are Slaves of America," and "Prince Sihanouk is the Father of Independence, Long Live the Nation." Following their rally, the protestors gathered in front of the royal palace to listen to a speech by Sihanouk. "The Thai have cheated us out of Preah Vihear," Sihanouk told his audience. "The Khmers must demand its return."[27] From this point on, the temple's recovery became an important plank in Sihanouk's nationalist political platform.

The public protest was followed by a flurry of press attacks portraying Cambodia as the target of a resurgent Thai imperialism. These articles were often penned by government officials who wanted to associate themselves with the cause of Preah Vihear as a nationalist symbol. The month after Sihanouk's speech, Cambodia's Department of Publicity printed an article on Preah Vihear written by Sam Sari, the ambassador to Great Britain. Sam Sari's piece begins by describing the temple as a beautiful edifice in the Dangrek Mountains, built by the ancient Khmers and left as an inheritance of all Cambodians. At one time, Thailand deceived the Cambodian king and acquired the territory surrounding the ruins, but later the Thai signed the treaty of 1904 returning the land to its rightful owners. Since they continually covet Cambodia's land and heritage sites, the Thai invaded in 1941 and again in 1953, when Thai soldiers seized the rocky outcropping around the temple. Bangkok's historical claims to the temple are invalid, Sam Sari argued, because if one goes far enough back into history, the entire Siamese kingdom once belonged to Cambodia. He concluded by pledging that Sihanouk would work tirelessly for the return of Preah Vihear and to make sure his nation was safe from the continual threat of Thai invasion.[28]

The Thai seizure of Preah Vihear also assisted the new national elite in Phnom Penh in reinterpreting the past seven centuries of their history as a legacy of Thai aggression and imperialism. One editorial in a Phnom Penh newspaper expressed this sentiment as follows: "Throughout the past seven centuries and even today we have paid a terrible price when swindled by the leader and government of this ravenous tiger of a nation, which should adopt the vulture as its national symbol rather than the garuda."[29]

Cambodian leaders used the appropriation of Preah Vihear as evidence that Thailand was in the process of launching both internal and external attacks against their country. The Khmer press accused General Phao, the Thai police chief, of supporting dissident Song Ngoc Thanh, who founded the Khmer Serei militia in an effort to overthrow the Sihanouk government. Sihanouk claimed the Thai army had briefly invaded Siem Reap Province.[30] Sam Sari wrote an article that compared Bangkok's use of military force at Preah Vihear to "Hitler tactics" and inferred that Cambodia faced a Thai invasion similar to when Germany swallowed up Czechoslovakia.[31] In a 1958 interview with a Japanese newspaper, Prime Minister Sim Var explained the Preah Vihear controversy using an Aesopian fable. The temple dispute, he argued, was merely a pretext designed to allow the Thai wolf to completely devour the Cambodian lamb.[32]

While the Thai government intended a quiet settlement between the two governments, Sihanouk had several reasons for escalating the dispute into an international matter. By proclaiming itself the victim early in the Preah Vihear controversy, Cambodia was able to seize the initiative and frame the debate on its own terms. Recovery of the temple became an issue Sihanouk would use to distance himself from his domestic rivals for power, one that resonated with ordinary people because it involved a potential loss of the country's ancient heritage. Substituting Thai for French imperialism as the enemy of Cambodian nationalism suited Sihanouk's purposes perfectly, as it detracted attention from the fact that he had once been an integral part of the French colonial apparatus. The image of Thai aggression was also essential to maintain Cambodia's foreign policy of nonalignment. Sihanouk used the threat of American-backed Thailand to solicit aid from the Chinese just as he used the threat of the Viet Cong to solicit military and economic assistance from the United States.[33] Cambodia used its media to make Preah Vihear an international incident because it realized only foreign pressure could convince Thailand to back down. When its public relations campaign failed to provoke a settlement during two-party negotiations, the Cambodian government turned to the United Nations. On September 4, 1958, Son San, the head of the Phnom Penh delegation, held a press conference at the Cambodian embassy in Bangkok, where he announced his government's decision to withdraw from the negotiations and instead settle the matter of Preah Vihear through an appeal to the ICJ.[34]

FRENCH WOLF, SIAMESE LAMB

Cambodia's announcement effectively pulled the rug from under the Thai state, forcing it to reevaluate its approach to the controversy. Prior to Cambodia's ICJ appeal, the Thai government resisted framing the temple dispute in irredentist terms. Based on its economic, political, and military strength in the region, Thailand possessed a great deal of leverage in two-party talks. The regime of Prime Minister Field Marshal Sarit Thanarat (1958–1963) appeared very confident it would prevail in the dispute and chose to ignore Sihanouk's attacks in the Cambodian press. While negotiations with Cambodia were in progress, the Ministry of Interior issued directives to several Bangkok newspapers, warning editors to avoid agitating relations with Cambodia with inflammatory coverage of the border negotiations.[35] Thai leaders understood that employing National Humiliation discourse was a strategy fraught with risk. Linking Preah Vihear with the *lost territories* would certainly make the temple a national issue and mobilize public support behind government policy. It could also destabilize Thai policy and intensify the conflict by encouraging irredentists to begin calling for the return of all of Monthon Burapha to Thailand.

The end of two-party talks eliminated Thailand's leverage and its confidence regarding the final outcome of the dispute. As the status of Preah Vihear became more uncertain, the use of National Humiliation discourse became more attractive. The Thai government dropped its attempts to restrain newspapers, whose pages were filled with strident nationalist voices portraying Cambodia's action as yet another attempt to dismember their country. Three days after Son San's press conference, over 10,000 people held a "Hyde Park" style rally at Sanam Luang in Bangkok to denounce Cambodia's withdrawal from negotiations. On September 7, 1958, in a reenactment of the original *lost territories* campaign of 1940, protestors once again marched down the city's Ratchadamnoen Avenue carrying posters featuring maps displaying the five sections of territory ceded to French Indochina. Other signs condemned Cambodian duplicity or proclaimed Thailand's rights to Preah Vihear. Despite receiving orders to disperse from Interior Minister Praphas, the protestors turned their march towards the Cambodian embassy. The march culminated in a riot. Police clashed with demonstrators trying to enter the compound, resulting in multiple injuries to both sides and making it the most violent public demonstration in Thailand's history prior to 1973.

These demonstrations marked a dramatic shift in the Thai government's approach to the controversy. The introduction of the ICJ as a variable in the struggle over sovereignty made Thailand confront for the first time the possibility that it might lose Preah Vihear. The shock of this possibility increased the state's willingness to associate the temple with the loss of the four provinces in 1946, as well as the original defeat and loss of territory to French Indochina in 1893. From these demonstrations in 1958 until the court handed down its decision in 1962, National Humiliation discourse would gradually transform Preah Vihear from a "pile of stones" into a new generation's opportunity to defend the nation's territory and honor, to succeed where past generations had failed. Thai irredentists expanded the concept of the *lost territories* to include Preah Vihear. In response to Sihanouk's narrative wherein Cambodia was the victim of Thai aggression, the Thai government promoted an alternative history centered on Thai suffering at the hands of Western imperialism. By framing the dispute within a binary of Franco-Thai border tensions, Bangkok hoped to deny Cambodia a voice in the dispute and avoid discussion of its own imperialist past. From this perspective, Thailand's recent expansion was anti- rather than neo-imperialist.

Acceptance of National Humiliation discourse requires one to also accept the romanticized belief that the Thai were once (and could become again) the masters of a mythical Golden Peninsula that existed before the arrival of the Europeans. The expansion of the British and French empires reduced the influence of Siam and eventually created independent states out of territories that had been vassals of Bangkok, such as Laos and Cambodia. From World War II onward, Thai irredentists used this narrative to criticize the notion of a territorial status quo as inherently biased towards European periodization. The Allies in 1945 and the ICJ in 1962 legitimized the boundaries established during the high colonial period, when European dominance of Southeast Asia was at its zenith. During the debate over Preah Vihear,

Bangkok newspaper editorials asked why, if we look to history as the basis of territorial sovereignty, must we always stop with the treaty of 1907? To do so privileges the European conception of state boundaries by according them a sense of permanence they did not deserve. If we are looking for a reference point, they asked, why not go back to a period five hundred years earlier when all of Cambodia was part of the Thai kingdom?[36]

The dispute thus opened up a Pandora's box of grievances and provided an opportunity to detail the injustices of the past century in front of the international community. It seemed outrageous and arbitrary to Thai irredentists that jurisdiction over the temple ruins, which they now possessed, could be up for discussion when the rest of its "stolen land" was off limits. "If this dispute goes to the World Court for consideration, and is decided on a historical basis without taking into account the matter of current jurisdiction, then why not also discuss the status of the Kong Island, Siam Rat, Battambang, and the way these territories were acquired? Why not wager these lands as well so that our Preah Vihear is not the only bet on the table?"[37]

The idea of *lost territories* dates back to the reign of Chulalongkorn, although the exact demarcation of this imagined geography has fluctuated along with memory of those events. During the Preah Vihear dispute, dozens of articles on the *lost territories* appeared in Bangkok newspapers, often accompanied by maps depicting Lan Na, Champassak, Battambang, and Phibun Songkhram provinces.[38] The events of the 1940s clearly reconstructed public memory of the *lost territories* and the events of the Franco-Siamese crisis. Newspaper editorials argued that Thailand should use the court case over Preah Vihear to reassert its historical claims over the four provinces that belonged to Thailand for centuries before being stolen by the French in 1946.[39]

As the media attempted to persuade a new generation of Thais that their nation had been swindled and disgraced over the past century, it raised the possibility of whether Thailand's tragic history of territorial forfeiture would repeat itself. For a newspaper columnist in the late 1950s, the trauma of 1893 had to be imagined, but the territorial loss in 1946 had taken place within their lifetime. Press accounts made no pretence of objectivity; instead they memorialized the events of the past by expressing a sense of grief over what was lost. Columnists wrote out of a sense of duty, explaining their generation's actions to those who had not experienced the event: "We will not describe here the conditions under which [the four provinces] were forcefully removed from our country's embrace. We will say only this: we would never willingly give these territories to anyone, but extraordinary circumstances dictated we must surrender our land with tears flooding our faces."[40]

Many Thai commentators were thrilled by the demonstrations of 1958, which manifested some opposition to any concession on Preah Vihear, suggesting the losses of the past had become meaningful to a new generation. Once again, the nation mourned its *lost territories,* this time in the form of the four provinces ceded in 1946. In an interview with reporters, Sarit expressed his own resentment that good men had fought and died for the four provinces, which Thailand later lost due to deception.[41] "Even though many years have passed, we have not forgotten," wrote one commentator. "We still taste the bitterness as though it happened yesterday."[42] Irredentists argued that Thailand had suffered more as a result of its encounter with French imperialism than any other country. In 1800, the Golden Peninsula was divided between Vietnamese, Siamese, and Burmese spheres of influence. While Vietnam and Burma regained all their territory lost to imperialism, the Lao and Khmer regions have never been restored to Thailand.[43] Thai perceptions of Preah Vihear are not based as much on its historical, cultural, or aesthetic value as on its symbolism regarding loss. To lose Preah Vihear would be to suffer the agony of territorial concession all over again.

Thai nationalists wanted to transform the contest over Preah Vihear into a contest over all of northwest Cambodia, or as they still referred to it—Monthon Burapha. In the opinion of the Bangkok press, Cambodia was an artificial construct, a geographical fraud perpetrated by the French using territory that really belonged to Thailand. This romanticized historical narrative depicted the battle for the Golden Peninsula as a two-nation contest between France and Siam. The Thai kings had sacrificed territory at their weaker moments, but in the twentieth century they had outlasted the French. It was only right, therefore, that these lands be returned to their former sovereigns. Cambodia, which was not a signatory in the treaties that determined the political status of this region, certainly had no claim to it now.[44] One columnist argued this point in an article titled, "The Thai Want Our Land Back," which listed seven reasons why Monthon Burapha should be returned to Thailand. "It is well known that the Thai signed the treaty ceding Monthon Burapha to France involuntarily, because it was an unjust treaty and therefore non-binding. However, when France relinquished its rights over those lands, it follows that the French also resigned their rights under that treaty, which is no longer enforceable. Therefore, according to the articles, the territory automatically returns to its original status and becomes part of Thailand."[45]

The article's claim, that Monthon Burapha belonged to Thailand because France had forced Siam to sign the treaties of 1904 and 1907,[46] illustrates how National Humiliation discourse depicts the Thai elite as naive victims rather than as agents actively negotiating a trade agreement. Chulalongkorn decided to sign because Chantaburi and Trat were more valuable to him than "a few Cambodian lands," but Thai irredentists condemned the treaty as a natural result of leverage gained by the French in 1893. This argument that France illegally transferred the disputed lands to Cambodia appears to have been a popular (although not universally accepted) opinion during the Preah Vihear dispute. In December 1959, a former member of parliament from the northeastern province of Khon Kaen gave a speech at the Royal Naval club titled "Thailand's Right to Monthon Burapha," in which he declared that France was obligated to transfer the territory back to Thailand upon its departure from Southeast Asia.[47] Many pundits wrote columns warning Sihanouk that Thailand's claim to the *lost territories* was much more legitimate than his petition concerning the temple site.[48] The prince would be wise not to continue his agitation over Preah Vihear lest an enraged Thailand respond by reconquering its former realm. As one writer observed, "As a nation that has long been civilized we have an enormous advantage over the Khmers, which we refrain from exploiting. But if we are harmless it is not out of fear. We warn Cambodia that 'if the tiger is asleep, do not say he is afraid.'"[49]

Thai pundits did not hesitate to point out the enormous military gap between Thailand and Cambodia, implying that Thailand could easily defeat its neighbors and take Monthon Burapha by force if it wished. They proudly recalled how the Thai army had already recaptured the *lost territories* once by defeating the mighty French. In describing the outcome of the 1941 border war, one columnist sardonically remarked, "It was fortunate [for Cambodia] that the Japanese intervened to take charge of the negotiations, otherwise the word 'Khmer' might never have been heard again."[50]

As the above comment suggests, an important strategy in the nationalist campaign to recover both the temple and the lost provinces involved the denial of a distinctive Cambodian identity. Luang Wichit's drama *Ratchamanu* claims that the Khmers were the brethren of the Thai and thus there should be no more war between them.[51] Thai chauvinists found Wichit's racial theory useful in arguing Thailand's case for Preah Vihear. In one of his many interviews on the progress of the dispute, Seni talked of how the Khmers were actually split into "high Khmer" and "low Khmer" races, but each constituted a branch of the Thai family tree. The similarity in dance, music, art, and culture of the two peoples proved the Khmers were really just Thais.[52] This genealogical narrative of the Khmers served to sever the historical link between modern Cambodia and its supposed heritage sites. When

Sihanouk claimed Cambodians were the rightful owners of Preah Vihear, because the temple had been built by their ancestors, Praphas corrected him, saying all the ancient temple complexes were built by the Khom, an extinct race of people separate from the Khmers. By absorbing Khmer identity within the boundaries of a Greater Thai race, Thai nationalists hoped to cement their claim to Preah Vihear and perhaps even more of Cambodia.

Amidst the expansionist clamor, there was the occasional voice that questioned whether Preah Vihear was worth the hassle of an international dispute. As Seni prepared to travel to The Hague, one member of parliament[53] publicly suggested Thailand would be better served by handing sovereignty over to Cambodia than allowing a prolonged dispute to affect foreign relations and international trade. Exercising political control over a "pile of stones" would not improve living conditions in either country.[54] Several newspapers denounced these comments as unpatriotic and accused the politician of wanting to sell out his country. It was detestable for an elected official to suggest giving away territory, when so many people were donating money and volunteering their time in an effort to preserve the nation. The Preah Vihear case was an opportunity for the country to demonstrate its unity before the world. It was ironic, wrote one columnist, that the ordinary citizens of this country understood this fact better than some of their leaders. This was not just a struggle for land; it was a contest for the sacred honor of Thailand.[55]

The reemergence of the National Humiliation narrative caused foreign relation headaches for the Thai government and complicated its legal strategy. Interior Minister Praphas made it clear from the outset of the dispute that the government would not request the return of any of the four provinces ceded in 1946.[56] With Laos already unstable, tensions growing between North and South Vietnam, and Cambodia developing closer ties with Beijing, the Sarit regime had no intention of allowing this border dispute to escalate into a military conflict. Also, from a purely legal standpoint the government lawyers argued that the lost provinces and Preah Vihear needed to be entirely separate issues. Thailand's official position, as explained by lead counsel Seni Pramoj, was that Preah Vihear had always been part of Thailand. The temple's status was not affected by the demarcation of 1904 or 1907. The border map completed by the French in 1908 was invalid in this case because the Thai members of the joint commission did not accept it. Unfortunately for Thai counsel, the Thai government had already put out publications contradicting this position. In 1941, the Department of Publicity published a book titled *Thai samai sarng chart* [Thailand in a Time of

Nation Building], which celebrated the return of Preah Vihear as part of the Tokyo Peace Accord.[57]

MOBILIZING CONTRIBUTIONS

One year after the press conference announcing Cambodia would seek the intervention of the United Nations in the Preah Vihear matter, Sihanouk made good his threat. In October 1959 he officially filed a petition to have the ICJ rule on the boundary between Thailand and Cambodia. As the press began predicting a long court battle, people began looking for ways to contribute to a legal defense fund. Once again it was the press that seized the initiative on the issue of donations. According to the Bangkok daily *Phim Thai,* the movement began in October 1959 with a letter to the editor regarding the expenses required for Thailand to present its case before the ICJ. Chan Witchanon, a private citizen, wrote to the newspaper proposing that *Phim Thai* begin accepting donations from ordinary citizens to help underwrite the legal costs of retaining Preah Vihear. If every person in Thailand donated only 1 baht, he reasoned, the resulting 21 million baht would surely help the nation to fight for this very important cause. Along with his letter, Chan contributed the sum of 5 baht, one for each member of his family.[58]

Inspired by this letter, the newspaper organized a "one person, one baht" campaign and announced that its main office would begin accepting donations towards the defense of Preah Vihear. A later article celebrated Chan Witchanon as an embodiment of the patriotism and self-sacrifice that would ensure Thailand's victory at the ICJ. It encouraged its readers to contribute by reminding them of the danger currently facing the nation. In the past, certain greedy nations had taken advantage of Thailand's peaceful nature by invading and stealing its territories. Today Sihanouk was trying to swindle the nation out of its land just as others had done. Donations for the Thai legal fund would constitute a powerful symbol of Thai resolve in this matter, demonstrating to the entire world that this time the country would not back down.[59]

The example of Chan Witchanon inspired thousands of people across Thailand. Letters flooded into *Phim Thai* offices with donations earmarked for the government's legal defense fund. Other newspapers such as *Siam nikorn, Sarn seri,* and *Thai* also announced their offices would begin accepting contributions. Not only could the newspapers claim to be performing an important service for the nation, but the various stories of self-sacrifice for the cause made great press and generated interest among readers. For weeks the news publications told readers of how ordinary Thais were contributing to the Preah Vihear defense fund. Taxi drivers set aside an entire day's earnings. A high school student donated the compensation he received from being hit by a car.[60] Elderly residents of a Bang Kae nursing home took up their own collection.[61]

As the spirit of giving swept across the country, people did not simply donate money but also various items that could be auctioned off by the newspaper or other organizations. Some gave blood so they could turn the proceeds over to the government. Thammasat University organized a ballroom dance and fashion show with a Preah Vihear theme. At the end of the evening, a large balloon was auctioned off for 10,000 baht.[62] Another auction held at Lumpini Park, which included items donated by the Thai Blood Party (Phak Lueat Thai), also raised several thousand.[63] The Sriratchawong Theater in Bangkok and the *Siam nikorn* newspaper teamed up to promote the premiere of a brand new movie, pledging that all revenues from ticket sales would go directly to the government.[64] This enthusiasm spread into the provinces, where patriotic citizens organized similar events in order to do their part. Soldiers who had spent their paychecks offered bottles of liquor, while one person brought in a transistor radio to be auctioned. In Songkhla Province, officials held an auction for the privilege of kissing the Miss Songkhla beauty queen.[65] By the end of November, total donations by patriotic citizens surpassed the 1 million baht mark.[66]

The success of the "one person, one baht" campaign spurred the government to become involved in fundraising also. At the end of October 1959, Sarit announced the creation of a special "Preah Vihear legal defense fund" that would accept private donations. Any monies already collected by the Bangkok press should be forwarded to this new office, which would operate under the jurisdiction of the Ministry of Interior. According to the new chain of command, donations should go to the district chief first, then to the provincial governor who would forward them on to Bangkok. Sarit ended his announcement by praising all those who had given so generously already, stating that the act of support was more important than the amount of the donation. He reminded the people that the nation's territory was an inheritance given by their ancestors, and that each person had a duty to protect and preserve it.[67]

Both the rhetoric surrounding the nationwide funding drive and the manner of donations suggested that a growing number of Thais associated the current prospect of losing Preah Vihear with Thailand's past losses. More specifically, donors envisioned the temple dispute as part of the ongoing legacy of French incursions into Thai territory. One elderly person expressed her conviction that France must be behind Cambodia's attempt to take Preah Vihear. "[The temple] has belonged to us for hundreds of years," she lamented. "How can they just take it away from us?"[68] Another man echoed this sentiment as he donated a postal stamp from 1895 for sale at a *Phim Thai* auction. The Chulalongkorn-era stamp featured a map that incorporated "Pattum bong" as part of Siam. "How can Preah Vihear possibly belong to Cambodia when all Battambang was ours?" he wondered.[69] The anxiety and excitement surrounding the Thai-Cambodian tension became intertwined with the public sense of grief involving the defeat and humiliation of past generations in a variety of ways. A Thammasat student took up a collection among her fellow classmates and donated the amount of 112 baht as a way of commemorating the Franco-Siamese crisis of 1893.[70] One auction item that received a considerable amount of press was a set of tennis racquets owned by one of Thailand's fallen patriots, an airman killed during the 1941 Indochina war. Because the *Sarn seri* newspaper was responsible for auctioning off the racquets, its editors reminded readers how Sanit Nuanmani had been one of Thailand's bravest warriors during a critical period in its history.[71] The nature of the donation campaign demonstrates how reaction to the idea of loss was the main motivating factor behind public response to the incident.

SIHANOUK THE UNGRATEFUL

Reports in Thai newspapers concerning the militant anti-Thai rhetoric and demonstrations coming out of Cambodia genuinely surprised observers in Bangkok. Why would a people so similar to the Thai in terms of religion, culture, and language express such strong resentment towards their neighbors? Government leaders appeared to solve this contradiction by pinning blame for the Preah Vihear dispute squarely on the shoulders of Norodom Sihanouk. As Seni Pramoj and others explained the issue in several radio and newspaper interviews, the controversy was not a quarrel between the people of Thailand and the people of Cambodia; it was a conflict between Thailand and the corrupt leaders in Phnom Penh. They reassured the public that Cambodians naturally respected the Thai as an elder sibling, and that the tension between the two peoples was the result of politicians such as Sam Sari and Sihanouk promoting their own interests by stirring up animosity towards their western neighbors. The Thai press often depicted Sihanouk as an ungrateful former ally who had betrayed his friends to become a pawn in the nefarious schemes of his French or Chinese patrons. Such rhetoric legitimized the Thai claim to Preah Vihear by explaining the dispute in anti-imperialist terms the public could easily understand. This was simply another attempt by powerful nations to steal land away from Thailand.

Thai leaders initially dismissed the news of Cambodia's petition to the World Court as simply a case of Sihanouk using Preah Vihear for political opportunism. In a 1959 press conference, Sarit discussed several possible reasons why Sihanouk had filed a World Court petition against Thailand. As Cambodia approached its upcoming election, he theorized, Sihanouk desperately needed to attract voters. If he was defeated at the polls, his enemies in Cambodia might even force him to go into exile.[72] He was creating a controversy over the temple to distract people from his shoddy record in office.[73] The petition could also be an attempt to avoid Thailand's repeated efforts to demarcate the border between the two countries out of fear Cambodia might be required to return territory to Thailand.[74] Also, Cambodia remained a very backward country and was likely jealous of Thailand's recent economic development. If that were the case, Sarit continued, Sihanouk would do better to learn from his neighbors instead of antagonizing them. The Thai press effectively used economic issues against Sihanouk, arguing that closed borders and severed diplomatic ties hurt Cambodians most, as they depended on access to Thai markets and shipping. One editorial suggested Sihanouk would eventually abandon the Preah Vihear issue following the election, but in the meantime his own citizens would pay the price.[75] Such rhetoric conveyed the idea that Bangkok was more concerned about the welfare of ordinary Khmers than the Cambodian government.

Portrayals of Sihanouk were patterned after historical narratives that often depicted Cambodian kings as inferior and untrustworthy.[76] In Thai royalist history, Cambodia appears as the younger sibling, dependent on an elder Siam. The benevolent Siamese monarch provides patronage to a Cambodian subordinate who ultimately proves ungrateful or even treacherous. In 1861, Sihanouk's ancestor King Norodom took refuge in Bangkok to avoid an internal rebellion in Cambodia. After being restored to his country under the protection of a Siamese armed guard, Norodom immediately began negotiations with the French in Cochin China that led to the establishment of a protectorate and the end of Siamese influence in Cambodia.[77] A more dramatic example is King Satha, a sixteenth-century ruler of the Khmer kingdom who paid tribute to Ayutthaya. The royal chronicles record that while Ayutthaya was busy fending off an invasion from Burma in the west, King Satha attacked the Siamese with his armies from the east. Enraged by this act of subversion, King Naresuan had Satha captured and executed, then proceeded to bathe his feet in the traitor's blood.[78]

This historical trope provided the framework of interpretation for Sihanouk's actions during the Preah Vihear controversy. As he rallied his country towards independence, many in Thailand were sympathetic to the Cambodian nationalist movement, or at least happy to see France leaving Southeast Asia. When the prince visited Bangkok briefly in June 1953, the *Standard* magazine showered him with praise, describing Sihanouk as a man who "leads his people calmly, wisely, with a full sense of responsibility, toward a complete independence."[79] That public goodwill disappeared five years later when Sihanouk denounced their country and filed a petition with the World Court demanding Thai soldiers withdraw from the temple site. In an interview on Bangkok radio, Kukrit Pramoj tried to explain the origins of the dispute in historical terms: "I believe that the reason behind all these actions is Sihanouk. In fact, if we look back at Thai history, we can see that all the Cambodian royal families were never thankful for the help Thailand offered them when they were in danger, but instead tried to hurt Thailand. Therefore, it's not surprising that Sihanouk would be just like them."[80]

Press coverage followed the same pattern of characterizing Sihanouk as a former ally turned bitter enemy. Thailand and Cambodia had been involved in negotiations for several months over the border issue, and many interpreted his sudden decision to refer the matter to the International Court of Justice as an act of betrayal. Journalists wrote that he was "two-faced" in his negotiations with Thailand, because his words conveyed a desire for friendly relations but his actions suggested the opposite. Thais were particularly enraged by comments made by Sihanouk about the Preah Vihear dispute while visiting other countries. Newspaper editorials denounced the prince for attempting to gain the sympathy of foreign nations by making false and inflammatory accusations against Thailand. Such displays of perfidy only confirmed to Thais that Sihanouk never had any intention of settling the issue amicably.[81] One article compared the prince with the Cambodian monarch who had betrayed Ayutthaya: "The name of Norodom Sihanouk will live forever in the memory of the Thai people as an evil enemy like King Satha. His treachery will never be forgotten."[82]

In the narrative being constructed on Preah Vihear, Sihanouk functioned as the lynchpin connecting the current border dispute to past confrontations with France. This narrative emphasizes that the quarrel is not with the Cambodian people but with political leaders who continue to act as sycophants of their former masters, the French. It did not escape the attention of journalists that each of the initial tirades against Bangkok was published in a French language newspaper. Commentators argued Sihanouk had always been more French than Cambodian; in fact, he was chosen to be king of Cambodia in 1941 only because he was a Francophile stooge who could be trusted to support the colonial administration. In his work on the history of Cambodia and Thailand, Manich Jumsai wrote that Sihanouk had been indoctrinated from a very young age to consider France the savior of Cambodia and the Thai their historical enemy. Due to the prince's erroneous belief that French colonization had preserved his country and culture from Siamese annexation, he felt gratitude towards France and a "perennial nervous fear" toward Thailand.[83] This historical misinformation was the source of all the political tension between Bangkok and Phnom Penh. Manich's portrayal of Sihanouk as French rather than Cambodian reinforced the suspicion that somehow France was behind the border controversy. It also allowed the Thai to remain the victims in their own modern narratives by avoiding a discussion of Siamese imperialist advances against the Khmer peoples dating back to the destruction of Angkor.

TRIAL AND VERDICT

From 1961 to 1962, The Hague became the new setting for the Preah Vihear dispute as Thai and Cambodian legal teams argued their country's case in front of the ICJ. The determining factor in the trial was the legitimacy of the famous Annex I map. The Cambodian delegation presented the map as evidence that the temple was situated within the borders of French Indochina, later Cambodia, since 1907. Attorneys requested that the World Court instruct Thailand to withdraw its soldiers from the complex and recognize Cambodian sovereignty over the site. In response, Thai attorneys argued that the map was solely the product of France's imagination, that it did not accurately depict the border region, and that it had never been accepted by Thailand. The international boundary had always been the watershed of the Dangrek Mountains as defined in the text of the 1904 Franco-Siamese treaty. This would place the ruins in Thailand. After careful deliberation on the legal and historical evidence, the court ruled 9 to 3 to recognize the Annex I map as the final authority on the border demarcation instead of the treaty clause. Bohdan Womarksi, president of the ICJ, gave his opinion that Thailand did indeed accept the map as an official representation of the boundary and had even published additional copies for use in Thailand.[84] Furthermore, if Thailand believed the map to be in error, it had multiple opportunities to protest its inaccuracy at Franco-Thai negotiations in 1937 and 1946, but it had not done so.[85] Therefore the court awarded sovereignty over the site to Cambodia and instructed Thailand to remove its soldiers from Preah Vihear.

The immediate reaction in Thailand to the court's ruling was disbelief and defiance. Stunned by the humiliating prospect of having to once again relinquish territory, and this time to a nation that had been a former vassal state, Thai leaders were defiant. The newspaper *Sarn seri*'s special edition on Preah Vihear carried the bold headline, "Thailand Will Fight to the Death," featuring an interview with Praphas. The army general summed up the country's mood by stating unequivocally that the Thai army would fight and die before it would allow another country to once again steal its territory. He later threatened to shoot any Cambodians who tried to enter the temple.[86] Deputy Prime Minister Thanom Kittikachorn scrutinized the verdict, saying Thailand had not received a fair hearing because some judges came from communist countries.[87] The reaction within the student community echoed these strong sentiments. Many wrote letters to newspapers beseeching the government to defy the court and pledging their willingness to fight to defend Preah Vihear from Cambodia. Students at Chulalongkorn University erected a banner that read, "Preah Vihear is ours, we must keep it."[88] One week after the verdict, undergraduates staged one of the biggest demonstrations in Thailand's history. Fifty thousand students from five different universities marched past the National Assembly carrying placards and shouting slogans in the hope of convincing the government to keep Preah Vihear. According to news reports, similar rallies took place in the provinces of Chonburi, Trat, Aranyaprathet, Phitsanulok, Ayutthaya, Nakhon Nayok, and Samut Prakan, with at least 10,000 people attending each rally.[89] In the aftermath of the court's decision, Sihanouk became public enemy number one for many Thais, who referred to the Cambodian head of state as "The Black Prince."[90]

For others, the verdict from the ICJ represented a rare opportunity for redemption. Believing that Thailand had been swindled and bullied throughout its history, irredentists hoped this was the moment when its leaders would assert themselves. Cambodia now had the backing of international law, but if the Thai army refused to vacate Preah Vihear it would be very difficult to dislodge them. Such a rare example of defiance would do much to dispel the legacy of humiliation and defeat in Thailand's past. Protestors in Bangkok captured the mood of the nation with a sign that read, "It is better to die fighting than to live with defeat."[91] A resurrected contingent of the Thai Blood Party began distributing leaflets encouraging the government to defy the ICJ judgment. "Isn't it time for us to stand up and fight in order to pull out the thorn that has for too long pierced the breast of the Thai nation? Only then can we assuage the bitter wounds of the past so that they can finally heal."[92]

Letters to newspapers argued the nation had brought its current dilemma upon itself through its policy of appeasement. One reader predicted a bleak future: "If we Thais agree to abide by the corrupt judgment of the ICJ, we can be certain to lose even more territory in the future. Today it was Preah Vihear, tomorrow it will be Lop Buri."[93] Irredentists played on the belief that Thailand's territory was a gift from the past to the present. If it was lost through neglect, future generations would denounce their ancestors as lacking the ability or willpower to protect their native soil. "History is being written," stated another letter. "How will our descendants feel if we give up such valuable territory? They will conclude that our generation lacked even the smallest amount of patriotism."[94] To defy the court would be to make a bold statement to the world that Thailand could no longer kowtow to the imperialist powers and allow the nation to recapture a little of its dignity and self-respect.

The publication of multiple examples of such extreme letters once again raises important questions regarding the relationship between the Thai media and public opinion. While these news outlets claimed to reflect the nation's mood, clearly they played an important role in shaping that mood in the years leading up to the court's decision. While reporting reactions to the verdict, certain newspapers functioned as an echo chamber. The sensationalist coverage of Preah Vihear helped spawn emotional reactions to the news of Cambodia's victory. Outraged readers wrote letters calling for armed conflict with Cambodia, which were then printed in the same newspapers as examples of popular opinion. The publication of these letters had the effect of making the spirit of confrontation seem universal rather than radical.

As these angry voices lobbied the Thai government to reject the verdict, there were also more moderate opinions urging caution and acceptance. Members of the business community in particular viewed the loss of Preah Vihear as insignificant in comparison to the potential damage to trade and Thailand's image abroad if the government defied the ICJ and continued to threaten Cambodia. This was also a major concern of the United States, which recognized the potential for escalating Thai-Cambodian tensions to jeopardize its relationship with both countries and further destabilize the region. Floyd Whittington, a State Department official stationed in Bangkok during the controversy, recalled his conversation regarding the Preah Vihear decision with Khun Yom Tansetthi, the newly appointed manager of the Industrial Finance Corporation of Thailand. Whittington's memo of their conversation reflected the concerns of the business elite regarding the fallout over the court's decision:

> I asked him what his reaction was to the Phra Viharn decision favoring Cambodia. He replied that his reaction was the same, he believed, as all other educated, intelligent, sensible and unemotional Thais. He stated he believed Thailand had rightfully submitted this case to the World Court. Such action obligated Thailand to accept gracefully the decision of the Court. Any untoward act by Thailand and the statements now being made in the heat of passion following the Court's determination were a discredit to the mature stature Thailand had achieved. Khun Yom said that if Thailand handled this problem well it would achieve status as a mature Southeast Asian country blessed with intelligent statesmen. If it blundered, challenged the decision in the press, threatened to prevent the decision from being effected, Thailand would lose friends, dignity, and international respect.
>
> I asked if this were the line he was taking with his friends and associates. His answer was, "Of course, and this is the line they are taking with me." I asked what he thought the men in the street would think. He said most men in the streets did no thinking and the few who did would know little about Phra Viharn and the World Court decision unless they were fired by sensationalists.[95]

Khun Yom's reaction to Thailand's handling of the Preah Vihear dispute raises several questions regarding the difficulty of analyzing public opinion. He stated that Thailand was right to submit the dispute to the World Court. Was that an indication that he supported his country's claim to the temple site? Perhaps not, as he says later that the man in the street knew little about Preah Vihear, suggesting that he recognized Cambodia's sovereignty. Second, he had discernible contempt for the sensationalist press and its uninformed readers, suggesting that the appeal of National Humiliation discourse was due to public ignorance of the site's actual history. Finally, he points out that the country's global prestige would be enhanced far more by peaceably relinquishing Preah Vihear than by retaining it through violence and disregard for international conventions.

These comments indicate that public reaction to the controversy was not monolithic. Not everyone supported Thailand's claim to Preah Vihear, and even among supporters many objected to the prospect of defying the ICJ and confronting Cambodia. Certainly there were dissenting voices regarding the temple dispute, just as there had been in 1940 during the buildup to war with French Indochina. But those who disagreed with the government's official position did so privately rather than pen editorials or letters published in newspapers or write their slogans on placards and march in the streets. This is one effect of National Humiliation discourse: not to force universal acceptance of an irredentist agenda but to create an environment in which expressing a contrary opinion was fraught with risk. Any suggestion that Thailand abandon its claims to Preah Vihear might be interpreted as an endorsement of Cambodian sovereignty, which could expose an individual to charges of disloyalty.

Given the media pressure to disregard the court ruling and the intimidating stance initially adopted by state leaders, Prime Minister Sarit surprised everyone by announcing in July 1962 that Thailand would comply with the court's ruling. In spite of the abundance of irredentist sentiment, there were many factors that compelled the Sarit regime to make such a decision. First, there was the opinion of the king to consider. It was well known that King Bhumibol was very concerned about the dispute and had advised the government to proceed with caution.[96] Despite its military advantage, Thailand did not dare provoke a conflict due to Cambodia's growing relationship with the People's Republic of China. Finally, Thailand's membership in the United Nations was an important source of international prestige.[97] Denouncing the ICJ as a neo-imperialist institution was one thing, but to defy the court's ruling might jeopardize Thailand's standing as a respected member of the community of nations. Sarit reminded the nation of this fact in his special address on Preah Vihear: "We are now living in a world society. Thai brethren must have been well aware of the recognition and esteem the Thai nation enjoys in the international society. Were we to lose our dignity and prestige on account of the ruins of Phra Viharn, how many more decades or centuries will be needed to restore the lost prestige?"[98]

Just as they had done in 1893 and again in 1946, the Thai elite were left with little choice but to embrace the role of martyr. Thai leaders claimed they were sacrificing the nation's own interests for the sake of international peace, but that they did so under protest. On July 15, 1962, military leaders gathered to ceremoniously cede sovereignty over Preah Vihear to Cambodia. Rather than remove the Thai flag, the color guard uprooted the flagpole and transplanted it to a spot on Thai soil designated to become a museum. Interior Minister Praphas presided over the ceremony, telling those in attendance, "One day we will bring this flag back to fly over Preah Vihear again."[99] The province of Sisaket planned to transform the event into a day of remembrance by mounting a plaque at the site that read, "We were robbed of Preah Vihear."[100]

WHY DID THAILAND LOSE?

As they dealt with their grief over losing Preah Vihear, irredentists began the process of assigning blame for the nation's defeat. Thailand's cause was just, they told themselves, yet it had failed. Why? The state also felt pressure to answer this question or it may have faced accusations of selling out the nation that would lead to problems for the Samak government in 2008. The state's response to this question once again demonstrated its attempt to package the Preah Vihear dispute as a reincarnation of the *chosen trauma*.

The narrative that emerged is reflected in the political cartoon by Prayoon Chanyawongse reproduced on page 184. "The Magic Carpet" attempted to explain the outcome of the border dispute, but it also reflects Thai anxieties concerning the long-term effects of the ICJ verdict. The real villain in the cartoon is the Annex I map, the expansionist tool of a deceitful imperialist power, which rolls indiscriminately over both the actual border and the bewildered Thai peasant. The boundary appears self-evident (to the viewer) in the form of a fence, but the bumbling judge is so intent on deciphering the chart that he doesn't notice he has crossed from Cambodia into Thailand. Together, the map and the judge have incapacitated Thailand and provided an entry point for communists such as the tiny Sihanouk backed by his Chinese patron, Mao. The sketch communicates the message that Thailand is still threatened by imperialism just as it was in the time of Chulalongkorn. Today, the injustices perpetrated on Thailand by old imperialism (the French map) have left it vulnerable to the intrusion of neo-imperialism (the World Court and Communism).

Because irredentists viewed the loss of Preah Vihear as the latest fruit borne by the seed planted in 1893, they held France partly responsible for their defeat at The Hague. French duplicity in 1907 had created the temple dispute, and documents from French archives proved essential to Cambodia's winning case. In the aftermath of the Thai government's decision to obey the court, *Sarn seri* invited its readers to share their reactions. All of the

Figure 7. **The Magic Carpet.** An international court judge violates the borders of Thailand as Sihanouk and Mao follow behind. (*Bangkok Post,* July 17, 1962)

published letters conveyed a strong anti-French sentiment. Several readers called for Thais to boycott French products, including medicine and cosmetics, saying this was the only way to make the French people reflect on all the hardship and suffering their government has caused Thailand today and in the past.[101] One columnist argued that France's current troubles in Algeria were proof that its many sins committed against Thailand were now being returned upon its own head.[102] Although France's cruelty might never be avenged, some believed the lessons of those painful events could still prove valuable. Newspapers encouraged the Ministry of Education to make the study of history a greater priority, so that students would never forget the bitterness of the past. "If not," wrote one pundit, "we can be sure to experience this sort of thing again and again."[103]

Now that the age of old imperialism was over, the new threat to Thai sovereignty was from neo-imperialist institutions such as the ICJ. The Thai press was extremely critical of the court's conduct during the trial, particularly its acceptance of the Annex I map as proof of France's sovereignty over Preah Vihear. The map used at the trial was not the original. Cambodia obtained a copy stored in France's archives, which led to speculation that the new map was forged for the purposes of the trial. This cartographical conspiracy theory fitted perfectly into the narrative of "French Wolf, Siamese Lamb" and demonstrated how little had changed since the first Franco-Siamese conflict. The ICJ was a tool employed by great countries to dominate lesser ones. Moreover, by inserting itself into the dispute and ruling in favor of Cambodia, the court had proved itself just as capable of imposing foreign influence in Thailand as any colonial power.[104] Thai leaders even accused the court of having communist sympathies and helping facilitate the spread of Communism. In an interview with the *Siam nikorn* newspaper, Thanom expressed his conviction that Thailand was cheated out of Preah Vihear because of the judges who came from communist countries.[105] Bangkok secretly believed that ICJ president Bohdan Winiarski, who was from Poland, was using the court in order to allow Communism to infiltrate Thailand through its eastern border with Cambodia. In response, the Thai government stopped issuing visas for Poles to enter Thailand, ordered members of Polish trade organizations to leave the country, and temporarily banned Polish imports.[106]

Thai irredentists also took aim at the United States, claiming they had been betrayed by their former ally. Since the end of World War II, when the United States dissuaded Britain from placing a protectorate over a defeated Thailand, Bangkok and Washington had developed a special relationship. Phibun and Sarit had pledged their commitment to democracy and their support of the Truman Doctrine in return for an American guarantee of protection against Communism. With the temple dispute occurring at the height of the Cold War, the Thai government naturally expected U.S. support against a neutralist Cambodia. They were sorely disappointed. Despite Sihanouk's flirtations with Beijing and attacks against Bangkok, the United States continued to supply Phnom Penh with increasing amounts of military and economic assistance. It appeared to Thailand as though their protector was sharpening the spearhead of a possible communist invasion. Nor did the United States meet expectations by using their influence in the UN to help Thailand's case. The Sarit government had originally appointed American attorney Phillip Jessup as one of its legal representatives at The Hague. In 1960, Jessup left the Thai Legation to serve as a justice on the ICJ, but because of his prior connection with the defense he recused himself from sitting in judgment on the Preah Vihear case. This denied Thailand both an important member of their legal counsel and a possible vote at the court. But most upsetting for

Bangkok was the fact that former U.S. secretary of state Dean Acheson agreed to serve as lead counsel for Cambodia. At this point, Acheson was practicing law at a private firm, but the media still viewed him as an official representative of the U.S. government. Thai observers interpreted his participation in the plaintiff's case as an American endorsement of Cambodia's claim to Preah Vihear.[107] For over a decade, Thailand had been a faithful client of U.S. foreign policy, but in the moment of reciprocation the patron failed to deliver. Outraged newspaper editorials compared America's abandonment of Thailand during the Preah Vihear trial with Great Britain's betrayal of Chulalongkorn in 1893. "This type of behavior," wrote a correspondent, "is a clear example of how Thailand always gets stabbed in the back."[108]

In the end, the Thai government bowed to international pressure, withdrew its forces from the temple site, and acknowledged Preah Vihear as part of Cambodia. The Sarit regime's message to the Thai people, however, conveyed the impression that the verdict represented a temporary setback rather than a permanent settlement. In his speech to the nation announcing Thailand's withdrawal from the ruins, Sarit reassured people that his government had not given up on the idea of reclaiming what it considered to be Thai territory:

> I know full well that the loss of Phra Viharn is a loss which afflicts the entire Thai nation. Therefore, even though Cambodia may have Phra Viharn, only the ruins and the piece of land on which the Temple is situated will be theirs. The soul of the Temple of Phra Viharn remains forever with Thailand. The Thai people will always remember that the Temple of Phra Viharn was robbed from us by the trickery of those who disregard honor and justice. As Thailand behaves in the world society as a member imbued with the highest sense of honor and morality, sooner or later the Temple of Phra Viharn shall revert once again to Thailand. . . . The incident of Phra Viharn will remain in the memory of the Thai people for generations to come and will leave an indelible mark on the nation's history as if it was a wound in the heart of each and everyone in the entire nation.[109]

Instead of facilitating the healing process, the Thai state worked to keep the wound open by insisting that the dispute had not been fully resolved. This task was made easier by a loophole in the ICJ's verdict. The court had awarded sovereignty over the temple site to Cambodia, but it made no ruling on the precise location of the border around it. Thai irredentists seized on this minor detail to argue that the temple structure might belong to Cambodia, but the surrounding land (including the disputed 4.6 km of territory) remained part of Thailand. From this perspective, the status of Preah Vihear could not be determined until a permanent border through the area was delineated. Sarit's speech to the nation clearly articulated the principles of National Humiliation discourse. Instead of attempting to heal the wounds from the conflict, his comments helped transform the memory of Preah Vihear into a painful scar on the body of the nation. His statement echoed the most chauvinist sentiments offered up by the Thai media—namely that Thailand had been betrayed by its friends and robbed of Preah Vihear by its enemies. This narrative on the temple, first articulated by the Phibun regime in the aftermath of the 1941 border conflict, has influenced Thai attitudes towards the temple question ever since. This explanation of events is very attractive to irredentist groups in Thailand because it cleverly conceals the country's expansionist ambitions and instead portrays the Thai as heroically resisting the neocolonial influence of the ICJ. While feigning compliance with the ICJ, the Sarit government adopted a policy on Preah Vihear that was designed to ensure future conflict.

CONCLUSION

By refusing to accept the finality of the ICJ decision, the Thai government constructed a historical narrative that associated Preah Vihear with the concept of *lost territory* and enabled the issue to resurface under the right circumstances. Sarit's implied suggestion that Thailand might one day regain Preah Vihear prevented the Thai nation from seeking closure on the issue and allowed the temple to become a potent symbol of National Humiliation in the hands of opportunists. Pavin Chachavalpongpun has argued that the 2008 protests over the World Heritage status of Preah Vihear represent exactly this type of political posturing. He accuses the People's Alliance for Democracy of raising the temple issue to shore up its faction's momentum and points out it is no coincidence that tensions with Cambodia erupted at a moment when the PAD was struggling to keep up the momentum of its demonstrations.[110] Both the PAD and the Democrat Party tried to connect the World Heritage status of Preah Vihear to Thailand's loss of territorial integrity and the failure of the state. This discourse splits the political world into two categories. The PAD presents itself as the defender of the nation and monarchy while denouncing its enemies—former prime minister Thaksin Shinawatra and his successor Samak Sundaravej—as amoral businessmen whose lust for profit supersedes love of country.[111] According to this paradigm, there is a "wall of righteousness" that separates good Thais from enemies, and those who disagree with policies on territorial integrity of the monarchy can be accused of selling out the nation. Pavin argues that this is the new face of Thai nationalism: nationhood defined by the sacredness and vulnerability of Thai territorial integrity, one that is permanently threatened by enemies, both inside and outside Thailand's borders.[112]

I argue here that the Thai-Cambodian border tensions beginning in 2008 have roots in the Thai irredentist narratives on *lost territory* dating back to the 1930s. The PAD's irredentist campaign was a rehashing of the discourse from the previous temple controversy of the 1960s, which in turn was a reiteration of the Franco-Thai border dispute of 1940; but all three episodes are firmly rooted in the fertile soil of National Humiliation discourse. As we have seen, the Thai irredentists have constructed a historiography that celebrates victimization, engenders a sense of collective shame, and produces periodic impulses towards expansion. By refusing to renounce territorial grievances, the Thai state created conditions wherein the legitimacy of its border becomes an issue of debate for each new generation. In 2008, Thailand's deeply divided politics created an ideal atmosphere for the issue of *lost territory* to return to prominence.

Conclusion

After the furor over Preah Vihear died down, the Thai state discontinued its use of National Humiliation discourse, which had once again became a liability. Sarit's pledge that one day Preah Vihear would belong to Thailand suggested that defeat was temporary, for the struggle was not over. Despite the ambiguous nature of the World Court's ruling on the boundary surrounding Preah Vihear, the Thai government did not request clarification for fear any resulting demarcation would cost them even more territory. For over four decades, the temple site functioned as a type of memorial, commemorating a dark anniversary. Then in 2005 the controversy flared up again when Cambodia submitted an application to have Preah Vihear listed as a World Heritage site. Initially, Bangkok objected to the submission on the grounds that sovereignty over the temple site was still contested. Two years later a Thai delegation traveled to Phnom Penh to propose that the heritage application be a joint venture between the two countries. The government of Hun Sen refused, saying that Preah Vihear was solely a Cambodian landmark. On June 24, 2008, Thai foreign minister Noppadon Pattama signed a joint communiqué supporting Cambodia's application to the World Heritage Committee.

The treaty signing initiated a firestorm of criticism and protest back in Bangkok. Many felt the country would lose face if Cambodia was permitted to list Preah Vihear as its own. Newspaper editorials accused the ruling People Power Party of "selling the country" in exchange for gas and casino concessions on Koh Kong, an island in the Gulf of Thailand. Worst of all, an opinion piece published in *The Nation* accused the government of abandoning Thailand's claim to the temple: "We question why the Thai government is so keen to endorse Cambodia's move on Preah Vihear in the absence of a joint application to UNESCO and in the absence of an amicable agreement on the territorial dispute. Most importantly, the endorsement is sending a signal that

Thailand will never try to reclaim Preah Vihear. The Samak government has committed a diplomatic blunder, which is unforgivable."[1]

The opposition Democrat Party called for a no-confidence vote against Prime Minister Samak Sundaravej and his entire cabinet, while the People's Alliance for Democracy filed a lawsuit in Thailand's Constitutional Court, claiming that the signing of the joint communiqué threatened the country's sovereignty and was therefore unconstitutional. Out in the streets, yellow-shirted PAD supporters demonstrated in front of the Ministry of Foreign Affairs before moving to the Government House. For his role as signatory of the joint communiqué, Noppadon Pattama faced an impeachment hearing in parliament and opted to resign.[2] The Thai cabinet eventually reversed its position and declared its opposition to Cambodia's application, but it could not stop the World Heritage Council from adding Preah Vihear to its list of sites. The World Heritage Council's decision made the Samak government look increasingly inept and lent credence to the PAD's accusations that the ruling party was engaged in selling the nation.

Why, after forty years, did the sovereignty of Preah Vihear suddenly reemerge as a controversial issue, and why was the PAD so effective at using the issue to throw the Samak government off balance? To answer this question we must analyze the PAD's dual-pronged discursive strategy: reconstructing Thai identity in ways that emphasize the nation's vulnerable position within a hostile world, then creating mechanisms to defend it. The PAD's rise to power has been based on this strategy of narrowly defining "Thainess," then hunting down and exposing those individuals or groups perceived as threatening that vision. The most sacred and vulnerable institution in Thai society, as the PAD describe it, is the monarchy. The past two decades have seen the proliferation and rigid enforcement of antidefamation laws. These laws, which ostensibly serve to defend the monarchy, have been deployed to silence political dissidents, intimidate academics, and establish the PAD's vision as a form of state nationalism. From their perspective, anyone accused of lése majestè has already failed the test of identity politics. The nation, whose culture and institutions are constantly threatened by outside interests, must deal harshly with those who would jeopardize its solidarity. As David Streckfuss has written, "Laws based on defamation principles see the world as a contest between those who want to unite the country and those who seek to divide it. Devilish characters speak evil of the throne, sow calumniation in the ears of foreigners, make dire prophecies, ridicule culture, and sell-out the nation by passing secrets to non-Thai."[3]

In a similar fashion, National Humiliation discourse, with its fabricated history of geospatial suffering, has been wielded by the PAD in its crusade of national defense. Like the monarchy, the state's boundaries constitute an endangered entity that requires protection. The PAD uses this narrative to alert the country to the potential dangers of disunity—namely loss of territory—then assigns blame to the groups or individuals responsible. These parties are branded as enemies looking to sell the nation for personal gain and threaten its unity. Who employs this discourse and who are its targets? In 2008, proponents of National Humiliation included factions in the military, powerful business interests, the Democrat Party, the PAD, and some Royalists. These groups went on the offensive, demonizing Thaksin, the Samak government, Hun Sen, or Cambodia as enemies who threaten the well-being of the nation. Pavin calls this strategy the "new face of Thai nationalism": nationhood defined by the sacredness and vulnerability of Thai territorial integrity, one that is permanently threatened by enemies, both inside and outside Thailand's borders.[4]

That sense of vulnerability is communicated using iconic images of Preah Vihear and the *lost territory* maps, which convey a message that Thailand's status in the world community has declined since the nineteenth century. The Thai National Memorial in Pathum Thani Province still has an exhibit on the 1941 Indochina war that includes a map of the five episodes when Thailand lost territories to France. At present, there are several versions of a PowerPoint slide presentation circulating on YouTube, which claims to educate Thais on the history of the *lost territories.* The presentation has expanded "The Loss" from the five episodes defined by Wichit Wathakan to eleven episodes, beginning with the transfer of Penang to British sovereignty during the reign of Rama I (1782–1809). These sensational images of Thai vulnerability are intended to shock viewers into rallying behind leaders or groups who make border protection a top priority. Anyone who disagrees with these leaders is quickly accused of sowing division within the nation, which might lead to foreign intervention and further loss of territory.

No government has been more effective at using historical memory as a source of political legitimacy than the People's Republic of China. Zheng Wang has studied the Communist Party's use of National Humiliation discourse to shore up its credibility in the wake of the Tiananmen Square massacre. The violent crackdown on student protests, combined with ongoing free market reforms, helped undermine the legacy of Maoism as the regime's governing philosophy. In an effort to build ties to the next generation, the Communist Party embarked on a patriotic education campaign designed to teach China's youth about the *chosen traumas* of the nation's past. In the 1990s, the state published new high school textbooks that downplayed the heroism of the party and instead focused on episodes of foreign invasion and oppression such as the Opium Wars or Japanese atrocities during World War II.[5] Zheng argues that this education campaign was an effort to redirect people's anger away from the party and domestic issues towards foreign policy and China's regional rivals. The constant emphasis of the phrase "Never Forget National Humiliation" has produced an increasingly patriotic generation of Chinese who appear to acutely feel the shame associated with China's past defeats.[6]

Like China, the Thai state has alternately defined itself either by focusing on the nation's supreme achievements or its greatest failures. These powerful memories act as the glue that binds the nation to the state. All historical narratives are composed of events a people choose to remember and those they choose to forget. Thailand's *chosen myth* is the assumption that the country was never colonized. This reading of history obscures Western subordination of Siam by focusing on the continuity of local royal power and ignoring how the Chakri monarchy both accommodated and profited from colonial intervention.[7] Thailand's *chosen trauma,* on the other hand, spotlights the dismemberment of the nation's geobody through the chronology of *lost territory.* It conceals how those very territorial concessions gave birth to the modern nation-state. Both narratives act as effective large-group markers and are represented by opposing symbols. In Thai culture today, Chulalongkorn symbolizes the *chosen myth,* while Preah Vihear represents the *chosen trauma.* According to Volkan, however, *chosen traumas* exert a more powerful influence on group behavior. Whereas *chosen myths* serve to elevate the collective esteem of a nation, *chosen traumas* initiate a much more profound psychological effect that can lead to mourning or reversal of humiliation. These actions in turn bind the group more tightly together.[8]

All of this helps explain why National Humiliation narratives have been so effective and durable as a means for constructing state identity. This was especially true during the first Phibun regime (1938–1944). Chai-anan Samudavanija suggests this period is often mischaracterized as a period of nation building; in actuality, the regime engaged in the construction of state-identity. After the 1932 military coup, the ideology of constitutionalism served to distinguish the new establishment from the monarchy, but due to its limitations it was replaced by militarism and a cult of personality after 1938.[9] I argue that the historical memory of *lost territory* was essential to this transition from constitutionalism to militarism. The geobody has always been a tool used to unify disparate groups, and it is most effective when it is perceived as having been attacked or injured. For example, Phibun's 1940 irredentist campaign led to unprecedented national unity by providing space for ordinary citizens to demonstrate their loyalty to the state.

The symbol of *lost territory* allowed the Thai state to reclassify certain minority groups as Thai while still excluding undesirables. Following the 1941 border conflict, the Phibun regime employed the traumatic memory of 1893 to invoke an imagined construct of the Golden Peninsula that huddled the Khmer, Lao, and Shan people under the umbrella of Thainess. The narrative of loss denied the Lao and Khmer status as distinct ethnic groups with corresponding cultures and instead categorized them as occupied regions of a Greater Thailand. Irredentists later interpreted Pan-Asianism as a Japanese version of National Humiliation discourse. For Bangkok, it was not religion or skin color that united Asians but the common experience of being humiliated by the West. Groups that placed personal, business, or religious affiliations ahead of state loyalty, however, would not be welcome in the new Thailand. Catholic Thais were accused of sympathizing with the imperialist power that had victimized Thailand. Today, politicians perceived as insufficiently committed to safeguarding the country's border are accused of selling the nation.

This study has attempted to trace the origins of National Humiliation discourse and explore its consequences, but the question remains as to how successful this discourse has been in shaping popular attitudes. People are not automatons incapable of interpreting or resisting the propaganda of the state. Granted, a great deal of evidence exists to suggest that the state's new historical narrative was well received by a large segment of the population. In the final months of 1940, with the Franco-Thai border dispute heating up, there were several examples of what could be considered popular anger over perceived past grievances and support for the government's policy of armed confrontation with French Indochina. Thai newspapers featured letters to the editor advocating war, collected donations to support irredentist causes, and reported marches by students and civil servants in favor of retaking the *lost territories*—all of which seem to suggest a popular embrace of National Humiliation narratives. There is similar evidence of popular resentment over the government's decision to return the four provinces to France, in 1958 at the outbreak of the Preah Vihear controversy, and again in 2008 after Cambodia applied to list the temple as a World Heritage site.

Evaluating public opinion in Thailand, especially during the first Phibun regime, is a very difficult task. Without access to polling data, historians must be creative in taking the pulse of the nation. Using the media to determine the popular mood is problematic. In 1941, Thailand's sole radio station was government controlled, and the state used its licensing restrictions and other means to wield influence over Bangkok newspapers.[10] Opposition to the state's irredentist agenda did exist, although it would not have been publicized in the media. Certainly religious and ethnic minorities quietly resisted Phibun's pan-Thai movement and the state's attempt to force conversions to Buddhism. The Seri Thai movement clandestinely worked to undermine confidence in the government and destabilize the Thai-Japanese alliance. Other political and business elites disagreed with the government's aggressive posturing towards French Indochina in the 1940s or Cambodia in the 1950s, but they did so privately.

One reason that it is difficult to analyze public response to state ideology is that Thailand lacks a space for public opinion. The state manufactures images that serve to legitimize its power and also creates channels for communicating them; but unlike many Western societies, there are no mechanisms in Thailand for assessing the popularity of those images. These mechanisms (polling, call-in radio shows) do not exist because the government has no interest in public opinion except at the elite level. Therefore, there are no ideological spaces wherein images created by the state can be challenged or evaluated.[11] I would further argue that during the 1940s, the state created images meant to simulate popular support but that were in fact part of the narrative rather than a response to that narrative. In particular, the marches and demonstrations in October 1940 were performances of a sort, orchestrated by the state and composed largely of teachers, students, and state employees, then reported in the newspapers as evidence of a popular groundswell. These marches were intended to demonstrate the unity of the Thai nation in the face of Western aggression. Letters to the editor also gave the appearance of a public forum and strengthened the democratic image of the government.

In recent years, much has been made of Thailand's ambivalent attitudes towards Western imperialism. The same could be said of Thailand's attitude towards its own past. For the most part, Thai history celebrates the *chosen myth* of perpetual independence from Western colonization. But periodically it becomes politically expedient to rehash the history of *chosen trauma*. National Humiliation involves the state's dissemination of a historical narrative designed to educate Thais regarding moments in their history where the state was defeated and degraded by foreign powers. It is used by political groups to communicate a sense of the nation's vulnerability. The message is one of unity: people are instructed to eliminate differences and unify behind the government's agenda. If they fail to do so, the discourse warns, then the current generation may reexperience the partition endured by their ancestors. The story of National Humiliation is usually told through the imagery of the *lost territories,* although there are many other examples of past trauma, including the Bowring Treaty, extraterritoriality, Preah Vihear, and even the 1998 Asian financial crisis. Each of these examples can be interpreted as an incident in which Thailand was attacked unjustly by foreigners. The recent temple dispute involving Cambodia indicates that National Humiliation discourse is still a powerful force in Thai politics.

NOTES

INTRODUCTION: THE IDEA OF "LOSS" IN THAI HISTORICAL NARRATIVES

1. *Bangkok Post,* March 1, 2001.
2. Rachel Harrison makes this point in her introduction. See Rachel V. Harrison and Peter A. Jackson (eds.), *The Ambiguous Allure of the West: Traces of the Colonial in Thailand* (Hong Kong: Hong Kong University Press, 2010).
3. Marc Askew (ed.), *Legitimacy Crisis in Thailand* (Chiang Mai: Silkworm Books, 2010), p. 14.
4. Thongchai Winichakul, "Siam's Colonial Conditions and the Birth of Thai History," in Volker Grabowsky (ed.), *Southeast Asian Historiography: Unraveling the Myths* (Bangkok: River Books, 2011), p. 21.
5. Ibid.
6. The word "Luang" is often included as part of Wichit's name to denote his royal title. Hereafter I will refer to him simply as Wichit. See Pra-onrat Buranamat, *Luang Wichitwathakan kap lakhon prawattisat* [The Historical Plays of Luang Wichitwathakan] (Bangkok: Thammasat University Press, 1985), p. 168.
7. Chris Baker and Pasuk Phongpaichit, *A History of Thailand* (Cambridge: Cambridge University Press, 2005), p. 45.
8. The notion of *bamboo diplomacy* is still quite popular among scholars of Thai foreign policy. For a recent example, see Arne Kislenko, "Bending with the Wind: The Continuity and Flexibility of Thai Foreign Policy," *International Journal* 57:4 (August 2002), pp. 537–561.
9. Thamsook Numnonda, *Thailand and the Japanese Presence, 1941–1945* (Singapore: Institute of Southeast Asian Studies, 1977), p. vi.
10. For an explanation of how Western spatial conceptions replaced traditional understandings of geography, see Thongchai Winichakul, *Siam Mapped: A History of the Geo-Body of a Nation* (Honolulu: University of Hawaiʻi Press, 1994).
11. Lysa Hong, "'Stranger within the Gates': Knowing Semi-Colonial Siam as Extraterritorials," *Modern Asian Studies* 38:2 (2004), p. 5.
12. William A. Callahan, "Beyond Cosmopolitanism and Nationalism: Diasporic Chinese and Neo-Nationalism in Thailand," *International Organization* 57:3 (2003), pp. 481–517.

13. Noel Alfred Battye, "The Military, Government and Society in Siam, 1868–1910: Politics and Military Reform during the Reign of Chulalongkorn" (Ph.D. diss., Cornell University, 1974), p. 315.
14. This is shorthand for "Rathanakosin Era 112," referring to the 112th year since the founding of the Chakri dynasty.
15. Thongchai, "Siam's Colonial Conditions," p. 30.
16. David K. Wyatt, *Thailand: A Short History* (New Haven, CT: Yale University Press, 2003), pp. 189–190.
17. It also confirms the perceived loss of territory as an embarrassing aspect of the royal legacy.
18. Vamik Volkan, *Bloodlines: From Ethnic Pride to Ethnic Terrorism* (New York: Farrar, Straus and Giroux, 1997), p. 147.
19. Ibid.
20. Volkan lists many such examples. The Czechs hold onto the memory of Bila Hora, the Lakota retain images of Wounded Knee, and Crimean Tartars define themselves by the shared experience of being deported from the Crimea. See Volkan, *Bloodlines,* p. 49.
21. The movie *Siamese Renaissance* is loosely based on the Thai novel *Thawiphob* (Between Worlds).
22. Rachel Harrison, "Mind the Gap: (En)countering the West and the Making of Thai Identities on Film," in Harrison and Jackson (eds.), *Ambiguous Allure of the West,* p. 114.
23. There are several accounts of this incident. See Lawrence Palmer Briggs, "The Aubaret versus Bradley Case at Bangkok, 1866–1867," *Far Eastern Quarterly* 6:3 (1947), pp. 262–282.
24. Baker and Pasuk, *A History of Thailand,* pp. 76–77.
25. Harrison and Jackson, *Ambiguous Allure of the West,* pp. 52–53.
26. Ibid., p. 12.
27. Benedict Anderson, "The State of Thai Studies: Studies of the Thai State," in Eliezer B. Ayal (ed.), *The Study of Thailand: Analyses of Knowledge, Approaches, and Prospects in Anthropology, Art History, Economics, History, and Political Science,* Southeast Asia series, no. 54 (Athens: Ohio University Center for International Studies, 1978), p. 197.
28. Harrison and Jackson, *Ambiguous Allure of the West,* p. 12.
29. See Kasian Tejapira, *Commodifying Marxism: The Formation of Modern Thai Radical Culture, 1927–1958* (Kyoto: Kyoto Areas Studies on Asia No. 3, 2001); Thongchai Winichakul. "The Quest for *'Siwilai'*: A Geographical Discourse of Civilizational Thinking in the Late Nineteenth and Early Twentieth-Century Siam." *Journal of Asian Studies* 59:3 (2002); Maurizio Peleggi, *Lords of Things: The Fashioning of the Siamese Monarchy's Modern Image* (Honolulu: University of Hawai'i Press, 2002).
30. Peleggi, *Lords of Things,* p. 6.

31. Harrison and Jackson, *Ambiguous Allure of the West.*
32. *Wan khru,* January 19, 1938.
33. Thamsook's argument is another example of the *bamboo diplomacy* explanation of Thai foreign policy. The insistence that Thailand remained independent through the conflict requires that we overlook Japan's invasion in 1941, Phibun's declaration of war on the Allies, and the presence of thousands of Japanese troops in Thailand during the war and British colonial troops following the war.
34. Callahan, "Beyond Cosmopolitanism and Nationalism," p. 497.

CHAPTER 1. CONSTRUCTING LOSS: REPEALING THE UNEQUAL TREATIES IN SIAM

1. Luang Nathabanja, *Extra-territoriality in Siam* (Bangkok: Bangkok Daily Mail, 1924), p. 5.
2. M. B. Hooker, *Laws of Southeast Asia,* vol. 2: *European Laws in Southeast Asia* (Singapore: Butterworth and Company, 1988), p. 535.
3. David Wyatt, *Thailand: A Short History* (New Haven, CT: Yale University Press, 2003), p. 168.
4. Lysa Hong, "'Stranger within the Gates': Knowing Semi-Colonial Siam as Extraterritorials," *Modern Asian Studies* 38:2 (2004), p. 350.
5. Luang Nathabanja, *Extra-territoriality in Siam,* pp. 2–3.
6. Ibid., p. 5.
7. Ibid., p. 6.
8. Ibid., p. 25.
9. Ibid., p. 38.
10. Kullada Kesboonchoo Mead, *The Rise and Decline of Thai Absolutism* (London: Routledge, 2009), pp. 1–3.
11. B. J. Terwiel, "The Bowring Treaty: Imperialism and the Indigenous Perspective," *Journal of Siam Society* 79:2 (1991), p. 43.
12. Ibid., p. 27.
13. Ibid., pp. 27–28.
14. Ibid., p. 30.
15. Ibid., pp. 30–31.
16. Ibid., p. 31 (italics mine).
17. Luang Nathabanja, *Extra-territoriality in Siam,* p. 25.
18. Constance Wilson, "State and Society in the Reign of Mongkut, 1851–1868: Thailand on the Eve of Modernization" (Ph.D. diss., Cornell University, 1970), p. 363.
19. Thongchai Winichakul, *Siam Mapped: A History of the Geo-Body of a Nation* (Honolulu: University of Hawai'i Press, 1994), p. 88.

20. Wilson, "State and Society," pp. 538–541.
21. Mathew Copeland, "Contested Nationalism and the 1932 Overthrow of the Absolute Monarchy in Siam" (Ph.D. diss., Australian National University, 1993), p. 14.
22. Ibid.
23. Patrick Tuck, *The French Wolf and the Siamese Lamb: The French Threat to Siamese Independence, 1858–1907* (Bangkok: White Lotus Press, 1995), p. 126.
24. Ibid., pp. 294–296.
25. Ibid., p. 179.
26. Ibid., p. 180.
27. Ibid.
28. Ibid.
29. Wyatt, *Thailand,* p. 191.
30. Ibid., p. 192.
31. By 1919, the United States had not signed an agreement comparable to the 1907 treaty with France or the 1909 agreement with Britain, so drafting a new treaty with the Americans was a high priority for Siam. See Peter B. Oblas, "A Very Small Part of World Affairs: Siam's Policy on Treaty Revision and the Paris Peace Conference," *Journal of Siam Society* 59:2 (1971), p. 58.
32. Ibid., p. 62.
33. Siam's motivation for declaring war was not solely a desire to revise the unequal treaties; it also reflected Rama VI's strategy for improving the country's status. See Walter F. Vella, *Chaiyo! King Vajiravudh and the Development of Thai Nationalism* (Honolulu: University of Hawai'i Press, 1978), pp. 109–110.
34. Oblas, "A Very Small Part of World Affairs," pp. 62–63.
35. Ibid., p. 65.
36. Pridi Phanomyong, *Pridi by Pridi: Selected Writings on Life, Politics, and Economy* (Bangkok: Silkworm Books, 2000), p. 180.
37. David Wyatt provides an example of this narrative. He describes the signing of the 1926 treaties in the following terms: "The long battle was finally won; Siam had finally regained its sovereignty." See Wyatt, *Thailand,* p. 219.
38. Stefan Hell, *Siam and the League of Nations: Modernization, Sovereignty, and Multilateral Diplomacy, 1920–1940* (Bangkok: River Books, 2010), pp. 43–44.

CHAPTER 2. THE BIRTH OF NATIONAL HUMILIATION DISCOURSE

1. The best-known example of this approach is Virginia Thompson's *Thailand: The New Siam* (New York: MacMillan, 1941). See also J. L. Christian and Nabutake Ike, "Thailand in Japan's Foreign Relations," *Pacific Affairs* 15 (June 1942): pp. 195–221.

2. E. Thadeus Flood, "The 1940 Franco-Thai Border Dispute and Phibun Songkhram's Commitment to Japan," *Journal of Southeast Asian History* 10:2 (September 1969), pp. 304–325.
3. Kobkua Suwannathat-Pian, *Thailand's Durable Premier: Phibun through Three Decades, 1932–1957* (Kuala Lumpur: Oxford University Press, 1995), p. 254.
4. NAT ก.ต. 1.2/8. *Singapore Free Press* interview, February 26, 1941.
5. France treated the Mekong as a French river and levied taxes on Thai commercial use. In 1935, French regulations prevented a Chiang Rai businessman from using the Mekong to float timber down to Saigon. See Direk Jayanama, *Thailand and World War II* (Chiang Mai: Silkworm Books, 2008), p. 11.
6. Flood, "1940 Franco-Thai Dispute," p. 307.
7. Kobkua, *Thailand's Durable Premier,* p. 255.
8. Direk, *Thailand and World War II,* p. 16.
9. Flood, "1940 Franco-Thai Dispute," pp. 309–310.
10. Direk, *Thailand and World War II,* p. 23.
11. Kobkua, *Thailand's Durable Premier,* pp. 257–258.
12. Soren Ivarsson, "Making Laos 'Our' Space: Thai Discourse on History and Race, 1900–1941," in Christopher E. Goscha and Soren Ivarsson (eds.), *Contesting Visions of the Lao Past: Lao Historiography at the Crossroads* (Copenhagen: Nordic Institute of Asian Studies, 2003), p. 256.
13. *Bangkok Chronicle,* September 14, 1940.
14. Flood, "1940 Franco-Thai Dispute," p. 325.
15. Krom Khosanakan, *Khamprasai khong phon than Nayok Rathamontri klaw kae muanchon chaw Thai thang withayu kracai siang wan thi 20 Tulakhom 1940 rueang kanprabprueng senkheddaen dan Indochin* [The prime minister's radio address to the Thai people on October 20, 1940, regarding the question of the border with French Indochina] (Bangkok: Krom Khosanakan).
16. Reynolds wrote that Phibun secretly (and without consent of his cabinet) promised the Japanese safe passage through Thailand to attack Singapore, provided the Japanese support his irredentist claims. Although he hoped to avoid fulfilling this pledge, Phibun would be forced to honor it in December 1942. See E. Bruce Reynolds, *Thailand and Japan's Southern Advance, 1940–1945* (New York: Palgrave MacMillan, 1994), p. 38.
17. Flood, "1940 Franco-Thai Dispute," p. 325.
18. Thamrongsak Phertlert-anan, "Kanriakrong dindaen P.S. 2483" [Requesting Territories in 1940], *Samut Sangkhomsat* 12:3–4 (1990), pp. 23–81.
19. Ivarsson, "Making Laos 'Our' Space," p. 242.
20. From the very beginning of their rule, the People's Party argued that the Thai would no longer be exploited by Western countries as in the past. See Charnvit Kasetsiri, "The First Phibun Government and Its Involvement in World War II," *Journal of the Siam Society* 62:2 (1974), pp. 48–49.

21. Suphaphorn Bumrungwong, "Kanriakrong lae kanbokrong dindaen thi khuen cak Farangsed, 2483–2491" [Requesting and Governing the Territories Returned from France, 1940–1948] (Ph.D. diss., Chulalongkorn University, 2003), p. 38.
22. Ivarsson, "Making Laos 'Our' Space," p. 243.
23. NAT ศธ. 0701.48/12.
24. *Thai rashdra,* October 18, 1940.
25. *Nikorn,* April 18, 1941.
26. *Bangkok Chronicle,* January 10, 1941.
27. *Thai rashdra,* October 4, 1940.
28. For a more complete discussion on the evolution of the *lost territories,* see Thongchai Winichakul, *Siam Mapped: A History of the Geo-Body of a Nation* (Honolulu: University of Hawai'i Press, 1994).
29. Ivarsson, "Making Laos 'Our' Space," p. 243.
30. Virginia Thompson, "Thailand Irredenta—Internal and External," *Far East Survey* 9:21 (October 23, 1940), p. 248.
31. After receiving protests from the British consulate, Phibun issued a memo instructing officials at the ministry to print only maps showing the territories lost to France. See NAT มท. 0201.2.1.14/1.
32. Suphaphorn, "Kanriakrong lae kanbokrong dindaen," p. 66.
33. *Bangkok Chronicle,* January 4, 1941.
34. Ivarsson, "Making Laos 'Our' Space," p. 245.
35. Wichit Wathakan, *Prathedthai: Rueang kansia dindaen kae Farangsed* [How Thailand Lost Its Territories to France] (Bangkok: Krom Khosanakan, 1940).
36. *Bangkok Chronicle,* January 4, 1941.
37. NAT ศธ. 0701.48/12.
38. NAT ศธ. 0701.48/8.
39. Thongchai, *Siam Mapped,* p. 152.
40. Patrick Tuck, The *French Wolf and the Siamese Lamb: The French Threat to Siamese Independence, 1858–1907* (Bangkok: White Lotus Press, 1995), p. 29. For a discussion of the contest for upper Laos, see p. 89.
41. David Streckfuss, "The Mixed Colonial Legacy in Siam: Origins of Thai Racialist Thought, 1890–1910," in Laurie J. Sears (ed.), *Autonomous Histories, Particular Truths: Essays in Honor of John R. W. Smail* (Madison: University of Wisconsin Center for Southeast Asian Studies, Monograph No. 11, 1993), pp. 123–153.
42. Ivarsson, "Making Laos 'Our' Space," p. 249.
43. William Clifton Dodd, *The Tai Race: Elder Brother of the Chinese* (Cedar Rapids, IA: Torch Press, 1923).
44. Scott Barmé, *Luang Wichit Wathakan and the Creation of a Thai Identity* (Singapore: Institute of Southeast Asian Studies, 1993), p. 125.
45. *Yudhakos* 47:11, August 10, 1939.

46. Sodsai Khantiwiraphongse, *Khwamsamphan khong Thai kab prathed tawantok* [Thailand's Relations with Western Countries] (Bangkok: Khled Thai Publishing, 1974), p. 79.
47. Ivarsson, "Making Laos 'Our' Space," p. 251.
48. *Bangkok Chronicle,* October 21, 1940.
49. Krom Khosanakan, *Khamprasai khong phon than Nayok Rathamontri.*
50. *Khaw phab,* October 19, 1940.
51. *Thai rashdra,* October 16, 1940.
52. *Sri krung,* October 29, 1940. See also *Khaw phab,* October 21, 1940.
53. *Bangkok Times,* November 22, 1940.
54. Barmé, *Luang Wichit Wathakan,* p. 168.
55. *Khaw phab,* November 5, 1940.
56. NAT สบ. 9.2.3/4.
57. Barmé, *Luang Wichit Wathakan,* p. 168.
58. *Khaw phab,* November 5, 1940.
59. *Nikorn,* March 14, 1941.
60. AOM Indochine/GG/CM 569, "Lettre de l'Okhna Kateanuraka, Chaukaykhet de Battambang á Minist. de l'Interieure et des Cultes" [A Letter from Okhna Kateanuraka of Chaukaykhet in Battambang Province to the Minister of the Religion and the Interior], January 17, 1941.
61. *Khaw phab,* October 19, 1940.
62. *Thai samit,* October 11, 1940.
63. *Bangkok Chronicle,* January 9, 1941.
64. Alexandre Varenne, "Indochina in the Path of Japanese Expansion," *Foreign Affairs* 27 (October 1938).
65. NAT FO/12/4059.
66. *Thai rashdra,* October 21, 1940.
67. AOM Indochine/GG/CM 563, note no. 9727.
68. AOM Indochine/GG/CM 604, no. 1090/2.SRM.
69. Ivarsson, "Making Laos 'Our' Space," p. 258.
70. *Bangkok Times,* October 21, 1940.
71. NAT ส.บ. 9.2.3/4.
72. AOM Indochine/GG/CM 563, "Lettre de M. Beaulieu á M. Le Resident Superieur au Laos" [A Letter from M. Beaulieu to the Resident Superior in Laos], December 19, 1940.
73. AOM Indochine/GG/CM 1159, "Traduction: Avis du Gouvernor de la province de Oubone" [A Notice from the Governor of Ubon Province], November 28, 1940.
74. *Bangkok Times,* December 14, 1940.
75. *Pramuan Wan,* October 23, 1940; *Varasab,* October 29, 1940; *Suphab burut,* October 30, 1940.
76. NAT มท. 2.2.9/9.

77. *Bangkok Times,* October 18, 1940.
78. Barmé, *Luang Wichit Wathakan,* p. 168.
79. Pridi even produced a historical drama titled "The King of the White Elephants" as part of his efforts to convince the country that a peaceful solution was best. See Suphaphorn, "Kanriakrong lae kanbokrong dindaen," pp. 53–54.
80. *Thai rashdra,* November 11, 1940.
81. *Bangkok Chronicle,* November 21, 1940.
82. *Nikorn,* January 13, 1941.
83. NAT PO/108.
84. *Nikorn,* April 11, 1941.
85. *Siam rashdra,* October 14, 1940.
86. *Bangkok Times,* October 21, 1940.
87. *Nikorn,* January 9, 1941.
88. *Khaw phab,* October 18, 1940.
89. AOM Indochine/GG/CM 604, no. 1090/2 SRM, November 12, 1940.
90. *Nikorn,* January 4, 1941.
91. *Bangkok Times,* October 5, 1940.
92. *Suphab burut,* October 7, 1940.
93. Suphaphorn, "Kanriakrong lae kanbokrong dindaen," p. 72.
94. *Bangkok Times,* October 9, 1941.
95. Ibid., October 16, 1940.
96. AOM Indochine/GG/CM 1159, note no. 1168289, "Letter from Inspector Georges Nadaud to Chef de Cabinet Militaire de Gouvernor General," November 7, 1940.
97. Direk, *Thailand and World War II,* p. 34.
98. NAT มท. 0201.2.14/4.
99. NAT มท. 2.2.9/14.
100. NAT มท. 2.2.9/17.
101. *Suphab burut,* October 3, 1940.
102. For examples of Catholic priests marching in the Yanawa district procession, see *Bangkok Times,* October 23, 1941. For a record of donations by Chinese merchants, see NAT มท. 2.2.9/12.
103. NAT มท. 2.2.9/6.
104. Barmé, *Luang Wichit Wathakan,* p. 167.
105. *Nikorn,* January 31, 1941.
106. To the great disappointment of Thai diplomats, the settlement did not include the town of Sisophon or the Angkor Wat–Angkor Thom temple complexes, which remained part of French Indochina. The Thai tried again, however, to acquire Preah Vihear (see chapter 6).
107. Kobkua, *Thailand's Durable Premier,* p. 261.
108. *Bangkok Times,* June 10, 1941.
109. NAT ศธ. 0701.48/12. See also *Khaw phab,* October 19, 1940.

110. *Bangkok Chronicle,* June 5, 1941.
111. *Nikorn,* April 2, 1941.
112. *Bangkok Chronicle,* June 23, 1941.
113. Taksin was a noble from Chantaburi Province and a general in the armies of the king of Ayutthaya. After Ayutthaya was destroyed by the Burmese, Taksin organized the remnants of the Siamese forces and established a new Thai capital at Thon Buri. In 1768 he was crowned as the new king of Siam.
114. NAP (National Assembly of Thailand Library, National Assembly Proceedings), *Raingan kanprachum Ratsapha,* May 9, 1941, pp. 118–119.

CHAPTER 3. NATIONAL HUMILIATION AND ANTI-CATHOLICISM

1. NAT มท. 3.1.2.10/6. Bishop Pasotti to Ministry of Interior, August 24, 1942.
2. The issue of sources deserves further treatment here. Admittedly, this chapter relies more heavily on Catholic perspectives than those representing the Thai government. There are a number of reasons for this, the most obvious being that the Thai state understood the postwar liabilities that might result from its actions and therefore took measures to limit documentation. Catholic sources are more readily available and describe the incidents in richer detail. I have included several eyewitness accounts of Catholics faced with various forms of violence and discrimination, and these voices speak with a power that cannot be equaled by any government memo. Bishop Pasotti's letters of appeal also figure prominently in this narrative. While they technically represent a Catholic perspective, they are part of the government record stored within the files of the Ministry of Interior.

    With regard to the Thai government's perspective, I was able to uncover three main groups of documents. These sources come almost exclusively from the archives of the Ministry of Interior, since this department had jurisdiction over religious affairs. The first involves the Ministry of Interior's responses to Bishop Pasotti. These letters are usually denials of Pasotti's requests; for example, a refusal to return Church property or end the government's ban on Catholic meetings. Although the memos do not explain government policy in sufficient detail, they indirectly confirm Pasotti's accusations that confiscations and meeting bans were in force.

    The second group of Interior Ministry documents includes correspondence from the provinces. The ministry's original directives regarding the Catholic Church are not available, but a few letters from provincial governors charged with enforcing that policy are still on file. This correspondence provides important details regarding the ministry's anti-Catholic policies and also indicates that local bureaucrats exerted a great deal of influence over implementation.

The final cache of government memos outlines the reversal of anti-Catholic policies. There are plenty of directives from the Interior Ministry, beginning after July 1944, requesting that local authorities make every effort to restore the prewar status of the Church. Thus, despite the fact that Catholic sources appear more visible in the subsequent narrative, every possible effort has been made to consult all available documentation from both sides and provide (to the extent that this is possible) a balanced interpretation of these events.

3. E. Thadeus Flood, "The 1940 Franco-Thai Border Dispute and Phibun Songkhram's Commitment to Japan," *Journal of Southeast Asian History* 10:2 (September 1969), p. 304.
4. Thamsook Numnonda, *Thailand and the Japanese Presence, 1941–1945* (Singapore: Institute of Southeast Asian Studies, 1977).
5. This fact is confirmed by an interview with former King Prajadhipok, who attested that Thailand's obsession with the *lost territories* was not a product of Japanese influence but that it had been a perpetual concern of the Chakri monarchs. NAT ก.ศ. 1.2/8. *Singapore Free Press* interview, February 26, 1941.
6. Eiji Murashima, "The Commemorative Character of Thai Historiography: The 1942–43 Thai Military Campaign in the Shan States Depicted as a Story of National Salvation and the Restoration of Thai Independence," *Modern Asian Studies,* 40:4 (2006), p. 1093.
7. E. Bruce Reynolds, "Phibun Songkhram and Thai Nationalism in the Fascist Era," *European Journal of East Asian Studies,* 3:1 (2004).
8. Michael Murdock, *Disarming the Allies of Imperialism: The State, Agitation, and Manipulation during China's Nationalist Revolution, 1922–1929* (Ithaca, NY: Cornell East Asia Series, 2006), p. 111.
9. Patrick Tuck, *French Catholic Missionaries and the Politics of Imperialism in Vietnam, 1857–1914: A Documentary Survey* (Liverpool: Liverpool University Press, 1987), p. 228.
10. Pussadee Chandavimol, *Wiatnam nai Mueang Thai* [The Vietnamese in Thailand] (Bangkok: Thailand Research Fund, 1998), p. 254.
11. James Patrick Daughton, *An Empire Divided: Religion, Republicanism, and the Making of French Colonialism, 1880–1914* (Oxford: Oxford University Press, 2006), p. 83.
12. Ibid., p. 256.
13. Ibid., p. 262.
14. Ibid.
15. Ibid., p. 256.
16. Ibid., p. 257.
17. Ibid., p. 263.
18. Ibid., p. 264.
19. Ibid., p. 265.

20. Jules Harmand, French Consul General in Siam, to Charles Le Myre de Villers, Governor of Indochina (Bangkok, March 4, 1882). Cited in Tuck, *French Catholic Missionaries,* p. 232.
21. Monseigneur Vey, Bishop of Geraza, Vicar Apostolic of Siam, to the directors of the Societés des missions étrangeres (Bangkok, September 27, 1881). Cited in Tuck, *French Catholic Missionaries,* p. 231.
22. The 250,000 francs was a portion of the indemnity received from Siam following the Franco-Siamese crisis of 1893. Tuck, *French Catholic Missionaries,* p. 239.
23. NAT มท. 3.1.2.10/6. Memo 1331/2485, September 17, 1942.
24. NAT มท. 3.1.2.10/6. Letter from Joseph Forlazzini to Bishop Pasotti, July 8, 1942.
25. "Khana Luead Thai Phanat Nikhom" [Thai Blood Party of Phanat Nikhom], January 24, 1941, *En Thailande de 1940 á 1945. Documents* (Bangkok: Assumption Cathedral Printing Press, unpublished manuscript).
26. Ibid.
27. "Khana Luead Thai Phrapradaeng" [Thai Blood Party of Phrapradaeng], *En Thailande de 1940 á 1945.*
28. Ibid.
29. Ibid.
30. Ibid.
31. NAT (1) มท. 3.1.2.10/6. Suk Anchanand to Ministry of Interior, July 19, 1942.
32. The official used the phrase, "Khonthai doei thaeching" [A true Thai]. NAT (1) มท. 3.1.2.10/6. Ministry of Interior to the Governor of Nakhon Phanom Province, August 26, 1942.
33. NAT (1) มท. 3.1.2.10/6. Governor of Nakhon Phanom to Ministry of Interior, July 31, 1942, p. 82.
34. NAT (1) มท. 3.1.2.10/6, Ministry of Interior to Isan and other governors, February 13, 1941, p. 207.
35. NAT (1) มท. 3.1.2.10/6, "Sanoe bladkrasuang" [An Offer from the Permanent Secretary], p. 18.
36. NAT (1) มท. 3.1.2.10/6. Letter from Nakhon Phanom provincial office to Ministry of Interior, March 14, 1943, p. 55.
37. NAT (1) มท. 3.1.4.19/10. Bishop Pasotti to Ministry of Interior, September 10, 1944, p. 7.
38. NAT (1) มท. 3.1.2.10/6. Letter from Nakhon Phanom provincial office to Ministry of Interior, March 14, 1943, p. 55.
39. Memo 1517/2486. "Athibidi Krom Tamruad to phukamkabkan lae phubangkhabkong nai Kanchanaburi, Ratchaburi, lae Samut Songkhram" [Message from Police Commissioner to Officials in Kanchanaburi and Samut Songkhram Provinces], October 5, 1943, cited in *En Thailande de 1940 á 1945.*
40. NAT (1) มท. 3.1.4.9/13. Governor of Nong Khai to Ministry of Interior, February 23, 1944.

41. NAT (1) มท. 3.1.2.10/6. "Nang Aw Yim" [Mrs. Aw Yim], January 2, 1941, p. 163.
42. NAT (1) มท. 3.1.2.10/6. Pasotti to Ministry of Interior, July 20, 1942.
43. NAT มท. 3.1.2.10/6. Ministry of Interior to Isan and other governors, February 13, 1941, p. 207.
44. The Vichy government signed the Tokyo Peace Accord in 1941, granting Thailand four border territories. At the conclusion of World War II, the new French government disregarded the treaty and informed Thailand that a state of war would exist between the two governments until the four provinces transferred to Thailand in 1941 were returned to French Indochina.
45. NAT (1) มท. 3.1.2.10/6. Bishop Pasotti to Ministry of Interior, July 20, 1942.
46. NAT (1) มท. 3.1.4.9/7. Governor of Nakhon Phanom to Ministry of Interior, September 4, 1944, p. 12.
47. NAT (1) มท. 3.1.4.9/6. Bishop Pasotti to Ministry of Interior, "Bai samkhan thi baed" [Memo No. 8], October 26, 1942.
48. NAT (1) มท. 3.1.2.10/6. Governor of Nakhon Phanom to Ministry of Interior, July 31, 1942, p. 75.
49. NAT (1) มท. 3.1.4.9/3. Petition from citizens of Tha Rae to Ministry of Interior, August 25, 1942.
50. Robert Gostae, *Prawad kanphoeiphrae Khritasasana nai Siam lae Lao* [A History of Christian Missionary Work in Siam and Laos] (Bangkok: Suemuanchon Catholic Prathedthai, 2006), p. 659.
51. "Temoignage de Monsieur klang kham, catechiste du Diocese d'Ubon (Thailand)" [Testimony of Mr. Klang Kham, Catechist of the Ubon Diocese (Thailand)], *En Thailande de 1940 á 1945*.
52. Ibid.
53. "Vexations contre la mission Catholique," *En Thailande de 1940 á 1945*, p. 145.
54. Ibid. Following the arrest of two priests, soldiers ransacked the church in nearby Lamkhot.
55. Gostae, *Prawad kanphoeiphrae*, p. 659.
56. Ibid., pp. 663–667.
57. Ibid., p. 660.
58. Ibid., p. 663.
59. Archbishop Lawrence Khai to Father Laraque, May 1, 1984, *En Thailande de 1940 á 1945*.
60. NAT (1) มท. 3.1.2.10/6. Pasotti to Ministry of Interior, July 20, 1942.
61. NAT (1) มท. 3.1.4.9/6. Pasotti to Charoenporn, October 26, 1942.
62. NAT (1) มท. 3.1.2.10/6. Nai Blang Thatsanapradit to Ministry of Interior, June 12, 1942, p. 118.
63. Ibid.
64. NAT (1) มท. 3.1.2.10/6. Nai Suphakidwilaekan to Ministry of Interior, August 2, 1943, p. 206.
65. NAT (1) มท. 3.1.2.10/6. R. P. Stocker to Monseigneur Drapier, pp. 229–230.

66. NAT (1) มท. 3.1.2.10/6. Guido Crolla to Nai Wichit, June 29, 1942, p. 200.
67. NAT (1) มท. 3.1.2.10/6. Correspondence from Ministry of Foreign Affairs to Ministry of Interior, June 20, 1942, p. 198.
68. NAT (1) มท. 3.1.2.10/6. Governor of Sakon Nakhon to Ministry of Interior, October 23, 1943, p. 223.
69. NAT (1) มท. 3.1.2.10/6. "Bai banthuk" [A Record of Events], July 21, 1942, p. 124.
70. NAT (1) มท. 3.1.2.10/6. Guido Crolla to Wichit, June 20, 1942, p. 123.
71. NAT (1) มท. 3.1.2.10/6. Thai Ambassador to Italy writing to Thailand's Foreign Affairs Office, September 10, 1942, p. 22. This memo reflects Thai concerns as to the level of independence Japan would grant Thailand once the Axis powers were victorious.
72. NAT (1) มท. 3.1.2.10/6. Bishop Pasotti to Ministry of Interior—"Bai samkhan thi hok" [Memo No. 6], July 20, 1942.
73. NAT (1) มท. 3.1.4.9/6. Bishop Pasotti to Charoenphorn Phana, October 26, 1942, p. 3.
74. Ibid.
75. *Bangkok Times,* October 20, 1940.
76. "Khamboklaw khong Nai Sanan Diawsiri" [The Testimony of Nai Sanan Diawsiri], *En Thailande de 1940 á 1945.*
77. "Khamboklaw khong Nai Thongma Phonprasoedmak" [The Testimony of Nai Thongma Phonprasoedmak], *En Thailande de 1940 á 1945.*
78. "Khamboklaw khong Nai Sanan Diawsiri" [The Testimony of Nai Sanan Diawsiri], *En Thailande de 1940 á 1945.*
79. Ibid. *Ka fak* is a fungus that destroys mango trees.
80. "Khamboklaw khong Nai Sanan Diawsiri" [The Testimony of Nai Sanan Diawsiri], *En Thailande de 1940 á 1945.*
81. "Khamboklaw khong Nang Sawnklin Phonprasoedmak" [The Testimony of Mrs. Sawnklin Phonprasoedmak], *En Thailand de 1940 á 1945. Documents.*
82. Ibid.
83. "Khamboklaw khong Nai Thongma Phonprasoedmak."
84. "Khian thi ban Tha Kwian amphoe Phanom Sarakham" [An Account Written at Tha Kwian Village in Phanoam Sarakham District], *En Thailande de 1940 á 1945.*
85. "Raingan hedkan thi thuk thamrai" [A Report of the Assault], *En Thailande de 1940 á 1945.*
86. Ibid.
87. "Khamboklaw khong Nai Thongma Phonprasoedmak."
88. Ibid.
89. NAT (1) มท. 3.1.4.5/19. Letter from Governor of Chachoengsao to Ministry of Interior, December 14, 1944.
90. Phibun's fall marked the ascendancy of Pridi Banamyong as the most powerful figure in Thai politics. Although he was very pro-Western and tried to restore

democracy to Thailand, Pridi was no friend of French imperialism, as evidenced by his secret support of the Viet Minh. See Christopher E. Goscha, *Thailand and the Southeast Asian Networks of the Vietnamese Revolution: 1885–1954* (Richmond, Surrey: RoutledgeCurzon, 1999).

91. NAT (1) มท. 3.1.4.9/7. Secretary of Interior Ministry to Bishop Pasotti, August 22, 1944, p. 20.
92. NAT (1) มท. 3.1.4.9/17. Pasotti to Governor of Loei Province, January 2, 1945.
93. NAT (1) มท. 3.1.4.9/7. Governor of Nakhon Phanom to district officials and police, November 14, 1944, p. 19.
94. NAT (1) มท. 3.1.4.9/9. Nai Roen Trisathan to Governor of Phitsanulok, September 16, 1944.
95. NAT (1) มท. 3.1.4.9/18. Pasotti to Ministry of Interior, December 10, 1944.
96. In 1944, the Thai government replaced the system of Islamic family courts and judges (which had functioned in Pattani since the region's annexation by Bangkok in 1902) with Thai civic law. Thanet Aphornsuwan argues that this was part of the state's larger program to convert Muslims into Buddhists. See Thanet Aphornsuvan, "Malay Muslim 'Separatism' in Southern Thailand," in Michael Montesano and Patrick Jory (eds.), *Thai North and Malay South: Ethnic Interactions on a Plural Peninsula* (Singapore: NUS Press, 2008), p. 107.
97. Government communications clearly distinguish between Catholics (Khristang) and Protestants (Khristian). Catholics were also referred to as "Roman Catholics" or "those who worship the Catholic religion." During reeducation meetings, local officials sometimes derided Catholicism as a "European religion" or a "religion for *farangs*." The Thai Blood propaganda went even further, denouncing Catholicism as "the religion of our enemies," meaning the French. The important thing to remember is that Thais understood Christian sects are not all the same.
98. NAT (1) มท. 3.1.2.10/6. Ministry of Foreign Affairs to Ministry of Interior, September 30, 1942, p. 20.

CHAPTER 4. THAILAND AND PAN-ASIANISM

1. Regarding Thailand's ideological commitment at the beginning of the war, Thamsook commented that the Thai government was neither pro-Western nor pro-Japanese, but pro-Thai. I would suggest that the prime minister was "pro-Phibun" more than anything, and in January 1942 his survival required that he explain how Thailand and Japan's interests were temporarily aligned.
2. E. Thadeus Flood, "Japan's Relations with Thailand: 1928–1941" (Ph.D. diss., University of Washington, 1967).
3. Thamsook Numnonda, *Thailand and the Japanese Presence, 1941–1945* (Singapore: Institute of Southeast Asian Studies, 1977), p. 30.

4. NAT มท. 2.2.6/3. "Kanprachum hai samphad rawang than akharathud Yipun pracam Prathedthai kab phuthaen nangsuephim Thai" [Meeting between the Japanese Ambassador to Thailand and Thai Newspaper Reporters], April 3, 1942. The ambassador warned reporters of writing stories about four sensitive issues: (1) the question of Thai independence under Japanese occupation; (2) Japanese citizens abusing their influence for personal gain; (3) abuses of power by Japanese soldiers; and (4) concerns about the state of the Thai economy.
5. Foreign Minister Direk Jayanama observed that Phibun's popularity from 1940 to 1942 made it almost impossible to oppose him. See Thamsook, *Thailand and the Japanese Presence,* p. 17.
6. Ibid., p. 44.
7. NAT สบ. 9.2.3/5. "Nayok Rathamontri wa cha mai thing prachachon nai yam thi kamlang dai thuk" [Prime Minister States He Will Not Abandon Nation in Its Hour of Need], December 11, 1941.
8. *Nikorn,* May 23, 1941.
9. Ibid., May 24, 1941.
10. NAT สบ. 9.2.7. "Khwampenma haeng songkhram Pacific" [The Origins of the Pacific War], *Santi rasadorn,* January 6, 1942.
11. *Sri krung,* December 16, 1941.
12. For examples of pre-1932 perceptions of Japan, see Mathew Copeland, "Contested Nationalism and the 1932 Overthrow of the Absolute Monarchy in Siam" (Ph.D. diss., Australian National University, 1993), p. 64.
13. NAT ศธ. 0701.28/27. "Thai Peace Brings New Foreign Issue," *Japan Times and Advertiser,* March 14, 1941.
14. Benjamin A. Batson and Shimizu Hajime, *The Tragedy of Wanit: A Japanese Account of Wartime Thai Politics* (Singapore: Institute of Southeast Asian Studies, 1977), p. 31.
15. NAT มท. 2.2.10/6. "The Kingdom of Thailand's Declaration of War on Great Britain and the United States," January 25, 1942. It is curious that, in this official document, the accusation is leveled at the United States and not Britain, as the former had no involvement in the region at the time. The same could be said of Japan.
16. *Nikorn,* February 21, 1942. The title of the article was "Cheb laew tong cham" [The Pain Helps Us Remember].
17. NAT ส.บ. 9.2.1/5. *Khaw reo,* January 1, 1942.
18. NAT ส.ธ. 0201.33/58. "Kham Nakhon sonthana khong Khana Ku Isaraphab India" [Broadcast of the Free India Party], August 17, 1942.
19. *Pramuan hedkan nai yuk mai khong Thai bodsonthana rawang Nai Man Chuchat kab Nai Khong Rak Thai tae 8 Thanwakhom 2484 thueng 28 Kumphaphan 2485* [Proceedings of the New Thai Era: The Conversations between Mr. Man Chuchat and Mr. Khong Rak Thai, December 8, 1941 to February 28, 1942], Samud thiraluek Nai Kanchapanakid sop nai hoksui sabsun nai Wat Traimit

Withayaram [cremation volume of Mr. Kanchapanakid], June 29, 1942. See transcripts from December 24, 1941, and January 23, 1942.

20. Ibid., December 31, 1941.
21. Ibid., January 7, 1942.
22. Ibid., December 22, 1942.
23. Ibid. For a more detailed account of these events, known as the Mergui Massacre, see Dirk Van Der Cruysse, *Siam and the West: 1500–1700* (Bangkok: Silkworm Books, 1999), pp. 412–414.
24. *Pramuan hedkan nai yuk mai khong Thai*, December 13, 1941.
25. Ibid., January 2, 1942. For a more complete assessment of the tributary relationship between Bangkok, Kedah, Penang, and the British, see Thongchai Winichakul, *Siam Mapped: A History of the Geo-Body of a Nation* (Honolulu: University of Hawai'i Press, 1994), pp. 86–94.
26. *Pramuan hedkan nai yuk mai khong Thai.* See broadcast transcripts from January 3, 1942, January 7, 1942, and January 8, 1942.
27. Ibid., January 7, 1942.
28. NAT มท. 0201.2.1.14/1. "Kanphim phaenthi sadaeng railaiad kansia dindaen" [Printing of Maps to Explain Our Loss of Territory], 5291/2483. Prime Minister to Department of Interior, December 30, 1940.
29. This explanation was offered to me by a museum curator at the National Memorial in Bangkok when I asked why a large irredentist map display did not include concessions to Britain.
30. Suphaphorn Bumrungwong, "Kanriakrong lae kanbokrong dindaen thi khuen cak Farangsed 2483–2491" [Requesting and Governing the Territories Returned from France, 1940–1948] (Ph.D. diss., Chulalongkorn University, 2003), p. 66.
31. Kullada Kesboonchoo Mead, *The Rise and Decline of Thai Absolutism* (London: Routledge, 2009), p. 31.
32. *Pramuan hedkan nai yuk mai khong Thai*, January 4, 1942.
33. Luang Nathabanja, *Extra-territoriality in Siam* (Bangkok: Bangkok Daily Mail, 1924), p. 5.
34. Patrick Tuck, *The French Wolf and the Siamese Lamb: The French Threat to Siamese Independence, 1858–1907* (Bangkok: White Lotus Press, 1995), p. 121.
35. *Yomiuri Shimbun,* quoted in the *Bangkok Times,* May 31, 1941.
36. *Pramuan hedkan nai yuk mai khong Thai*, January 13, 1942.
37. *Nikorn,* July 11, 1942.
38. Ibid. The article neglects to mention how Japan also demanded extraterritorial privileges for its own citizens in Thailand.
39. *Japan Times and Advertiser,* March 12, 1941.
40. The United States responded to Thai aggression in Indochina by refusing delivery of warplanes, for which the Thai military had already paid.
41. The Thai public was disappointed in the Japanese mediation because they had been misled by propaganda to believe that the Thai army could have taken

much more territory (including Angkor Wat and the city of Siem Reap) if the border war had continued a few more weeks. See E. Bruce Reynolds, *Thailand and Japan's Southern Advance, 1940–1945* (New York: Palgrave MacMillan, 1994), pp. 49–51.

42. NAT ศธ. 0701.28.27. "Thai Regards Nippon as True Friend: States Bangkok Minister in Interview."
43. Ibid.
44. Ibid.
45. *Pramuan hedkan nai yuk mai khong Thai*, December 14, 1941.
46. Reynolds, *Thailand and Japan's Southern Advance*, p. 154.
47. NAT มท. 2.2.6/10. "Chomphon Phibun Songkhram Nayok Rathamontri Prathedthai klaw kae thahan Yipun nai okad wan khuen pi mai" [Prime Minister Phibun Songkhram Gives New Year's Address to Japanese Troops], January 1, 1942.
48. NAT มท. 2.2.6/3. "Kanprachum hai samphad rawang than akharathud Yipun pracam Prathedthai kab phuthaen nangsuephim Thai" [Japanese Ambassador to Thailand Gives Interview to Thai Media), April 3, 1942.
49. Robert S. Ward, *Asia for the Asiatics: The Techniques of Japanese Occupation* (Chicago: University of Chicago Press, 1945), p. 189.
50. Okawa Shumei, "The Establishment of the Greater East Asian Order," in Joyce C. Lebra (ed.), *Japan's Greater East Asia Co-Prosperity Sphere in World War II* (Kuala Lumpur: Oxford University Press, 1975), pp. 39–40.
51. Martin W. Lewis and Kären E. Wigen, *The Myth of Continents: A Critique of Metageography* (Berkeley: University of California Press, 1997).
52. E. Bruce Reynolds, "The Indian Community and the Indian Independence Movement in Thailand during World War II," in Paul H. Kratoska (ed.), *Southeast Asian Minorities in the Wartime Japanese Empire* (London: RoutledgeCurzon, 2002), p. 172.
53. *Sunsap khongphon than Chomphon Phibun Songkhram Nayok Rathamontri haeng Prathedthai tob sunsap khongphon than Nai Phonek Tojo Nayok Rathamonti haeng prathed Yipun thang withayu kracai siang* [A Radio Address from Prime Minister Phibun Songkhram of Thailand and Prime Minister Tojo of Japan] (Bangkok: Krom Khosanakan, December 23, 1941).
54. *Pramuan hedkan nai yuk mai khong Thai*, February 14, 1942.
55. Ibid., February 11, 1942.
56. Ibid., December 16, 1941.
57. Ibid., December 20, 1941.
58. Ibid., January 17, 1941.
59. *Japan Times and Advertiser*, March 14, 1941.
60. Ibid., March 12, 1941.
61. *Pramuan hedkan nai yuk mai khong Thai*, February 14, 1942.
62. Ibid., December 18, 1941.

63. NAT มท. 2.2.6/3. "Kanprachum hai samphad rawang than akharathud Yipun pracam Prathedthai kab phuthaen nangsuephim Thai" [Press Conference of Thai Reporters with the Japanese Ambassador to Thailand], April 3, 1942.
64. Eiji Murashima, "The Thai-Japanese Alliance and the Chinese of Thailand," in Kratoska, *Southeast Asian Minorities,* p. 197.
65. *Pramuan hedkan nai yuk mai khong Thai,* January 7, 1942.
66. NAT สบ. 9.2.3/4. "Kamakan Samakhom Chin khawphob than Nayok" [Chinese Commerce Group Meets with Prime Minister], *Prachamit,* December 28, 1941. Also see Eiji Murashima, "Opposing French Colonialism: Thailand and the Independence Movements in Indochina in the Early 1940s," *Southeast Asia Research* 13:3 (2005), and Reynolds, "The Indian Community and the Indian Independence Movement."
67. NAT FO/12/4059.
68. Support for Lao Issara and the Viet Minh will be discussed in the next chapter. See also Christopher E. Goscha, *Thailand and the Southeast Asian Networks of the Vietnamese Revolution: 1885–1954* (Richmond, Surrey: RoutledgeCurzon, 1999).
69. Reynolds, "The Indian Community and the Indian Independence Movement," p. 183.
70. NAT สร. 0201.33/58. "Sonthana phak India," p. 5.
71. Reynolds, "The Indian Community and the Indian Independence Movement," p. 176.
72. NAT สร. 0201.33/58. "Khamplae sonthana khong Khana Ku Issaraphab India" [Translation of the Free India Broadcast], p. 3.
73. Ibid., p. 6.
74. Ibid., p. 12.
75. Ibid., p. 13.
76. Ibid., p. 29.
77. Ibid., p. 34.
78. Ibid., p. 15.
79. *Pramuan hedkan nai yuk mai khong Thai,* January 12, 1942.
80. Reynolds, "The Indian Community and Indian Independence Movement," p. 174.
81. Kesar Singh Giani, *Indian Independence Movement in East Asia: The Most Authentic Account of the I.N.A. and the Azad Hind Government* (Lahore: Singh Bros., 1947), pp. 61–62.
82. Eiji Murashima, "The Thai-Japanese Alliance and the Chinese of Thailand," p. 202.
83. Ibid.
84. NAT PO/38. J. Crosby to Lord Halifax, "French Report on Japanese-Siamese Plan for Joint Attack on British Burma and French Indochina," October 17, 1939.

85. Mary P. Callahan, *Making Enemies: War and State Building in Burma* (Ithaca, NY: Cornell University Press, 2003), pp. 52–53.
86. *Pramuan hedkan nai yuk mai khong Thai*, February 2, 1942.
87. Ibid.
88. NAT สบ. 9.2.3/5. "Nayok Rathamontri wa cha mai thing prachachon nai yam thi kamlang dai thuk," December 10, 1941.
89. Ibid., January 21, 1942.
90. NAT มท 2.2.10/5. "Sunsap khong Nayok Rathamontri klaw kae prachachon chaw Thai thang withayu kracai siang muea wan thi 27 November 1941" [Prime Minister Gives Radio Address to Thai People, November 27, 1941].
91. *Pramuan hedkan nai yuk mai khong Thai*, January 22, 1942.
92. The Thai military was so eager to possess the Shan states that, according to E. Bruce Reynolds, it accepted the humiliating conditions placed on it by Japanese forces. See Reynolds, *Thailand and Japan's Southern Advance,* p. 116. See also Murashima, "The Commemorative Character of Thai Historiography: The 1942–43 Thai Military Campaign in the Shan States Depicted as a Story of National Salvation and the Restoration of Thai Independence," *Modern Asian Studies* 40:4 (2006), p. 1067. Tenasserim Province had once belonged to Ayutthaya before becoming a possession of the British East India trading company.
93. Murashima, "The Commemorative Character of Thai Historiography," p. 1085.
94. Ibid., p. 1074.
95. *Nikorn,* June 17, 1942.
96. Ibid. The article also contains descriptions of the natural resources surrounding Keng Tung and how they would benefit Thailand.
97. *Nikorn,* June 24, 1942.
98. Kukrit Pramoj, *Four Reigns* (Chiang Mai: Silkworm Books, 2005), p. 583.
99. E. Bruce Reynolds, "Phibun Songkhram and Thai Nationalism in the Fascist Era," *European Journal of East Asian Studies* 3:1 (2004), p. 133.
100. *Pramuan hedkan nai yuk mai khong Thai*, February 6, 1942.
101. Phibun and Wichit did not address the apparent contradiction in claiming that Thailand was on the verge of complete independence when the country still hosted thousands of Japanese troops.

CHAPTER 5. 1946: POSTWAR RECONCILIATION AND THE LOSS REIMAGINED

1. Thamsook Numnonda, *Thailand and the Japanese Presence, 1941–1945* (Singapore: Institute of Southeast Asian Studies, 1977), p. vi.
2. E. Bruce Reynolds, "Phibun Songkhram and Thai Nationalism in the Fascist Era," *European Journal of Asian Studies* 3:1 (2004).
3. *Nakorn sarn,* November 21, 1946.

4. Siam was the name of the country from 1946 to 1948, when Phibun changed it back to Thailand. In accordance, this chapter will use the name "Siam" when discussing the immediate postwar era.
5. Songsri Foran, "Thai-British Relations during World War II and the Immediate Postwar Period, 1940–1946" (Paper No. 10, Thai Khadi Research Institute, Thammasat University, 1981), p. 154.
6. NAT US/1. "General Report on Conditions in Thailand," American Legation, Bangkok, Thailand, August 18, 1942.
7. Ibid.
8. Larry A. Niksch, "United States Foreign Policy in Thailand's World War II Peace Settlement with Britain and France" (Ph.D. diss., Georgetown University, 1976), p. 53.
9. NAT (2) สร. 0201.18.2/4. *Samnakngan Khosanakan khad lae tad khaw* [Ministry of Public Relations and Information].
10. *New York Times,* August 21, 1945.
11. NAT (2) สร. 0201.18.2/4. This quote is from the article, "Siam Was U.S. Friend Not Foe," featured in the *New Yorker* magazine.
12. *New York Times,* August 21, 1945.
13. Ibid., August 29, 1945.
14. NAT US/4. "Phibun Songkhram Circular Letter Addressed to Editors of Various Newspapers" (Translation), 1945.
15. Songsri, "Thai-British Relations during World War II," p. 171.
16. Ibid., pp. 213–214.
17. Ibid., p. 277.
18. *Sri krung,* September 3, 1946.
19. Songsri, "Thai-British Relations during World War II," p. 281.
20. Sodsai Khantiwiraphongse, "Prathedthai kab panha Indochin khong Farangsed" [Thailand and the Problem of French Indochina] (MA thesis, Chulalongkorn University, 1977), p. 301.
21. Ibid., p. 297.
22. Many American officials, including Kenneth Landon, sympathized with the claim that the people of the border provinces were ethnic Thai. See Niksch, "United States Foreign Policy," p. 161.
23. Songsri, "Thai-British Relations during World War II," p. 239.
24. *Bangkok Post,* October 16, 1946.
25. *Nakorn sarn,* October 14, 1946.
26. Ibid., p. 143.
27. Niksch, "United States Foreign Policy," p. 153.
28. Sodsai, "Prathedthai kab panha Indochin khong Farangsed," p. 333.
29. Niksch, "United States Foreign Policy," pp. 238–239.
30. *New York Times,* June 2, 1946.
31. Niksch, "United States Foreign Policy," p. 209.

32. Christopher E. Goscha, *Thailand and the Southeast Asian Networks of the Vietnamese Revolution: 1885–1954* (Richmond, Surrey: RoutledgeCurzon, 1999), p. 124.
33. Ibid., pp. 122–123.
34. Ibid., p. 194.
35. Niksch, "United States Foreign Policy," p. 179.
36. NAT (2) ก.ต. 1.1.8/157. "Khaw kiawkab Lao Issara" [Report on the Lao Issara], August 6, 1946. This same group held political meetings in a local movie theater in order to recruit young men to join the Lao Issara. Ministry of Interior memos condoned these activities but stressed that they should be done in a more secretive manner to avoid problems with France.
37. Ibid., p. 189.
38. Ibid., p. 166.
39. NAT (2) ก.ต. 7.1.8/124. "Hedkan thi koed khuen chaidaen Indochin" [Thai-French Indochina Border Events], March 18, 1946.
40. NAT (2) ก.ต. 7.1.8/127. "Kanluang khaw khong nangsuephim Thai kiawkab kankratham khong rathaban Wiatmin" [Thai Newspaper Coverage of the Government of Vietnam], December 20, 1945.
41. Goscha, *Thailand and the Southeast Asian Networks,* p. 122.
42. NAT (2) ก.ต. 7.1.8/132. "Siam-French Indochina Border Incidents," p. 17.
43. The bombardment of Nakorn Phanom was especially galling, since Thais viewed France's bombing of this city in late November 1940 as the beginning of border hostilities between Thailand and French Indochina.
44. NAT ส.ป. 9.2.1/2. *Seri,* May 21, 1946.
45. NAT ส.ป. 9.2.1/2. *Thamthada,* June 1, 1946.
46. Sodsai, "Prathedthai kab panha Indochin khong Farangsed," p. 329.
47. Goscha, *Thailand and the Southeast Asian Networks,* p. 165.
48. *New York Times,* August 27, 1946.
49. NAT (1) ม.ท. 3.1.2.10/190. "Kho boed phromdaen kancharachan thang nam Maenam Khong" [Request to Reopen Commerce across the Mekong River]. See also *Bangkok Times,* August 14, 1946.
50. *Tawan,* October 17, 1946.
51. Direk Jayanama, *Thailand and World War II* (Chiang Mai: Silkworm Books, 2008), pp. 283–284.
52. NAT สบ. 9.2.1/2. "Tadsin anakhod si changwad nai wanni" [Future of the Four Provinces to Be Decided Today], *Phim Thai,* October 15, 1946.
53. NAP (National Assembly of Thailand Library, National Assembly Proceedings), *Raingan kanprachum Ratsapha,* October 14, 1946, p. 201.
54. In one of his many speeches before the assembly, Foreign Minister Direk Jayanama revealed that once Thailand had suggested the possibility of the United Nations ordering it to return the four provinces when signing the peace agreement with the Allies. See NAP, *Raingan kanprachum Ratsapha,* p. 241.

55. Ibid., p. 232. Also see the comments of Thon Buri representative Saw Sethabut on the principles of self-determination in the Atlantic Charter, p. 309.
56. For example, Dusit Buntham suggested that perhaps Siam should simply do nothing and wait for France's response. Thamnun Thianngen argued that waiting for France to invade Siam would at least get the United Nations involved in the dispute. NAP, *Raingan kanprachum Ratsapha,* pp. 276–281.
57. Niksch, "United States Foreign Policy," p. 225.
58. NAP, *Raingan kanprachum Ratsapha,* October 15, 1946, p. 278.
59. *Democracy,* October 19, 1946.
60. *Nakorn sarn,* October 19, 1946.
61. *Thai rashdra,* October 19, 1946.
62. *Democracy,* October 20, 1946.
63. *Democracy,* December 11, 1946.
64. *Naew na,* October 19, 1946.
65. *Tawan,* October 21, 1946.
66. *Phim Thai,* October 26, 1946. See also *Nakorn sarn,* October 31, 1946.
67. *Bangkok rai wan,* October 21, 1946. This sentiment would be repeated, almost verbatim, after the loss of Preah Vihear in 1962.
68. *Siam nikorn,* August 14, 1946.
69. *Sri krung,* October 22, 1946.
70. *Siam nikorn,* October 21, 1946.
71. *Democracy,* October 23, 1946.
72. Ibid.
73. *Siam nikorn,* October 22, 1946.
74. *Democracy,* October 16, 1946.
75. *Nakorn sarn,* September 2, 1946. See also *Bangkok Post,* October 16, 1946.
76. *Prachakorn,* September 23, 1946.
77. *Bangkok Post,* September 6, 1946.
78. *Suwannaphum,* November 19, 1946.
79. *Nakorn sarn,* November 22, 1946.
80. *Democracy,* October 18, 1946.
81. Suphaphorn Bumrungwong, "Kanriakrong lae kanbokrong dindaen thi khuen cak Farangsed 2483–2491" [Requesting and Governing the Territories Returned from France, 1940–1948] (Ph.D. diss., Chulalongkorn University, 2003), p. 204.
82. Ibid., p. 206.
83. The government printed 500 copies in Thai and 100 copies in both English and French.
84. *Bangkok Post,* August 12, 1947.
85. Ibid., September 1, 1947.
86. Suphaphorn, "Kanriakrong lae kanbokrong dindaen thi khuen cak Farangsed," p. 206.

87. Krom Khosanakan, *Raingan kansangsueng prathan kamakan kan chad sang anusawari Chai Samoraphum an sanoe phana than Nayok Rathamontri nueang nai rathaphiti boed anusawari nai wanchad* [A report from the president of the Victory Monument construction task force presented to the prime minister at the Victory Monument dedication ceremony on National Day] (Bangkok: Krom Khosanakan, June 24, 1942).
88. Ka Fai Wong, "Visions of a Nation: Public Monuments in Twentieth Century Thailand" (MA thesis, Chulalongkorn University, 2000), p. 83.
89. Krom Khosanakan, *Sunsap khong phana than Nayok Rathamontri nai kanboed anusawari Chai Samoraphum* [The prime minister's speech at the Victory Monument dedication ceremony] (Bangkok: Krom Khosanakan, June 25, 1942).
90. Ibid.
91. A Siamese expeditionary force did participate in World War I, but it served only in a secondary capacity. See Walter F. Vella, *Chaiyo! King Vijiravudh and the Development of Thai Nationalism* (Honolulu: University of Hawai'i Press, 1978).
92. Apinan Poshyananda, *Modern Art in Thailand: Nineteenth and Twentieth Centuries.* (Singapore: Oxford University Press, 1992), p. 46.
93. E. Bruce Reynolds, "The Indian Community and the Indian Independence Movement in Thailand During World War II," in Paul H. Kratoska (ed.), *Southeast Asian Minorities in the Wartime Japanese Empire* (London: RoutledgeCurzon, 2002).
94. *Bangkok Post,* August 14, 1947.
95. This information comes from a biographical sketch of Prayoon Chanyawongse by the Ramon Magsaysay foundation when Prayoon won the award for journalism in 1971.
96. *Democracy,* October 16, 1946.

CHAPTER 6. PREAH VIHEAR: A THAI SYMBOL OF NATIONAL HUMILIATION

1. *Nation,* July 10, 2008.
2. Chamrat Duangthisan, *Khwammueang rueang Khaw Phrawihan* [The Politics of Preah Vihear] (Bangkok: Sadsawan Press, 1962), p. 151. Thai journalists were asking the same question in 2011. One columnist recently wrote, "I'm not a pacifist. There are reasons to fight. But 4.6 square kilometres of dirt is not one of them." See Voranai Vanijaka, "The Plague of Fanaticism," *Bangkok Post,* February 6, 2011.
3. Charnvit Kasetsiri, "Thailand-Cambodia: A Love-Hate Relationship," *Kyoto Review of Southeast Asia* 3 (March 2003).

4. Volker Grabowsky (ed.), "The Preah Vihear Conflict and the Current Political Debate in Thailand," *Informal Northern Thai Group Bulletin* 2, September 2011, p. 4.
5. John Tully, *France on the Mekong: A History of the Protectorate in Cambodia, 1863–1953* (Lanham, MD: University Press of America, 2002), p. 428.
6. Charnvit Kasetsiri argues that the monarchy viewed France's annexation of the eastern territories as an acceptable price for maintaining independence. See Charnvit Kasetsiri, *Prasart Khaw Phra Viharn: Lum dam latthi chart-niyom prawattisart phlae kao prawattisart tat ton kap ban-mueang khong raw* [Preah Vihear: A Black Hole-Nationalism Wounded History and Our Country: Siam-Thailand] (Bangkok: Foundation for the Promotion of Social Sciences and Humanities Textbooks Project, 2008).
7. Luang Wichit Wathakan, *Thailand's Case* (Bangkok: Department of Publicity, 1941), pp. 35–37. If the boundary had followed the watershed without deviation, Preah Vihear would have been located on the Thai side.
8. P. Cuasay, "Borders on the Fantastic: Mimesis, Violence, and Landscape at the Temple of Preah Vihear," *Modern Asian Studies* 32:4 (1998), p. 855. Among them was a map known as Annex I, later used by Cambodia to claim sovereignty over Preah Vihear.
9. Thongchai Winichakul, *Siam Mapped: A History of the Geo-Body of a Nation* (Honolulu: University of Hawai'i Press, 1994), p. 113.
10. International Court of Justice (ICJ), "Case Concerning the Temple of Preah Vihear (Cambodia v. Thailand)," in *Pleadings, Oral Arguments, Documents,* vols. 1–2 (The Hague, Netherlands, 1964), p. 215.
11. Manich Jumsai, *History of Thailand and Cambodia: From the Days of Angkor to the Present* (Bangkok: Chaloemnit Press, 1987), p. 214.
12. NAT PO/8. British Legation, Bangkok, "Siam Frontier Incident," March 3, 1930.
13. ICJ, "Case Concerning the Temple of Preah Vihear," pp. 89–91.
14. Pussadee Chandavimol, *Wiatnam nai Mueang Thai* [The Vietnamese in Thailand] (Bangkok: Thailand Research Fund, 1998), p. 262.
15. Cuasay, "Borders on the Fantastic," p. 852.
16. NAT PO/8. British Legation, Bangkok, "Siam-Indochina Frontier Incident," March 3, 1930.
17. ICJ, "Case Concerning the Temple of Preah Vihear—Merits," Judgment of June 15, 1962.
18. Cuasay, "Borders on the Fantastic," p. 869.
19. Manich, *History of Thailand and Cambodia,* p. 214.
20. *Nikorn,* March 28, 1941.
21. Ibid., May 28, 1941.
22. Ibid.

23. Maurizio Peleggi, *The Politics of Ruins and the Business of Nostalgia* (Bangkok: White Lotus Press, 2002), p. 39.
24. Ibid.
25. L. P. Singh, "The Thai-Cambodian Temple Dispute," *Asian Survey* 2:8 (October 1962), pp. 23–26. Volker Grabowsky argued that the Thai never withdrew their troops in the aftermath of the 1946 treaty with France. See Grabowsky, "The Preah Vihear Conflict," p. 7.
26. Chamrat Duangthisan, *Khwammueang rueang Khaw*, pp. 129–131.
27. Ibid., pp. 96–98.
28. Sam Sari, *La Cambodge aujourd'hui* (Phnom Penh: Department of Publicity, 1958).
29. *La Dépêche du Cambodge,* June 19, 1958.
30. Chamrat, *Khwammueang rueang Khaw Phrawihan,* p. 115.
31. Sam Sari, *La Cambodge aujourd'hui.*
32. Chamrat, *Khwammueang rueang Khaw Phrawihan,* p. 187.
33. Historians of Thailand often celebrate the country's unique diplomatic ability to protect its own interests by playing the great powers against each other. This strategy obviously did not apply during the Cold War, when military rulers committed Thailand to following U.S. foreign policy. Instead, it was Cambodia that used this tactic to extract maximum concessions from both sides.
34. Chamrat, *Khwammueang rueang Khaw Phrawihan,* p. 157.
35. Ibid., p. 141.
36. *Sarn seri,* June 20, 1962. See also *Siam nikorn,* October 16, 1959.
37. Ibid.
38. *Sarn seri,* October 19, 1959.
39. Ibid., October 11, 1959.
40. Ibid.
41. *Chaw Thai,* October 23, 1959.
42. *Siam nikorn,* October 26, 1959.
43. *Chaw Thai,* October 25, 1959.
44. *Siam nikorn,* October 16, 1959.
45. *Chaw Thai,* October 27, 1959.
46. We should note that France had already used this argument to nullify the 1941 Tokyo Peace Accord.
47. *Sarn seri,* October 25, 1959.
48. Ibid., October 11, 1959.
49. Ibid., November 12, 1959.
50. Ibid.
51. Scott Barmé, *Luang Wichit Wathakan and the Creation of a Thai Identity* (Singapore: Institute of Southeast Asian Studies, 1993), pp. 125–126.
52. *Siam nikorn,* October 29, 1959.

53. This individual is not identified in *Sarn seri's* original story (April 5, 1961), but a later column in *Siam rat* (May 26, 1970) claimed it was Suthi Puwaphan, former representative of Surin Province.
54. *Sarn seri,* May 5, 1961.
55. Ibid.
56. *Siam rat,* October 17, 1959.
57. Krom Khosanakan, *Thai samai sang chat* [Thailand in a Time of Nation-Building] (Bangkok, 1941). The Cambodian legal team used this publication as evidence that the 1946 treaty restored Preah Vihear to the control of French Indochina.
58. *Phim Thai,* October 25, 1959.
59. Ibid.
60. *Sarn seri,* October 31, 1959.
61. Ibid., November 5, 1959.
62. *Thai,* November 3, 1959.
63. *Sarn seri,* November 21, 1959. For more information on the Thai Blood Party and its activities during the 1940 irredentist campaign, see Shane Strate, "An Uncivil State of Affairs: Fascism and Anti-Catholicism in Thailand, 1940–1944," *Journal of Southeast Asian Studies* 42:1 (2011), pp. 59–87.
64. *Siam nikorn,* November 5, 1959.
65. *Sarn seri,* November 18, 1959.
66. Ibid., November 20, 1959.
67. Ibid., October 26, 1959.
68. Ibid., November 5, 1959.
69. *Phim Thai,* October 31, 1959.
70. *Phim Thai,* October 30, 1959. The students collected 112 baht because the Franco-Siamese crisis occurred in the 112th year of the Chakri dynasty, or RS 112.
71. *Sarn seri,* November 11, 1959.
72. *Phim Thai,* October 11, 1959.
73. *Siam rat,* October 9, 1959.
74. *Sarn seri,* October 9, 1959.
75. *Siam rat,* October 11, 1959.
76. Thongchai Winichakul, "Trying to Locate Southeast Asia from Its Navel," in Paul Kratoska, Remco Raben, and Henk Schulte Nordholt (eds.), *Locating Southeast Asia: Geographies of Knowledge and Politics of Space* (Singapore: Singapore University Press, 2005), p. 120.
77. Tully, *France on the Mekong,* p. 17. According to Tully, Thai historians neglect to mention that Norodom had been held as a prisoner in Bangkok until 1858 to help ensure that his father, Ang Duong, complied with the wishes of the Siamese monarchy.
78. Charnvit Kasetsiri, "Thailand-Cambodia: A Love-Hate Relationship."

79. John P. Armstrong, *Sihanouk Speaks* (New York: Walker and Company, 1964), p. 70.
80. Kukrit Pramoj, radio address from March 10, 1962. Transcript in Chamrat, *Khwammueang rueang Khaw Phrawihan,* p. 625.
81. *Sarn seri,* December 1, 1959.
82. Ibid., October 20, 1959.
83. Manich, *History of Thailand and Cambodia,* p. 202.
84. Singh, "The Thai-Cambodian Temple Dispute," p. 24.
85. *Sarn seri,* June 17, 1962.
86. *Phim Thai,* July 19, 1962.
87. Ibid.
88. *Thai,* June 20, 1962.
89. *Bangkok Post,* June 22, 1962.
90. David Chandler recalled riding in a taxi in Bangkok months after the ruling on Preah Vihear. When he mentioned that he had just come from Cambodia, the taxi driver responded in his broken English, "The Black Prince—I want to kill him!" Personal e-mail correspondence with David P. Chandler, December 17, 2009.
91. *Thai,* June 20, 1962. Another poster contained the question, "Will we let them come up?" above a cartoon of a Cambodian man trying to climb the cliff to Preah Vihear and an armed Thai soldier kicking the man in the face, causing him to fall back down again.
92. *Sarn seri,* July 19, 1962.
93. Ibid.
94. Ibid., June 19, 1962.
95. NACP RG 59, Southeast Asia Lot Files; Bureau of Far Eastern Affairs, Office of Southeast Asian Affairs, Thailand Files, 1960–1963; Thai-Cambodian Relations; Memorandum of conversation between Floyd Whittington and Khun Yom Tantsetthi, June 19, 1962.
96. *Sarn seri,* July 19, 1962.
97. Ironically, Thailand gained entrance to the UN only after giving the four provinces to French Indochina in return for France's promise not to veto their application.
98. Department of Publicity, "The Prime Minister's Address on the Temple of Prah Viharn Case" (Bangkok: Department of Publicity), July 1962.
99. *Thai,* July 17, 1962.
100. Ibid., July 15, 1962.
101. *Sarn seri,* July 22, 1962.
102. Ibid., June 20, 1962.
103. *Phim Thai,* July 14, 1962.
104. *Siam nikorn,* June 19, 1962.
105. Ibid., June 17, 1962.

106. *Bangkok Post,* June 21, 1962.
107. Ibid., June 18, 1961.
108. *Phim Thai,* July 14, 1962.
109. Department of Publicity, "Prime Minister's Address," July 1962.
110. Pavin Chachavalpongpun, "Temple of Doom: Hysteria about the Preah Vihear Temple in the Thai Nationalist Discourse," in Marc Askew (ed.), *Legitimacy Crisis in Thailand* (Chiang Mai: Silkworm Books, 2010), p. 92.
111. The PAD contrasts Thaksin with the revered Chulalongkorn. They claim that while both Thai leaders surrendered territory, Chulalongkorn did it to save the nation, while Thaksin was motivated strictly by personal financial incentives—that is, the sale of Shincorp or gas concessions in Koh Kong Province.
112. Pavin, "Temple of Doom," p. 84.

CONCLUSION

1. *Nation,* June 25, 2008.
2. Ibid., July 10, 2008.
3. David Streckfuss, *Truth on Trial in Thailand: Defamation, Treason, and Lése Majesté* (New York: Routledge, 2011), p. 305.
4. Pavin Chachavalpongpun, "Temple of Doom: Hysteria about the Preah Vihear Temple in the Thai Nationalist Discourse," in Marc Askew (ed.), *Legitimacy Crisis in Thailand* (Chiang Mai: Silkworm Books, 2010), p. 84.
5. Zheng Wang, *Never Forget National Humiliation: Historical Memory in Chinese Politics and Foreign Relations* (New York: Columbia University Press, 2012), p. 101.
6. Ibid., p. 3.
7. Peter A. Jackson, "The Performative State: Semi-Coloniality and the Tyranny of Images in Modern Thailand," *Sojourn* 19:2 (2004), p. 233.
8. See Vamik Volkan, *Bloodlines: From Ethnic Pride to Ethnic Terrorism* (New York: Farrar, Straus and Giroux, 1997), and Zheng Wang, *Never Forget National Humiliation,* p. 68.
9. Chai-ana Samudavanija, "State Identity Creation, State-Building and Civil Society, 1939–1989," in Craig J. Reynolds (ed.), *National Identity and Its Defenders: Thailand Today* (Bangkok: Silkworm Books, 2002), p. 298.
10. After coming to power in 1932, the People's Party periodically shut down newspapers in response to political commentary, speculation over foreign policy, or even criticism on the monarchy. Phibun used World War II as a pretext for taking even tighter control over the newspapers. From 1942 to 1944, all news had to be approved by the government. See Phanphirom Lamtham, *Bodbat thang kanmeuang khong nangseu phim Thai tangtae kan blian blaeng kan bok khrong PS*

2475 theung sinsud songkhram lok khrang thi song [The Political Role of Thai Newspapers from the 1932 Coup until the End of World War II] (Bangkok: Samakhom Sangkhomsat haeng Prathet Thai [Social Science Association of Thailand Press], 2002), pp. 40–63.

11. Annette Hamilton, "Rumours, Foul Calumnies and the Safety of the Thai State," in Reynolds, *National Identity and Its Defenders,* p. 298.

BIBLIOGRAPHY

ARCHIVES

AOM: Les Archives d'Outre Mer, Aix-en-Provence, France.
    Fond: Indochine
        Sous-fond: Gouvernor General
            Collection: Cabinet Militaire
NAP: National Assembly of Thailand Library, National Assembly Proceedings.
NAT: National Archives of Thailand, Bangkok, Thailand.
    กต. Ministry of Foreign Affairs
    มท. Ministry of Interior
    ศธ. Ministry of Education
    สบ. Private Collections
    สร. Office of the Prime Minister
PO Public Record Office, London, England.
US National Archives of the United States.
National Archives at College Park, Maryland.

NEWSPAPERS

English
Bangkok Chronicle
Bangkok Post
Bangkok Times
Democracy
Japan Times and Advertiser
Nation
New York Times
Osaka Mainichi and Tokyo Nichi Nichi
Singapore Free Press

Thai
Bangkok rai wan
Chaw Thai
Ekkaraj

Khaw phab
Naew na
Nakorn sarn
Nikorn
Phim Thai
Prachachad
Prachakorn
Pramuan Wan
Santi rasadorn
Sarn seri
Seri
Siam nikorn
Siam rashdra
Siam rat
Sri krung
Suphab burut
Suwannaphum
Tawan
Thai
Thai rashdra
Thai samit
Thamthada
Varasab
Wan khru
Yudhakos

French
La Dépêche du Cambodge

PRIMARY AND SECONDARY SOURCES

Aldrich, Richard J. *The Key to the South: Britain, the United States, and Thailand during the Approach of the Pacific War, 1929–1942.* Oxford: Oxford University Press, 1993.

Apinan Poshyananda. *Modern Art in Thailand: Nineteenth and Twentieth Centuries.* Singapore: Oxford University Press, 1992.

Armstrong, John P. *Sihanouk Speaks.* New York: Walker and Company, 1964.

Askew, Marc (ed.). *Legitimacy Crisis in Thailand.* Chiang Mai: Silkworm Books, 2010.

Assumption Cathedral Printing Press. *En Thailande de 1940 á 1945. Documents.* Bangkok: Assumption Cathedral Printing Press (unpublished documents).

Asvabhahu. *A Siam Miscellany*. Bangkok: Siam Observer Press, 1912.

Atkins, Nicholas, and Frank Tallet (eds.). *The Right in France, 1789–1997*. London: I. B. Tauris Publishing, 1997.

Ayal, Eliezer B. (ed.). *The Study of Thailand: Analyses of Knowledge, Approaches, and Prospects in Anthropology, Art History, Economics, History, and Political Science*. Papers in International Studies, Southeast Asia series, no. 54. Athens: Ohio University Center for International Studies, 1978.

Baker, Chris, and Pasuk Phongpaichit. *A History of Thailand*. Cambridge: Cambridge University Press, 2005.

Barmé, Scott. *Luang Wichit Wathakan and the Creation of a Thai Identity*. Singapore: Institute of Southeast Asian Studies, 1993.

———. *Woman, Man, Bangkok: Love, Sex and Popular Culture in Thailand*. New York: Rowman & Littlefield, 2002.

Batson, Benjamin A. "The Fall of the Phibun Government, 1944." *Journal of the Siam Society* 62(2), 1974, 89–120.

Batson, Benjamin A., and Shimizu Hajime. *The Tragedy of Wanit: A Japanese Account of Wartime Thai Politics*. Singapore: Institute of Southeast Asian Studies, 1977.

Battye, Noel Alfred. "The Military, Government and Society in Siam, 1868–1910: Politics and Military Reform during the Reign of Chulalongkorn." Ph.D. diss., Cornell University, 1974.

Bell, Morag, Robin Butler, and Michael Heffernan. *Geography and Imperialism, 1820–1940*. Manchester: Manchester University Press, 1995.

Briggs, Lawrence Palmer. "The Aubaret versus Bradley Case at Bangkok, 1866–1867." *Far Eastern Quarterly* 6(3), 1947.

Callahan, Mary P. *Making Enemies: War and State Building in Burma*. Ithaca, NY: Cornell University Press, 2003.

Callahan, William A. "Beyond Cosmopolitanism and Nationalism: Diasporic Chinese and Neo-Nationalism in Thailand." *International Organization* 57(3), 2003.

Chaiwat Khamchoo and E. Bruce Reynolds (eds.). *Thai-Japanese Relations in Historical Perspective*. Bangkok: White Lotus Press, 1988.

Chamrat Duangthisan. *Khwammueang rueang Khaw Phrawihan* [The Politics of Preah Vihear]. Bangkok: Sadsawan Press, 1962.

Chandler, David. *A History of Cambodia*. Boulder, CO: Westview Press, 2007.

Charnvit Kasetsiri. "The First Phibun Government and Its Involvement in World War II." *Journal of the Siam Society* 62(2), 1974.

———. *Prasart Khaw Phra Viharn: Lum dam latthi chart-niyom prawattisart phlae kao prawattisart tat ton kap ban-mueang khong raw* [Preah Vihear: A Black Hole-Nationalism Wounded History and Our Country: Siam-Thailand]. Bangkok: Foundation for the Promotion of Social Sciences and Humanities Textbooks Project, 2008.

———. "Thailand-Cambodia: A Love-Hate Relationship." *Kyoto Review of Southeast Asia* 3, March 2003.

Christian, J. L., and Nabutake Ike. "Thailand in Japan's Foreign Relations." *Pacific Affairs* 15, June 1942.

Cooper, Nicola. *France in Indochina: Colonial Encounters.* Oxford: Berg Publishing, 2001.

Copeland, Mathew. "Contested Nationalism and the 1932 Overthrow of the Absolute Monarchy in Siam." Ph.D. diss., Australian National University, 1993.

Crosby, Sir Josiah. *Siam at the Crossroads.* London: Hollis and Carter, 1945.

Cuasay, P. "Borders on the Fantastic: Mimesis, Violence, and Landscape at the Temple of Preah Vihear." *Modern Asian Studies* 32(4), 1998.

Daughton, James Patrick. *An Empire Divided: Religion, Republicanism, and the Making of French Colonialism, 1880–1914.* Oxford: Oxford University Press, 2006.

Direk Jayanama. *Thailand and World War II.* Chiang Mai: Silkworm Books, 2008.

Dixon, C., and M. J. G. Parnwell (eds.). "Thailand: The Legacy of Non-Colonial Development in South East Asia." In C. Dixon and M. Hefferman (eds.), *Colonialism and Development in the Contemporary World.* London: Manswell, 1991.

Dodd, William Clifton. *The Tai Race: Elder Brother of the Chinese.* Cedar Rapids, IA: Torch Press, 1923.

Duke, Pensri. *Les Relations entre la France et la Thailande.* Bangkok: Chulalongkorn University Press, 1962.

Duus, Peter, Ramon H. Myers, and Mark R. Peattie (eds.). *The Japanese Wartime Empire.* Princeton, NJ: Princeton University Press, 1996.

Fishel, Wesley R. *The End of Extraterritoriality in China.* Berkeley: University of California Press, 1952.

Flood, E. Thadeus. "The 1940 Franco-Thai Border Dispute and Phibun Songkhram's Commitment to Japan." *Journal of Southeast Asian History* 10(2), September 1969, 304–325.

———. "Japan's Relations with Thailand: 1928–1941." Ph.D. diss., University of Washington, 1967.

Gallagher, John, and Ronald Robinson. "The Imperialism of Free Trade." In Anil Seal (ed.), *The Decline, Revival, and Fall of the British Empire.* Cambridge: Cambridge University Press, 1982.

Galli, Henri. *Gambetta et l'Alsace-Lorraine.* Paris: La Fondelle, 1911.

Garnier, Francis. *Travels in Cambodia and Part of Laos: The Mekong Exploration Commission Report (1866–1868).* Vol. 1. Bangkok: White Lotus Press, 1996.

———. *Travels in Laos and in Yunnan: The Mekong Exploration Commission Report (1866–1868).* Vol. 2. Bangkok: White Lotus Press, 1996.

Gellner, Ernest. *Nations and Nationalism.* Oxford: B. Blackwell, 1983.

Giani, Kesar Singh. *Indian Independence Movements in East Asia: The Most Authentic Account of the I.N.A. and the Azad Hind Government.* Lahore: Singh Bros., 1947.

Gildea, Robert. *The Past in French History.* New Haven, CT: Yale University Press, 1994.

Godlewska, Anne, and Neil Smith. *Geography and Empire.* Oxford: Blackwell Publishing, 1994.

Goodman, Grant K. (ed.). *Japanese Cultural Policies in Southeast Asia during World War II.* New York: St. Martin's Press, 1991.

Goscha, Christopher E. *Thailand and the Southeast Asian Networks of the Vietnamese Revolution: 1885–1954.* Richmond, Surrey: RoutledgeCurzon, 1999.

Goscha, Christopher E., and Soren Ivarsson (eds.). *Contesting Visions of the Lao Past: Lao Historiography at the Crossroads.* Copenhagen: Nordic Institute of Asian Studies, 2003.

Gostae, Robert. *Prawad kanphoeiphrae Khritasasana nai Siam lae Lao* [A History of Christian Missionary Work in Siam and Laos]. Bangkok: Suemuanchon Catholic Prathedthai, 2006.

Grabowsky, Volker (ed.). "The Preah Vihear Conflict and the Current Political Debate in Thailand." *Informal Northern Thai Group Bulletin* 2, September 2011.

———. *Southeast Asian Historiography: Unraveling the Myths.* Bangkok: River Books, 2011.

Harrison, Rachel V., and Peter A. Jackson (eds.). *The Ambiguous Allure of the West: Traces of the Colonial in Thailand.* Hong Kong: Hong Kong University Press, 2010.

Hell, Stefan. *Siam and the League of Nations: Modernization, Sovereignty, and Multilateral Diplomacy, 1920–1940.* Bangkok: River Books, 2010.

Hobsbawm, Eric. *Nations and Nationalism since 1780: Programme, Myth, Reality.* Cambridge: Cambridge University Press, 1990.

Hong, Lysa. "'Stranger within the Gates': Knowing Semi-Colonial Siam as Extraterritorials." *Modern Asian Studies* 38(2), 2004.

Hooker, M. B. (ed.) *Laws of Southeast Asia.* Vol. II: *European Laws in Southeast Asia.* Singapore: Butterworth and Company, 1988.

International Court of Justice (ICJ). "Case Concerning the Temple of Preah Vihear (Cambodia v. Thailand)." *Pleadings, Oral Arguments, Documents.* Vols. 1–2 (The Hague, Netherlands, 1964).

Ivarsson, Soren. "Making Laos 'Our' Space: Thai Discourse on History and Race, 1900–1941." In Christopher E. Goscha and Soren Ivarsson (eds.), *Contesting Visions of the Lao Past: Lao Historiography at the Crossroads.* Copenhagen: Nordic Institute of Asian Studies, 2003.

Jackson, Peter A. "The Performative State: Semi-Coloniality and the Tyranny of Images in Modern Thailand." *Sojourn* 19(2), 2004.

Jiraphorn Sathabanawathana. "Wikrithakan Siam R.S. 112" [Siam's 1893 Crisis]. Ph.D. diss., Srinakharinwirod University, 1976.

Jones, F. C. *Extraterritoriality in Japan and the Diplomatic Relations Resulting in Its Abolition.* New Haven, CT: Yale University Press, 1931.

Ka Fai Wong. "Visions of a Nation: Public Monuments in Twentieth-Century Thailand." MA thesis, Chulalongkorn University, 2000.

Kasian Tejapira. *Commodifying Marxism: The Formation of Modern Thai Radical Culture, 1927–1958.* Kyoto: Kyoto Areas Studies on Asia No. 3, 2001.

Kerneis, Georges-Marie. *La vérité sur la conflit entre la France et la Thailande* [The Truth about the Conflict between France and Thailand]. Hanoi: Imprimerie G. Taupin & Cie, 1941.

Kislenko, Arne. "Bending with the Wind: The Continuity and Flexibility of Thai Foreign Policy." *International Journal* 57(4), August 2002, 537–561.

Klein, Ira. "Salisbury, Rosebery, and the Survival of Siam." *Journal of British Studies* 8(1), 1968.

Kobkua Suwannathat-Pian. *Thailand's Durable Premier: Phibun through Three Decades, 1932–1957.* Kuala Lumpur: Oxford University Press, 1995.

Kratoska, Paul H. (ed.). *Southeast Asian Minorities in the Wartime Japanese Empire.* London: RoutledgeCurzon, 2002.

Kratoska, Paul, Remco Raben, and Henk Schulte Nordholt (eds.). *Locating Southeast Asia: Geographies of Knowledge and Politics of Space.* Singapore: Singapore University Press, 2005.

Krom Khosanakan. *Khamprasai khong phon than Nayok Rathamontri klaw kae muanchon chaw Thai thang withayu kracai siang wan thi 20 Tulakhom 1940 rueang kanprabprueng senkheddaen Indochin* [The prime minister's radio address to the Thai people on October 20, 1940, regarding the question of the border with French Indochina]. Bangkok: Krom Khosanakan, 1940.

———. *Raingan kansangsueng prathan kamakan kan chad sang anusawari Chai Samoraphum an sanoe phana than Nayok Rathamontri nueang nai rathaphiti boed anusawari nai wanchad* [A report from the president of the Victory Monument construction task force presented to the prime minister at the Victory Monument dedication ceremony on National Day]. Bangkok: Krom Khosanakan, June 24, 1942.

———. *Sunsap khong phana than Nayok Rathamontri nai kanboed anusawari Chai Samoraphum* [The prime minister's speech at the Victory Monument dedication ceremony]. Bangkok: Krom Khosanakan, June 25, 1942.

———. *Sunsap khong phon than Chomphon Phibun Songkhram Nayok Rathamontri haeng Prathedthai tob sunsap khong phon than Nai Phonek Tojo Nayok Ratham-onti haeng prathed Yipun thang withayu kracai siang* [A Radio Address from Prime Minister Phibun Songkhram of Thailand and Prime Minister Tojo of Japan]. Bangkok: Krom Khosanakan, December 23, 1941.

———. *Thai samai sang chat* [Thailand in a Time of Nation-Building]. Bangkok: Krom Khosanakan, 1941.

Kukrit Pramoj. *Four Reigns.* Chiang Mai: Silkworm Books, 2005.

Kullada Kesboonchoo Mead. *The Rise and Decline of Thai Absolutism.* London: Routledge, 2009.

Lambert, Susan. *The Franco-Prussian War and the Commune in Caricature, 1870–1871.* London: Thanet Press, 1971.

Landon, Margaret. "Thailand under the Japanese." *Asia and the Americans* 44(9), 1944.

Leach, Edmund. "The Frontiers of Burma." *Comparative Studies in Society and History* 3, 1960.

Lebra, Joyce C. (ed.). *Japan's Greater East Asia Co-Prosperity Sphere in World War II.* Kuala Lumpur: Oxford University Press, 1975.

Lewis, Martin W., and Kären E. Wigen. *The Myth of Continents: A Critique of Metageography.* Berkeley: University of California Press, 1997.

Ling, Trevor. *Buddhism, Imperialism and War.* London: George Allen & Unwin, 1979.

Li Narangoa and Robert Cribb (eds.). *Imperial Japan and National Identities in Asia, 1895–1945.* London: RoutledgeCurzon, 2003.

Luang Nathabanja. *Extra-territoriality in Siam.* Bangkok: Bangkok Daily Mail, 1924.

Luang Satkhornkhotkhet. *Chodmayhed khwamsongcam samai Farangsed yued Chanthaburi* [Memories of France's Occupation of Chantaburi]. Bangkok: Tono Kraemi Ltd., 1996.

Luang Wichit Wathakan. *Prathedthai: Rueang kansia dindaen kae Farangsed* [How Thailand Lost Its Territories to France]. Bangkok: Department of Publicity, 1940.

———. *Prawatisat sakon* [A Universal History]. Bangkok: Thai Mai Printing Company, 1932.

———. *Thailand's Case.* Bangkok: Department of Publicity, 1941.

Manich Jumsai. *Ekasan prawathisad R.S. 112: Reuang Farangsed wangphaen yued isan* [A History of R.S. 112: France's Conspiracy to Invade the Isan]. Bangkok: Chaloemnit Press, 1976.

———. *History of Thailand and Cambodia: From the Days of Angkor to the Present.* Bangkok: Chaloemnit Press, 1987.

Manit Nuallaor. "Political Symbols in Thai Politics: A Case Study of the Political Symbolic Uses During Field Marshall Phibulsongkhram's Government (1938–1944)." Ph.D. diss., Chulalongkorn University, 1990.

McCoy, Alfred W. (ed.). *Southeast Asia under Japanese Occupation.* New Haven, CT: Yale University Southeast Asian Studies, Monograph series no. 22, 1980.

Mitchell, Alan. *German Influence in France after 1870: The Formation of the French Republic.* Chapel Hill: University of North Carolina Press, 1979.

Mouhot, Henri. *Travels in Siam, Cambodia, and Laos, 1858–1860.* Singapore: Oxford University Press, 1989.

Murashima, Eiji. "The Commemorative Character of Thai Historiography: The 1942–43 Thai Military Campaign in the Shan States Depicted as a Story of

National Salvation and the Restoration of Thai Independence." *Modern Asian Studies* 40(4), 2006, 1053–1096.
———. "Opposing French Colonialism: Thailand and the Independence Movements in Indochina in the Early 1940s." *South East Asia Research* 13(3), 2005, 333–383.
Murdock, Michael. *Disarming the Allies of Imperialism: The State, Agitation, and Manipulation during China's Nationalist Revolution, 1922–1929*. Ithaca, NY: Cornell East Asia Series, 2006.
Myers, Ramon H., and Mark R. Peattie (eds.). *The Japanese Colonial Empire.* Princeton, NJ: Princeton University Press, 1984.
Nathabanja: *See* Luang Nathabanja.
Newell, William H. (ed.). *Japan in Asia, 1942–1945*. Singapore: Singapore University Press, 1981.
Niksch, Larry A. "United States Foreign Policy in Thailand's World War II Peace Settlement with Britain and France." Ph.D. diss., Georgetown University, 1976.
Nithi Aeusrivongse. *Pakkai lae bayruea* [Pen and Sail]. Bangkok: Ammarin Printing, 1986.
Nora, Pierre (ed.). *Realms of Memory.* Vol. 2. New York: Columbia University Press, 1997.
Oblas, Peter B. "A Very Small Part of World Affairs: Siam's Policy on Treaty Revision and the Paris Peace Conference." *Journal of Siam Society* 59(2), 1971.
Okawa Shumei. "The Establishment of the Greater East Asian Order." In Joyce C. Lebra (ed.), *Japan's Greater East Asia Co-Prosperity Sphere in World War II.* Kuala Lumpur: Oxford University Press, 1975, 39–40.
Osborne, Milton. *Fear and Fascination in the Tropics: A Reader's Guide to French Fiction on Indochina*. Madison: Wisconsin Papers on Southeast Asia (Occasional Paper No. 11), 1986.
———. *The French Presence in Cochinchina and Cambodia: Rule and Response (1859–1905)*. Ithaca, NY: Cornell University Press, 1969.
———. *River Road to China: The Mekong River Expedition, 1866–1873*. New York: Liveright Press, 1975.
Pavin Chachavalpongpun. "Temple of Doom: Hysteria about the Preah Vihear Temple in the Thai Nationalist Discourse." In Marc Askew (ed.), *Legitimacy Crisis in Thailand.* Chiang Mai: King Prajadhipok's Institute Year Book No. 5, Silkworm Books, 2010.
Peleggi, Maurizio. *Lords of Things: The Fashioning of the Siamese Monarchy's Modern Image.* Honolulu: University of Hawai'i Press, 2002.
———. *The Politics of Ruins and the Business of Nostalgia*. Bangkok: White Lotus Press, 2002.
Phanphirom Lamtham. *Bodbat thang kanmeuang khong nangseu phim Thai tangtae kan blian blaeng kan bok khrong PS 2475 thueng sinsud songkhram lok khrang*

thi song [The Political Role of Thai Newspapers from the 1932 Coup until the End of World War II]. Bangkok: Samakhom Sangkhomsat haeng Prathet Thai [Social Science Association of Thailand Press], 2002.

Pramuan hedkan nai yuk mai khong Thai bodsonthana rawang Nai Man Chuchat kab Nai Khong Rak Thai tae 8 Thanwakhom 2484 thueng 28 Kumphaphan 2485 [Proceedings of the New Thai Era: The Conversations of Mr. Man Chuchat and Mr. Khong Rak Thai, December 8, 1941–February 28, 1942]. Samud thiraluek Nai Kanchapanakid sop nai hoksui sabsun nai Wat Traimit Withayaram [Cremation volume of Mr. Kanchapakanid]. June 29, 1942.

Pra-onrat Buranamat. *Luang Wichitwathakan kap lakhon prawattisat* [The Historical Plays of Luang Wichitwathakan]. Bangkok: Thammasat University Press, 1985.

Pra-Phicanphonkid. *Chodmayhed khwamsongcam samai Farangsed yued mueang Trat* [Recollections of France's Occupation of Trat Province]. Bangkok: Department of Police, 1960.

Prasoed Patmasukon. *Rathsapha Thai nai rob sisib songpi (2475–2517)* [Proceedings of the Thai National Assembly (1932–1974)]. Bangkok: Hang Hun Suan, 1964.

Pridi Phanomyong. *Pridi by Pridi: Selected Writings on Life, Politics, and Economy.* Bangkok: Silkworm Books, 2000.

Proschan, Frank. "Peoples of the Gourd: Imagined Ethnicities in Highland Southeast Asia." *Journal of Asian History* 60(4), 2001.

Pussadee Chandavimol. *Wiatnam nai Mueang Thai* [The Vietnamese in Thailand]. Bangkok: Thailand Research Fund, 1998.

Reid, Anthony. *Imperial Alchemy: Nationalism and Political Identity in Southeast Asia.* Cambridge: Cambridge University Press, 2010.

Reynolds, Craig J. *National Identity and Its Defenders: Thailand Today.* Bangkok: Silkworm Books, 2002.

Reynolds, E. Bruce, "The Indian Community and the Indian Independence Movement in Thailand during World War II." In Paul H. Kratoska (ed.), *Southeast Asian Minorities in the Wartime Japanese Empire.* London: RoutledgeCurzon, 2002.

———. "Phibun Songkhram and Thai Nationalism in the Fascist Era." *European Journal of East Asian Studies* 3(1), 2004.

———. *Thailand and Japan's Southern Advance, 1940–1945.* New York: Palgrave MacMillan, 1994.

Ryan, James. *Picturing Empire: Photography and the Visualization of the British Empire.* London: Reaktion Books, 1997.

Said, Edward. *Orientalism.* London: Routledge and Kegan Paul, 1978.

Sam Sari. *La Cambodge aujourd'hui.* Phnom Penh: Department of Publicity, 1958.

Sawan Suwanachod. "Prathedthai kab panha mueang Chanthaburi lae Trat thi Farangsed yuedkhrong rawang pi P.S. 2436–2449" [Thailand and the Problem of French Occupation of Chantaburi and Trat, 1893–1906]. Ph.D. diss., Phetchabun Teacher's University, 1975.

Sears, Laurie J. (ed.) *Autonomous Histories, Particular Truths: Essays in Honor of John R. W. Smail.* Madison: University of Wisconsin, Center for Southeast Asia Studies, Monograph No. 11, 1993.

Seni Pramoj. "Thailand and Japan." *Far Eastern Survey* 12(21), 1943.

Singh, L. P. "The Thai-Cambodian Temple Dispute." *Asian Survey* 2(8), October 1962.

Sivaram, M. *Mekong Clash and the Far East Crisis.* Bangkok: Thai Commercial Press, 1941.

Skinner, William. *Chinese Society in Thailand: An Analytical History.* Ithaca, NY: Cornell University Press, 1957.

Smith, Anthony D. *Theories of Nationalism.* London: Duckworth & Company, 1983.

Sodsai Khantiwiraphongse. *Khwamsamphan khong Thai kab prathed tawantok* [Thailand's Relations with Western Countries]. Bangkok: Khled Thai Publishing, 1974.

———. "Prathedthai kab panha Indochin khong Farangsed" [Thailand and the Problem of French Indochina]. MA thesis, Chulalongkorn University, 1977.

Songsri Foran. "Thai-British Relations during World War II and the Immediate Postwar Period, 1940–1946." Paper No. 10, Thai Khadi Research Institute, Thammasat University, 1981.

Sorasan Phaengsapha. *Songkhram Indochin: Thai rop Farangsed P.S. 2483* [The Indochina War: Thailand versus France, 1941]. Bangkok: Sarakhadee Press, 1984.

Stowe, Judith A. *Siam Becomes Thailand: A Story of Intrigue.* Honolulu: University of Hawai'i Press, 1991.

Strate, Shane. "An Uncivil State of Affairs: Fascism and Anti-Catholicism in Thailand, 1940–1944." *Journal of Southeast Asian Studies* 42(1), 2011.

Streckfuss, David. "The Mixed Colonial Legacy in Siam: Origins of Thai Racialist Thought, 1890–1910." In Laurie J. Sears (ed.), *Autonomous Histories, Particular Truths: Essays in Honor of John R. W. Smail.* Madison: University of Wisconsin Center for Southeast Asian Studies, Monograph No. 11, 1993.

———. *Truth on Trial in Thailand: Defamation, Treason, and Lése Majesté.* New York: Routledge, 2011.

Stuart-Fox, Martin. *The History of Laos.* Cambridge: Cambridge University Press, 1997.

Suphaphorn Bumrungwong. "Kanriakrong lae kanbokrong dindaen thi khuen cak Farangsed 2483–2491" [Requesting and Governing the Territories Returned from France, 1940–1948]. Ph.D. diss., Chulalongkorn University, 2003.

Tambiah, S. J. *World Conqueror and World Renouncer.* Cambridge: Cambridge University Press, 1976.

Terwiel, B. J. "The Bowring Treaty: Imperialism and the Indigenous Perspective." *Journal of Siam Society* 79(2), 1991.

Thak Chaloemtiarana. *Thailand: The Politics of Despotic Paternalism.* Ithaca, NY: Cornell Southeast Asian Program, 2007.

Thamrongsak Phertlert-anan. "Kanriakrong dindaen P.S. 2483" [Requesting Territories in 1940]. *Samut Sangkhomsat* 12(3–4), 1990.

Thamsook Numnonda. "Negotiations Regarding the Cession of the Siamese Malay States, 1907–1909." *Journal of the Siam Society* 55, July 2, 1967.

———. "Phibun Songkhram's Thai Nation-Building Campaign during the Japanese Military Presence of 1941–1945." *Journal of Southeast Asian Studies* 9(2), 1978.

———. *Thailand and the Japanese Presence, 1941–1945.* Singapore: Institute of Southeast Asian Studies, 1977.

Thanet Aphornsuvan. "Malay Muslim 'Separatism' in Southern Thailand." In Michael Montesano and Patrick Jory (eds.), *Thai North and Malay South: Ethnic Interactions on a Plural Peninsula.* Singapore: NUS Press, 2008.

Thompson, Virginia. *Thailand: The New Siam.* New York: MacMillan, 1941.

———. "Thailand Irredenta—Internal and External." *Far East Survey* 9(21), October 23, 1940.

———. "Undeclared War along the Mekong." *Far Eastern Review,* January 28, 1941.

Thongchai Winichakul. "The Quest for *'Siwilai'*: A Geographical Discourse of Civilizational Thinking in the Late Nineteenth and Early Twentieth-Century Siam." *Journal of Asian Studies* 59(3), 2002.

———. *Siam Mapped: A History of the Geo-Body of a Nation.* Honolulu: University of Hawai'i Press, 1994.

———. "Siam's Colonial Conditions and the Birth of Thai History." In Volker Grabowsky (ed.), *Southeast Asian Historiography: Unraveling the Myths.* Bangkok: River Books, 2011.

———. "Trying to Locate Southeast Asia from Its Navel." In Paul Kratoska, Remco Raben, and Henk Schulte Nordholt (eds.), *Locating Southeast Asia: Geographies of Knowledge and Politics of Space.* Singapore: Singapore University Press, 2005.

Tombs, Robert (ed.). *Nationhood and Nationalism in France: From Boulangism to the Great War.* London: HarperCollins, 1992.

Tuck, Patrick. *French Catholic Missionaries and the Politics of Imperialism in Vietnam, 1857–1914: A Documentary Survey.* Liverpool: Liverpool University Press, 1987.

———. *The French Wolf and the Siamese Lamb: The French Threat to Siamese Independence, 1858–1907.* Bangkok: White Lotus Press, 1995.

Tully, John. *Cambodia under the Tricolour: King Sisowath and the "Mission Civilisatrice," 1904–1927.* Clayton, Australia: Monash Asia Institute, Monash University, 1996.

———. *France on the Mekong: A History of the Protectorate in Cambodia, 1863–1953.* Lanham, MD: University Press of America, 2002.

Van Der Cruysse, Dirk. *Siam and the West: 1500–1700.* Bangkok: Silkworm Books, 1999.

Varenne, Alexandre. "Indochina in the Path of Japanese Expansion." *Foreign Affairs* 27, October 1938.
Vella, Walter F. *Chaiyo! King Vajiravudh and the Development of Thai Nationalism.* Honolulu: University of Hawai'i Press, 1978.
———. *The Impact of the West on Government in Thailand.* Berkeley: University of California Press, 1955.
Viollis, Andrée. *S.O.S. Indochine.* Gallimard, 1935.
Volkan, Vamik. *Bloodlines: From Ethnic Pride to Ethnic Terrorism.* New York: Farrar, Straus and Giroux, 1997.
Ward, Robert S. *Asia for the Asiatics: The Techniques of Japanese Occupation.* Chicago: University of Chicago Press, 1945.
Warner, Charles K. (ed.). *From the Ancien Regime to the Popular Front: Essays in the History of Modern France in Honour of Shephard B. Clough.* New York: Columbia University Press, 1969.
Weber, Eugen. *Peasants into Frenchmen: The Modernization of Rural France, 1870–1914.* Stanford, CA: Stanford University Press, 1976.
Well, David, and Sandra Wilson. *The Russo-Japanese War in Cultural Perspective, 1904–05.* London: MacMillan Press, 1999.
Wilson, Constance. "State and Society in the Reign of Mongkut, 1851–1868: Thailand on the Eve of Modernization." Ph.D. diss., Cornell University, 1970.
Wolters, O. W. *History, Culture, and Region in Southeast Asian Perspectives.* Singapore: Institute of Southeast Asian Studies, 1982.
Wright, Joseph J., Jr. *The Balancing Act: A History of Modern Thailand.* Oakland, CA: Asia Books, 1991.
Wyatt, David K. *Politics of Reform in Thailand: Education in the Reign of Chulalongkorn.* New Haven, CT: Yale University Press, 1984.
———. *Thailand: A Short History.* New Haven, CT: Yale University Press, 2003.
Young, Louise. *Japan's Total Empire: Manchuria and the Culture of Wartime Imperialism.* Berkeley: University of California Press, 1998.
Zheng Wang. *Never Forget National Humiliation: Historical Memory in Chinese Politics and Foreign Relations.* New York: Columbia University Press, 2012.

INDEX

Page numbers in **boldface** refer to illustrations and maps.

ABOUT THE AUTHOR

Shane Strate is assistant professor of history at Kent State University.

OTHER VOLUMES IN THE SERIES

PRINT AND POWER:
Confucianism, Communism, and Buddhism in the Making of Modern Vietnam
Shawn Frederick McHale

INVESTING IN MIRACLES:
El Shaddai and the Transformation of Popular Catholicism in the Philippines
Katherine L. Wiegele

TOMS *AND* DEES:
Transgender Identity and Female Same-Sex Relationships in Thailand
Megan J. Sinnott

IN THE NAME OF CIVIL SOCIETY:
From Free Election Movements to People Power in the Philippines
Eva-Lotta E. Hedman

THE TÂY SƠN UPRISING:
Society and Rebellion in Eighteenth-Century Vietnam
George Dutton

SPREADING THE DHAMMA:
Writing, Orality, and Textual Transmission in Buddhist Northern Thailand
Daniel M. Veidlinger

ART AS POLITICS:
Re-Crafting Identities, Tourism, and Power in Tana Toraja, Indonesia
Kathleen M. Adams

CAMBODGE:
The Cultivation of a Nation, 1860–1945
Penny Edwards

HOW TO BEHAVE:
Buddhism and Modernity in Colonial Cambodia, 1860–1931
Anne Ruth Hansen

CULT, CULTURE, AND AUTHORITY:
Princess Liễu Hạnh in Vietnamese History
Olga Dror

Khmer Women on the Move:
Exploring Work and Life in Urban Cambodia
Annuska Derks

The Anxieties of Mobility:
Migration and Tourism in the Indonesian Borderlands
Johan A. Lindquist

The Binding Tie
Chinese Intergenerational Relations in Modern Singapore
Kristina Göransson

In Buddha's Company:
Thai Soldiers in the Vietnam War
Richard A. Ruth

Lục Xì
Prostitution and Venereal Disease in Colonial Hanoi
Vũ Trọng Phụng
Translated by Shaun Kingsley Malarney

Refiguring Women, Colonialism, and Modernity in Burma
Chie Ikeya

Natural Potency and Political Power:
Forests and State Authority in Contemporary Laos
Sarinda Singh

The Perfect Business?
Anti-Trafficking and the Sex Trade along the Mekong
Sverre Molland

Seeing Beauty, Sensing Race in Transnational Indonesia
L. Ayu Saraswati

Potent Landscapes:
Place and Mobility in Eastern Indonesia
Catherine Allerton

Forest of Struggle:
Moralities of Remembrance in Upland Cambodia
Eve Monique Zucker

Sounding Out Heritage:
Cultural Politics and the Social Practice of Quan Họ Folk Song in Northern Vietnam
Lauren Meeker

Caged in on the Outside:
Moral Subjectivity, Selfhood, and Islam in Minangkabau, Indonesia
Gregory M. Simon

Ghosts of the New City:
Spirits, Urbanity, and the Ruins of Progress in Chiang Mai
Andrew Alan Johnson

Essential Trade:
Vietnamese Women in a Changing Marketplace
Ann Marie Leshkowich

Saving Buddhism:
The Impermanence of Religion in Colonial Burma
Alicia Turner

Embodied Nation:
Sport, Masculinity, and the Making of Modern Laos
Simon Creak